8500

AERINX HALL LIBRARY
550 E. LOCKWOOD
WEBSTER GROVES, MO. 63119

PROPERTY
HALL LIBRARY

JUL 25 '98

222   Kuschel, Karl-Josef
KUS   Abraham:

8500

AERINX HALL LIBRARY
E. LOCKWOOD
WEBSTER GROVES, MO. 63119

Abraham

ABRAHAM

Sign of Hope for Jews, Christians and Muslims

Karl-Josef Kuschel

8500

NERINX HALL LIBRARY
530 E. LOCKWOOD
WEBSTER GROVES, MO. 63119

CONTINUUM · NEW YORK

1995

The Continuum Publishing Company
370 Lexington Avenue, New York, NY 10017

Translated by John Bowden from the German *Streit um
Abraham, Was Juden, Christen und Muslime trennt –
und was sie eint*, published 1994 by Piper Verlag
Munich.

© R. Piper GmbH & Co KG, Munich 1994
Translation © John Bowden 1995

All rights reserved. No part of this book may be reproduced,
stored in a retrieval system, or transmitted, in any form or by
any means, electronic, mechanical, photocopying, recording or
otherwise, without the written permission of
The Continuum Publishing Company.

Library of Congress Cataloging-in-Publication Data

Kuschel, Karl-Josef, 1948–
    [Streit um Abraham. English]
    Abraham: sign of hope for Jews, Christians, and Muslims / Karl-
Josef Kuschel.
        p.   cm.
    Includes bibliographical references and index.
    ISBN 0–8264–0808–7
    1. Abraham (Biblical patriarch).   2. Abraham (Biblical patriarch)
in the New Testament.   3. Abraham (Biblical patriarch) in rabbinical
literature.   4. Abraham (Biblical patriarch) in the Koran.
5. Christianity and other religions–Judaism.   6. Christianity and
other religions–Islam.   7. Judaism–Relations–Christianity.
8. Islam–Relations–Christianity.   9. Judaism–Relations–Islam.
10. Islam–Relations–Judaism.   I. Title.
BS 580.A3K87   1995
222'.11092–dc20   95–10650
                                                                            CIP

Printed in Great Britain

Contents

*To my Jewish, Christian and Muslim partners
in the 'International Scholars' Annual Trialogue'
sponsored by the
National Council of Christians and Jews in New York
in gratitude for a tangible 'Abrahamic ecumene'*

Abraham's house was open to all the children of men,
those going past and those returning,
and day by day they came
to eat and drink with Abraham.
To those who were hungry he gave bread,
and the guests ate and drank and were filled.
Those who came naked to his house
he clothed,
and helped them to experience God,
the creator of all things.

(*The Sagas of the Jews*)[1]

As it is written, 'I have made you the father of many nations'. Abraham is the father of us all – in the presence of the God in whom he believed, who gives life to the dead and calls into existence the things that do not exist.

(Romans 4.17)

O followers of earlier revelation! Why do you argue about Abraham, seeing that the Torah and the Gospel were not revealed till after him? Will you not, then, use your reason? Abraham was neither a 'Jew' nor a 'Christian', but was one who turned away from all that is false, having surrendered himself unto God.

(Surah 3.65–67).

Why this book was written

It may seem somewhat rash to write a book at this particular time about the ecumene between Jews, Christians and Muslims. 'Too late!', some people will exclaim. In Germany, the houses of Muslims are being set on fire, Jewish cemeteries are again being desecrated with Nazi symbols, and Jews and Muslims are being violently assaulted. Perhaps years ago it might have been possible to prevent these devastating atrocities and riots by right-wing extremists by means of ecumenical networks of Christians, Jews and Muslims. Perhaps a spirit of ecumenical brotherhood and sisterhood could have been achieved by large-scale educational campaigns in schools, churches and associations. But now, 'Too late!' Who is interested in idealistic theological and ecumenical concepts any more?

'Too early!', others exclaim. 'Radical Muslims, Christians and Jews are on the march':[2] that seems to be the sign of our time. 'The vengeance of God' is called down on all liberalism, on 'lily-livered toleration', on compromise over religious profiles, and this attitude is backed up by allegedly infallible sacred scriptures and traditions. Those are the slogans all round the world, of politicizing Jewish radical rabbis, of fundamentalist Christian television preachers or fanatical Islamic mullahs. Instead of co-existence with modernity there is a fight against modernity; instead of aggiornamento there is re-Catholicization; instead of the modernizing of Islam there is the Islamicization of modernity.

There is 'a fraternal feud in the house of Abraham' instead of ecumenical brotherhood and sisterhood: that in fact – if we look round the world – is the brutal reality of today. One need only mention Bosnia, Palestine and the Caucasus. All these scenes of bloody conflict are certainly not scenes of directly religious wars. But who could dispute that in all these crisis regions religion plays an important role and often makes things worse? 'Catholic' Croats,

'Orthodox' Serbs and 'Muslim' Bosniacs in Europe; Israelis and Palestinians in the Near East; 'Christian' Armenians and 'Muslim' Azerbaijanis in the Caucasus – all are entangled in murderous conflicts, not merely as nations but also as Jews, Christians and Muslims. They are tearing one another apart, not least because by virtue of their religious self-understanding they cannot or will not make peace. As recently as February 1994 in Hebron – deliberately, as a provocation, by the tomb of Abraham and Sarah – twenty-nine Muslims who had gathered for prayer were murdered by a fanatical religious Jewish settler in order to torpedo the peace process between Jews and Palestinians which had begun so hopefully.

That is where this book begins – in full awareness of the appalling difficulties on all sides. It deliberately sets out to provide a counterpoint. This is first a counterpoint to a violent fanaticism which is incapable of peace, and which in most countries has social, economic and psychological causes. Secondly, it is also a counterpoint against a resigned and paralysing fatalism. So it is a counterpoint in particular to the attitude that when it comes to Judaism, Christianity and Islam there is 'no more to be done', and the 'seizure of power' by right-wing extremists or fundamentalists is unstoppable.

Instead, this book insists that all three religions have not yet used up their energies for peace; indeed, in all probability they have yet to discover them fully. But at the beginning of all three religions lies a source of peace which time and again has been and still is obscured on all sides by fanaticism and exclusiveness. This source is called Abraham. It is called Abraham, Hagar and Sarah, the progenitors of three religions: Judaism, Christianity and Islam. The Jewish theologian from Jerusalem, Shalom Ben-Chorin, is therefore right in remarking: 'I know of no political conflict whose roots go back four thousand years: but that is the case in the land of promise, and is indissolubly connected with the election of Israel. The problems of the present need to be understood from here, from the primal history of Jews and Arabs, the hostile brothers, so that we can see that this is not just archaic saga material but at the same time an account of the ongoing tension between kindred peoples. Ishmael and Isaac were not well disposed to each other, but they united over the body of their father Abraham, and together they buried him in the cave of Machpelah in Hebron, which Abraham himself had bought as a family burial place after the death of his wife Sarah.'[3]

Indeed this book sets its hope on this. The violent fraternal feud in the house of Abraham can only be ended by reflection on common origins. So this book dares to present an ecumenical vision: the vision of an Abrahamic ecumene of Jews, Christians and Muslims. Here it should be made clear from the start that 'Abrahamic ecumene' is not a magic word which can make all the differences between the religions disappear, nor even an imperialistic straitjacket, invented in the West, which is meant to rob Jews, Christians and Muslims of their religious independence. The theology of an Abrahamic ecumene which I shall sketch out here seeks to take seriously the differences between these three great monotheistic religions and yet canvass for a process of peace and understanding out of theological and religious conviction. Here, with objectivity, passion and proportion, I shall outline a real vision, not a fantasy. For we shall be tracing two quite different currents. There is a cold current: Jews, Christians and Muslims are doggedly persisting in their exclusivisms and are therefore incapable of ecumenical brotherhood and sisterhood. But at the same time, as we shall see, there is a warm current: Jews, Christians and Muslims are in search of peace, as peacemakers capable of recognizing the presence of the primal father and primal mother in each other's brothers and sisters within the Abrahamic family.

The kind of theology which will be done here is not an end in itself. The attempt at an Abrahamic ecumene made here is to be seen as an investigation of foundations which leads to action. For here we shall be uncovering the foundations of the particular traditions, with the aim of analysing how they came to be consolidated, looking behind false claims to possession in order to develop theological perspectives for the future. So the theology practised here is applied research into foundations. And here the Bible plays a key role, since it is Holy Scripture for both Jews and Christians and is also highly respected by Muslims as 'revelation'. There can be no ecumenical theology of the other religions in any of the traditions without biblical or Qur'anic foundations and criteria. With biblical or Qur'anic scholarship where they are today, such a theology of religions is still no more than something to be hoped for in ecumenical research.[4] Today, for example, inter-religious dialogue is either censured in a 'fundamentalistic' way by Christians who with reference to the Bible regard it as an encouragement to syncretism, or is carried on 'pluralistically', largely at the expense of the biblical framework. This is a crazy alternative which needs to be overcome, and the present book is meant to be a first effort in this direction. In the not too distant future I then hope to be able to produce a comprehensive theology of the religions on a biblical basis.

For I am convinced that without this critical work on the foundations, on the sources of revelation, there will be no peace between religions worthy of the name. In particular there will be no peace between Jews, Christians and Muslims. Only out of a deep religious conviction can that change of heart come about which is so necessary in the face of all the political, social and religious conflicts. And this change of heart can come about above all if we listen again to the primal history, the history of Abraham, Hagar and Sarah. In its spirit the religions should show the way for politics, instead of constantly limping behind the politics of the day. In its spirit Realpolitik and spirituality are not opposites, but a fruitful unity for the well-being of peoples and religions.

Abraham – Hagar – Sarah: we need to take this situation seriously. We are not just concerned with Abraham; Sarah and Hagar also belong here. Without these primal mothers there would be no Jewish, Christian or Islamic civilization. Nevertheless, for pragmatic reasons and by virtue of the evidence, we cannot avoid the abbreviated phrase 'Abrahamic ecumene', since the primal mothers do not play the same role as Abraham in the various revealed writings. Only Abraham is common to all three religions and has similar theological relevance. Hagar and Sarah play a marginal role in the New Testament; Hagar is not even mentioned in the Qur'an, and Sarah is not mentioned by name. Of course we need to ask critical questions about this state of affairs. The misuse of tradition by a patriarchal approach, as though the primal mothers were once and for all of secondary or incidental significance, cannot go on. This situation must not encourage the marginalization of women or even the suppression of women's traditions, as unfortunately still continues to happen when Old Testament scholars talk of the 'patriarchal narratives'. So wherever possible, we need to think not only of 'father' Abraham, but also of the wives and mothers, Hagar and Sarah.

Whether such an ecumene comes about will depend on whether Jews, Christians and Muslims are prepared to stop dismissing one another with polemic as 'unbelievers', 'apostates', or 'superseded'; in other words, whether they are positively ready to accept one another as brothers and sisters, in faith in the God of Abraham, and thus engage in the 'pilgrimage of hope' which the British ecumenist Marcus Braybrooke has described so impressively in connection with the inter-religious dialogue of the past century.[5] The present book, also written by a Christian theologian, can only serve as an introduction here. It sets out to be a programmatic theological work which, aware of its limitations, seeks to do as much justice as possible to all three traditions. But it will have achieved its aim only if in future all three work together in order to attain a common theology of peace and understanding in the spirit of Abraham, Hagar and Sarah. So it would be ideal if this book were to spark off an 'Abraham, Hagar and Sarah project' in which Jews, Christians and Muslims engaged together — with an eye towards the third millennium.[6]

Tübingen, July 1994
Karl-Josef Kuschel

Prelude

Reflecting with Nelly Sachs on the Man from Ur

How do we begin to talk about Abraham? How do we establish a relationship with man from Ur, the 'Ur-man', as Thomas Mann called him in his great novel *Joseph and His Brothers*, with a word play which is possible only in German? How do we overcome the distance of around 3500 years between the world of the son of Terah, which is so remote and strange, and the reality of the twentieth century, which is so near and familiar to us? If we shake off the dust of millennia, what becomes visible? Does he come to meet us from the shades of time?

None of the great authors of the twentieth century has raised these questions in such a penetrating and passionate way as the German Jewish poet Nelly Sachs, who won the Nobel prize for literature in 1966 and has left us a unique collection of poems and plays.[7] No one has understood as well as she, both in her Abraham poems and her 'scenic poem' entitled 'Abram in the Salt', how to conjure up and interpret the mystery of Abraham specifically for our time – a time stamped by the mass murder of the European Jews and the return of the people to the land once promised to Abraham. Nelly Sachs, the Jewish poet from Berlin, can tell us what can become visible of Abraham, despite the dust of the millennia.

Nelly Sachs began work on her Abram drama at a time when her poetic gift first came to life, a few years before the end of the war, in 1943, three years after her flight from Nazi Germany. Since then she had been living in Stockholm, where in Bergsundstrand 23 she had to share the tiny flat provided for her by the Jewish community with her mother, who was sick and needed care. Well informed about the cruel events in the death camps, which she herself had barely escaped, thanks to the help of the Swedish writer Selma Lagerlöf, she now began, in numerous poems and smaller 'plays', to sound out and identify the mysterious destiny, indeed the mission, of Israel for the nations: 'Eli, A Mystery Play of the Suffering of Israel', 'In the Dwellings of Death', 'The Darkening of the Stars'.

Amazingly enough, the experience of the Shoah was not an occasion for Nelly Sachs, as it was for other intellectuals and writers, to stop believing in God and regard Israel's special mission as one of pious self-deception. She knew that the literary scene was dominated by a young generation of poets who in the spirit of Jean-Paul Sartre had a 'very sceptical, almost nihilistic attitude, utterly without faith in the religious sense'.[8] She suffered from the fact that 'the atheists, including the genius Gide', regarded 'believers only as good and convenient uncles', who 'sleepily' repeated what had already been said. Nowhere in her day from this side had she found even a hint 'of fearful, indeed demonic, prostration before the mystery'.[9]

But this prostration was what she wanted to express with her texts. Religion for her was the opposite of 'convenience' and 'sleepiness'. As early as July 1944 she wrote: 'All the longing that made Jewish people once again set out for their God, as in the time of the Hasidim, has come alive among the few who perhaps may survive this terror.'[10] Or in January 1946: 'I have only the deep feeling that it had to be that Jewish artists had once again to begin to listen to the voice of their blood, so that the primeval source could awaken to new life.'[11] Amazingly enough, in fact for Nelly Sachs the deadly doom of Israel became the occasion for a new grappling with God, Israel's God, the God of the Bible, who is fearful because enigmatic and mysterious. With her texts she wanted to arouse people from religous apathy and a dulling of the senses and seize the crisis as an opportunity for once again setting out towards God and making the age-old source spring again. She passionately protested against the extinguishing of the biblical traditions by modern secularism, because secularism leads to forgetfulness of God.

So because Nelly Sachs was concerned to uncover age-old sources that had been buried, sources from which the people of Israel had been drawing spiritual energy for millennia, time and again the great figures of the Bible keep appearing in her texts: Jacob, Job, Daniel, David, Saul and Jesus. Because she sought a new approach to God, she looked for a link above all with Abraham, the Ur-man, who was the first man to renounce the false idols and set out for the one true God. Thus for her Abraham was also the primal embodiment of the role of Israel for humankind. In April 1946 she wrote: 'I think so often that light must be kindled again somewhere in Israel's world, kindled with its own candles, refreshed with its own spring water. The lands where we enjoyed hospitality, even Palestine with the dust of the patriarchs, all must once again retreat in the face of the eternal communion with God which bids us together. Through it the Jews will still have things to give humanity; I cannot think of another future than this.'[12]

Nelly Sachs finally called her drama 'Abram in the Salt' (it had first been called 'Man from Ur' and 'The Burning Hair'). Its final form took her almost ten years' work. We can follow parts of this formative process through numerous letters: the process itself is highly dramatic. For in grappling with Abraham, Nelly Sachs found autobiography and contemporary history, private life and politics mixed. Not only are the recollections of the Nazi death camps omnipresent; at this time the poet also experienced the slow dying of her mother, who was only released from her suffering in 1950. And she experienced from afar the political conflicts over the foundation of the state of Israel, over 'Palestine with the dust of the patriarchs'. At this time the religious mission of Israel and political reality in Israel were in harsh conflict, a conflict which Nelly Sachs recorded, deeply oppressed. Thus in September 1946, at a time when clashes between Jews and Arabs were reaching a new climax in what was then the British Mandate of Palestine, she wrote to a friend: 'You must remember, my dear, that here too one is often lonely. If I did not have dear mother, I too would sometimes love to close my eyes. The disaster in Palestine. I attempted to put it into words, but it almost breaks one's heart . . . I have no land and basically also no language. Only the ardour of a heart which wants to hasten away beyond all frontiers.'[13]

But Nelly Sachs would not stop uncovering the source of Abraham, despite her unhappiness. At least one voice must ring out, she thought; someone must be able 'to collect the bloody footprints of Israel from the sand and show them to humankind – and not just in the form of protocols'.[14] In other words, Nelly Sachs was quite clear that more was needed for her message than protocols which only registered the cruelty and the bloody footsteps of Israel. She wanted literally more than statistics. Another form was needed to give expression to the earnestness and dignity of this 'message'. Nelly Sachs chose the form of the old 'cult theatre' and wrote a 'play of

words, mime and music' in which when words reached their limits
they could be replaced and supplemented by gestures and movement
or by tones and sounds. She herself would later write of this choice of
form that what she had intended was 'a kind of cult theatre in which
the arts could combine, without one swamping the other. The chorus
muttering darkly and looking forward; as in antiquity accompany-
ing events from afar. The dialogue spoken . . . the music always
beginning where the words fall silent.'[15] She not only knew the
Abraham material from the Bible, but also used for the play the
well-known Jewish legend about Abraham's childhood in Ur
(Chaldaea) under the cruel despot Nimrod, which she had learned in
the translation by Johann Gottfried Herder.[16]

So how does one speak of Abraham in the middle of the twentieth
century without flat illustrations, without the result being a simply
illustrated 'story of Abraham'? How does one express Abraham in
the theatre of the twentieth century without historicizing naivety;
without flat naturalism; without acting as though one knew how
things were with Abraham? Nelly Sachs chose first the picture
language of dreams, secondly a rock-bottom situation, and thirdly a
radical reduction of material which is posible only in the cult theatre,
along with a mythical stylization of the legend. What that means in
practice is this.

The picture language of dreams: the drama begins by taking up the
twentieth-century situation. For many people the relationship of our
century to Abraham is now a historical and archaeological one:
excavations in Ur. But at the same time Nelly Sachs makes it clear
that by this means at best one finds prints in the dust of the millennia
of people or objects which have long disappeared. To be touched by
Abraham it is necessary to penetrate to true reality. However, that
does not happen with the help of the spade but only with the dream,
the royal way into the depths of the soul. So at the beginning of the
play Nelly Sachs makes one of the excavators fall asleep, his dusty
hand reaching into the air as if it wanted to hold something. As
though in a framework formed by the distance between his two
hands, the following seven scenes of the 'play' arise 'like a
tapestry'.[17] So the dream bridges the millennia and is meant at the
same time to form a link with the depth of truth which rests in the
soul of every human being. The excavator becomes an archaeologist
of the soul who is once again to open up the inner springs which have
for so long been covered over, thus making possible an approach to

the invisible God. The history of the human soul is to be depicted from its beginnings: a new start, a situation of breakthrough to God in the consciousness. 'And the way to "Him" is not clear. It is fearful. And the patriarchs and the prophets in the Bible are those "smitten" by God, so that they are in "grace".'[18]

Rock-bottom situation: at the beginning of the drama a 'salty landscape after the flood' is sketched out, with a temple tower in the middle and a giant idol in honour of the moon god Sin. The king of the land and the supreme servant of this god of death who requires human sacrifices is the cruel and bloody hunter king Nimrod. Blood lust prevails and the thirst for ever new blood. The action is driven forward by Abram, accompanied by a chorus which often admonishes or interprets. As a fifteen-year-old boy, along with 150 other boys Abram is condemned to be a human sacrifice in the tomb of the king's son, who has just died. But as though by a miracle he is able to free himself from this cave of death and thus escape the power of the false god. Abram is the 'elect' from his birth. He alone dares to rebel against the rule of the moon god, despite all warnings. He is equipped with nothing but pure longing for the invisible God.

This is precisely what Nelly Sachs wanted to show in her drama from the 'Ur time': the moon cult may be able to satisfy blood lust, but not the thirst which already in the Bible itself symbolizes the longing for God (Ps.42.2). So the 'ascent of Abraham from the night to the surprises of the God event' can be shown, the 'climbing of the Invisible':[19] 'I saw the young Abraham as the saga tells, banished by Nimrod to a stony cave, and at the same time, woven from stones and stars, there arose in me the longing of Abraham as the first man for the sole deity, which then leads him to destroy the wood of the artificial gods, whereas Nimrod as a hunter would be the counterpart and adversary who could lead to the form of the fiend in our time.'[20]

'The fiend in our time'? The scene and action of the play unmistakably contain allusions to the experience of Israel with Nazi Germany. The 'salty landscape after the flood'? Associations with the Shoah experience will be aroused here for the twentieth-century spectator. Nimrod? He is a mythical figure who has returned in Adolf Hitler: a primal tyrant who is the archetype of death. In this way the Abraham-action becomes an anticipation of events in Germany, a variation on the theme of executioner and victim, hunter and pursued.[21] What this implies is that even today – as at the primal begining of all history in Ur – the people of Israel is again at rock bottom in a salty landscape after a flood, in a landscape of death, having had to pay homage to the god of death for years during which a bloody ruler has been able to revel in his power. The Ur time and the present time melt into each other in a mysterious way. As Nelly Sachs writes: 'I see countless bodies of dead animals on the way, that oven which has to swallow up those who do not believe in the god of the tyrant. The weak and doubting father of Abraham, who would gladly worship everything if only he were given a tranquil everyday existence, and who resolves to flee only when they want to throw his son in the oven. And the departure of Abraham, the first homeless one, to God and to the eternal mission of the Jewish people.'[22] This also indicates that in this salty landscape not all have succumbed to delusion: there is at least one person who does not let go of the longing for God and who is in a position to break out of the dead, false world:

> One time is fulfilled,
> another begins,
> longing in thirst.[23]

Reduction and mythicization: Nelly Sachs aims at pathos and dignity by radically reducing the Abraham material and at the same time stylizing it as myth. A critic of her play has rightly pointed out: 'The legend is interpreted mythologically; figures and objects are seen as models for human possibilities at all times and from the perspective of eternity. So it is possible for Nelly Sachs to keep to the historical and cultural location of the legend and simultaneously to transfer the narratives to her own time.'[24] The reduction of the Abraham material to Abraham's childhood also had the advantage of showing that here we do not have the complete hero of Israel's faith, the bearer of the promise and God's preferred covenant partner. For Nelly Sachs, Abraham is still 'Abram', the young man on the way to God, who out of longing sets out for an unknown land — thus reflecting the twentieth-century person who has lost any relationship to God and must rediscover it. Moreover the key word 'longing' is repeated like a mantra in the scene which is decisive for Abram, without heed to any personal psychology, in a way that is permissible only in dream language and which can be achieved only by cult theatre with its rituals of repetition. Moreover this circling round a word also has a meditative force and can thus produce a link with certain laws of the unconscious, of the soul:[25]

> You have called me, Abram,
> and I long so much for you.
> Starry teeth bite through the tomb
> and I long so much for you.
> With his horns the ram broke through the wall
> and I long so much for you.
> You tear open death
> like a pea-pod,
> and I long so much for you.
> With the leaf of the night
> you protect my eyes from the light,
> and I long so much for you.[26]

All this already shows that Nelly Sachs sought to depict Abraham, not as a historical individual figure, but as the embodiment of a basic human attitude. She understands Abraham as an archetypal figure, as the Ur man of the Ur longing for the divine which is beyond stone and star, endowed with the possibility of transcending the provisional and transitory for the mystery of the invisible and eternal. In short, 'Abram in the Salt', according to Nelly Sachs herself, is 'written as an attempt to bring new life to the age-old cultic theatre which once began to give expression to elemental human feelings . . . All attempt to break out of a mysterious captivity. Nimrod, the hunter king, embodies the thirst of the hunt to the sleep-walking moonstruck choir. The quest for something "beyond" has begun. The earthly zodiac, Nimrod's bloody booty, begins to shine in heaven when the fifteen-year-old Abram emerges from the cave of death into which he had been thrown. At the same time blood is as it were exchanged for the stars. Out of a longing which almost tears his body apart he is pursued into spheres without images.'[27]

Thus for Nelly Sachs, grappling with Abraham is at the same time:
— Assuring herself of the primal determination of human beings. Under the surface and the false images of life it is important to seek the true God, to retain the longing for a homeland which is not already identical with the here and now. It is important to be ready to deny communities of blood and destiny (family and people) and set off afresh into the unknown. Abraham? For Nelly Sachs, he is the

'first to be set aflame with longing',[28] the 'divining rod' with which one can 'smite the eternal spring which changes death into life'.[29] And her Abraham drama? It is 'not primarily an external dramatic event but a spiritual one. The dawning of an invisible concept of God in the midst of a people which is still looking around in a state of trance, wandering around in the dark.'[30]

— Keeping alive the direction of the people of Israel. Abraham is Israel's legacy to the peoples of the world. For in this Ur-man from Ur the primal image of human being has been preserved: being human is being on the way to God, is exodus from false belief, breaking out from the ties of destiny in trust in a God who directs people to an unknown land. It is Israel's mission to remind the peoples of the world that the umbilical cord to this eternal and mysterious God has not been cut — despite all the floods. The races of humankind will have a share in Abraham's blessing if they themselves set out, i.e. if they put into practice the departure for God which is prefigured in the person of Abraham.[31]

The present book, too, seeks to do justice to the great poet Nelly Sachs's experiences of Abraham, and at the same time to meet specifically inter-religious interests which Nelly Sachs did not have in view, but which are very much in line with her thought.

— Keeping alive the longing for the true God and freeing all religious Abraham traditions from their rigidities and exclusivist encapsulations.

— Reviving the age-old sources from which the energies of religious peace can be drawn.

— Rekindling Israel's light in the awareness that despite all the experiences of the flood, Israel's mission for the world of the nations is not yet finished, and that this light burns on in other great religious traditions like Christianity and Islam.

— Rediscovering the 'imprints' of Abraham in the patriarchal dust of Palestine, not in order to divide this land again but in order to reconcile it anew in the spirit of Abraham's readiness for peace. Here nothing can be discovered about Abraham that one can 'excavate' and 'grasp'. Abraham only lives (for Nelly Sachs and for us) if his history, preserved by Israel as holy scripture, touches the souls of human beings. It awakens to new life from the dust only if what he stands for seizes human hearts.

So it is important for the well-being of the divided nations to keep alive the memory of the man from Ur who abjured false gods and idols and made his way into the unknown. All this in the awareness that among many people today, nationalism, xenophobia, religious fanaticism and exclusivism have attained the status of gods and idols, become the objects of idolatry, which has to be combatted for the sake of the true and living God.

A. Abraham as the Possession of Judaism, Christianity and Islam

I. Abraham and Judaism

Why are Jews, Christians and Muslims so much at odds? One answer is that they are so much at odds because this is a real family dispute. And as is well known, family disputes tend to be carried on with particular passion. What is this family dispute about? Each of the three faiths believes that it has preserved the paternal or maternal heritage in the purest form. And this heritage is the heritage of Abraham, Hagar and Sarah. The dispute between Jews, Christians and Muslims is above all also a dispute over who are the true children of Abraham.

1. The birth of Judaism

But can we as believers speak about Abraham as the poets do? Surely Abraham poetry is one thing and Abraham theology another? As men and women of the twentieth century, used to the historical verification of events, can we simply leave aside the question whether the stories about Abraham, particularly in the book of Genesis, have any historical value at all? Was there ever such a person as Abraham? Do the stories describe what really happened to him? More precisely, was Abraham merely a figure who had some influence on history (which is indisputable), or was he also a historical figure: a person with a biography which can be verified by modern historians? Did the events which are reported in connection with him take place in history? His conversations with God, God's promise of descendants and land, God's 'eternal' covenant with Abraham? And if the answer to this is 'no', then does it make sense to want to use Abraham for theology, for an ecumenical theology of peace today? With legends as a basis? With the products of pious fantasy as a starting point? 'Don't touch Abraham,' a British friend once warned me, 'No one knows whether there ever was such a person.'

How do we speak of Abraham?

All these questions must be taken seriously, but they can be answered with two arguments.

1. For a long time during this century there was indeed a dispute as to whether Abraham actually was a historical figure. 'Abraham' was thought rather to be a fictitious literary figure, projected by later popular fantasy on to earliest times, typical of tribal or clan societies without any political head like a king or a chieftain.[1] We may appeal to a widespread consensus and say that a concrete historical person Abraham may have stood behind the stories, and not just a mythical ancestor figure. For why should stories of this kind, clearly different from classical myths, have been 'invented'? At all events, the burden of proof lies with those who assert, contrary to the texts, that these are mythical or fictitious narratives, and such proof has not been produced so far. Furthermore, the time of Abraham may be put in the first half of the second millennium before Christ: 2000-1500. At that time there was the kind of social and cultural milieu which is described here, nomads in the hill country or on cultivated land who did not live in houses but in tents; who reared sheep, goats, oxen and asses and perhaps even camels; who remained with their flocks and herds in the cultivated land and on its borders, 'as a non-sedentary population between the towns and villages, preferably in places where towns and villages were not too concentrated'.[2]

But can we do Abraham theology with these dry bones of a few facts which are historically more or less probable? The answer has to be 'no'. In strictly historical terms Abraham largely remains once and for all in the shadows of history. And those who have only a historical relationship to his story, who want to 'grasp' him historically, will literally find the dust of the millennia running through their fingers. Hardly anything will remain. But at the same time the truth of Abraham is not to be found on a purely historical level. Anyone who wants to 'grasp' Abraham purely historically will not understand anything about him. For what Nelly Sachs showed through poetry and archetypes, Genesis shows in the form of theology. The Abraham stories are the stories of the faith of a people which is explaining to itself God's relationship with it by means of these stories. So:

2. The Abraham stories in the Hebrew Bible call for a com-

mitment of faith. They are 'proclamation', not historiography. They contain above all deep religious truth, and only a little of the truth of historical facts. They speak only to those who do not see in them merely the fortuitous words of human beings, but God's eternal Word. And today, too, we have to be prepared to follow the people of Israel in taking this primal decision (or we can forget the Abraham stories): these texts are 'Holy Scripture', God's revelation to men and women. At all events, Christianity and Islam have followed the people of Israel in making this primal decision. They, too, have affirmed that the stories of Abraham are God's word in human words, not just flights of fantasy. They express something of God's history with creation and humankind, and are not just random sagas from primeval times. They seek to move the heart, so that people recognize the truth about themselves, rather than offering historical proof.

So whatever dispute there may be over Abraham; whatever dates, circumstances and self-understanding of this man may be covered over once and for all by the dust of the millennia, one thing is certain: Abraham was, is and remains in Israel a theological and political figure. In other words, the recollection of Abraham, the recollection of a long-distant 'prehistory' when the 'fathers' and 'mothers' were still alive: Noah and his wife; Abraham, Hagar and Sarah; Isaac and Rebecca; Jacob, Leah and Rachel; Joseph and his brothers, this recollection had a concrete function in the confusing yet utterly consistent life of this people. What function? In brief, it helped towards coping with crises and assuring the people that it continued to have a bond with God. Recollection of the stories of Abraham has always been part of theology for a specific community of faith; it has been a creative theological reaction to ever new historical demands which the people of Israel was not spared in its tremendous history. Christianity and Islam were simply to continue to write creative Abraham theology on their own account.

So we shall not begin 'historically'. We can leave the question of the 'historical Abraham' on one side. We shall begin where the memories of Abraham literally became a life-and-death matter for the people of Israel.

The Torah as an instrument for coping with crises

There is no greater catastrophe in the history of Israel before the Holocaust than the deportation of large sections of the people from Palestine to Babylon in 587 BCE. The 'Babylonian exile' then began, and was to last almost fifty years. What it meant can be summed up very briefly: with the destruction of the capital, Jerusalem, the people of Israel had lost its centre – both its political and its religious centre. For the end of Jerusalem was also the end of a form of political life which had been familiar for almost 500 years: the Davidic monarchy, which was never to exist in Israel again.

Even worse: the end of Jerusalem was also the end of the great temple which had been built under King Solomon. It, too, was a good 400 years old. And the end of the temple was also the end of a whole religious form of life: the end of the state sacrificial cult, the end of the priesthood, the end of those commandments which had guaranteed the functioning of the temple.

No wonder that after the return from exile in Babylon the first concern was to rebuild the temple. In the year 538 the great Persian king Cyrus, now also ruler over Babylon, had issued an edict allowing the Jews to return to Palestine and rebuild the temple, which could be consecrated in 515. All now seemed set for a renewal in the old, 'promised land': the temple was no longer the property of the king but of the whole people, whose head was now a 'high priest'. Israel had become a kind of church state in which the law of God ruled, supervised by the high priest as the representative of Yahweh on earth.

When the impetus to reform had run out of steam two generations later, there was another wave of reform. The great kings of Persia sent commissioners, Nehemiah and Ezra, two Jews from influential families, who had commended themselves to the Persian authorities, to Jerusalem to ensure internal and external order. Moreover both indeed worked hard to restore order; here the priest Ezra is portrayed as having been particularly harsh. Fanatically and inexorably he took action against 'mixed marriages', i.e. marriages which Israelites had entered into with non-Israelites. Furthermore, in 398 BCE Ezra had 'all the people' assembled in Jerusalem. In public, he formally read aloud 'the book with the law of Moses', which at the same time he explained to the people: 'And they read from the book, from the laws of God, clearly; and they gave the sense, so that the people understood the reading' – at any rate this is what the book of Nehemiah (8.8) tells us, probably with some degree of authenticity.[3]

It should be noted that this sort of thing had not happened in the land of Israel before, and was very much in accord with the experiences of the exile:

– All at once there was no longer just 'a law' (Torah); all at once this law also existed in the form of a 'book', written down, fixed in writing. All at once God's will had become a book. We are experiencing the birth of the religion of the book, the religion of the law of God codified in writing.

– All at once there was no longer merely the temple in which one encountered God, but a public reading of the law of God, not in the temple, but in a public place, so that all who could hear had unhindered access. All at once the worship of God was no longer identical with temple sacrifice and temple worship; all at once worship consisted in the reading of scriptural texts and their exegesis and application. We are experiencing the birth of the liturgy of the word of God in the popular assembly, as from now on it was to be practised in synagogues (which already came into being during the exile).

– All at once it was no longer enough, as before, to delegate religious tasks to an official priesthood. All at once the whole people underwent religious instruction: the explanation of the law of God, the teaching and inculcation of the many commandments which from then on were to structure everyday life for everyone, i.e. point them towards God: commandments about killing animals and eating meat; about sexual intercourse, about food, cleanness, the holiness of the temple, sabbath rest and the annual festivals. We are experiencing the birth of study of the Torah, of learning the Torah, of Torah piety.

No Judaism without Abraham

We can call these measures a way of overcoming the crisis and guarding against crises which had been practised during the exile. Now the people were to know once and for all what they had to observe. They now used this scheme to read their own history. Indeed it may have been the wisest political ploy of the reformers of

the time finally to establish an interpretation of history which had
already existed in other circles, in the circles which stood behind the
book of 'Deuteronomy' and the Deuteronomistic history (the books
of Joshua, Judges, Samuel and Kings). This scheme of interpretation
went: obedience to the law leads to blessing, apostasy from the law
to curse, to catastrophe, to divine judgment. From our perspective
we can see this as a type of simplification.

However, this scheme was extraordinarily successful. With it,
history could be made so to speak transparent for anyone (as we can
also read in Nehemiah 9). On the one hand we have the 'clear
ordinances' of God, the 'reliable laws' and 'good precepts and
commandments' which God the Lord had decreed on Sinai (9.13).
And on the other there is the arrogance of the 'fathers', their
contempt for the commandments, their wickedness – time and again,
despite all the warnings which the prophets had already uttered. The
consequence was one misery after another: misery in Egypt, misery
in the wilderness, misery in exile. And yet time and again in his
patience God had kept liberating the people from its misery. Why?
Because God had thought of the covenant which he once made with
Abraham.

Abraham: at the beginning of the interpretation of history in
Nehemiah, at the beginning of the birth of Judaism, he is also there.
Literally,

> You are the Lord, the God who chose Abram and brought him
> forth out of Ur of the Chaldeans and gave him the name Abraham;
> and you found his heart faithful before you, and made the
> covenant with him to give to his descendants the land of the
> Cananite, the Hittite, the Amorite, the Perizzite, the Jebusite and
> the Girgashite, and you fulfilled your promise, for you are
> righteous (Neh.9.7).

It is striking how in this early post-exilic text the role of Abraham in
Israel has already become a matter of unshakable certainty, which
now seems to have been written in cast-iron formulae:

1. The God who is invoked in Israel is identified as the God who
dealt with Abraham.

2. God's action in Abraham is defined more closely as both
election and leading out of an old land into a new one. In this way
Abraham becomes the instrument of God's plan for Israel. Indeed,

Abraham is so much God's possession that God gives him a new name (and thus a new identity, cf. Gen.17.5).

3. The election of Abraham, the leading out of Abraham and his gift of an identity come to a climax in the making of the covenant. Abraham now becomes God's favoured partner in the covenant. The content of the covenant is the promise of a land, the promise of Canaan.

We can say without exaggeration that all the Abraham theology of post-exilic Judaism is here in a nutshell. Here Israel assured itself that because Abraham stands at the beginning of history as the elect of God, the partner in the covenant and the guarantor of the promise of the land, in the end the further history of the people of Israel cannot fail either. However much the people may sin against Yahweh and his commandments and thus time and again end up in distress, God does not repent of his covenant. God keeps on rescuing the people. Why? Because he keeps to the promise that he once gave to Abraham. Thus the basic formulae of a creative Abraham theology in Israel become historically tangible for us for the first time. Abraham became important because he helped people to cope spiritually with the great crisis of the exile, the loss of the land. We shall now look at that more closely

2. Abraham's role in the great catastrophe: exile

It is striking that the great representatives of creative theology before the exile, the prophets Amos and Hosea in the northern kingdom of Israel and Isaiah in the southern kingdom of Judah, are completely silent about Abraham. Evidently they presented their theological programme without reference to the 'fathers' and 'mothers' of the earliest times. Yet the knowledge of the theological significance of Abraham was already deeply rooted in the people – above all in respect of the promised land. At all events, the prophet Ezekiel reports, not without a critical undertone, about people who despite the destruction of Jerusalem by the Babylonians in 587/6 remained in the land of Israel and evidently justified remaining in the 'ruins' by saying: 'Abraham was only one man, yet he got possession of the land; but we are many; the land is surely given us to possess' (33.24; cf. Isa.63.16).

Even prophets refer back

Here we already have the expression of a scheme which will also shape the great Abraham narratives: at the beginning the individual man – at the end the whole land. The fact that something has a tiny, weak beginning does give any indication about its end. It is permissible to hope. Moreover this hope is explictly nourished by Deutero-Isaiah ('Second Isaiah'), the prophet of the exile, specifically with reference to Abraham. For it is Deutero-Isaiah in particular, a prophet about whom we know nothing, and whose message is contained in Isaiah 40-55, who shortly before the downfall of the Babylonian empire emphasizes with an unprecedented wealth of imagery the might and power of God to change the fate of the downtrodden and exiled people for the better. Indeed this prophet does not hesitate to make God himself recall Abraham in an oracle of salvation, in order to goad the people on to persevere. The God of this prophet had already spoken beforehand of exiled Israel as the 'seed of my friend Abraham' in order to assure the people of his abiding faithfulness even in the distress of the exile. Now the prophet even makes God exclaim with an oath:

> Look to Abraham your father
> and to Sarah who bore you;
> for when he was but one I called him,
> and I blessed him and made him many.
> For the Lord will comfort Zion;
> he will comfort all her waste places,
> and will make her wilderness like Eden,
> her desert like the garden of the Lord;
> joy and gladness will be found in her,
> thanksgiving and the voice of song (51.2f.).

Abraham the 'friend of God'; Abraham and Sarah as father and mother of Israel: it becomes clear how much a prophet like Deutero-Isaiah is able to use the recollection of Abraham and Sarah both theologically and as a piece of crisis psychology. Moreover the story of Abraham and Sarah and the 'promise of land' and 'assurance of the covenant' which is given to them by God is also to be set against 'the crisis and lack of perspective in their own situation as a potential of hope which will overcome it'.[4] Or to put it another way, the fact that 'interest in Abraham revived in the exilic and post-exilic age reflects the mood of crisis which was caused by the loss of the land and the fall of the Davidic monarchy. It was natural for people to refer to the covenant tradition which assured Israel the possession of the land by a divine oath.'[5]

The collection of the 'Five Books of Moses'

It is in keeping with this that already during the exile a beginning was made on gathering together into five books the stories from the creation of the world and of the first human being (Gen.1) to the exodus of the people from Egypt and the death of Moses (Deut.34), which had been in circulation for centuries, fixing them in writing and finally editing them. We do not know precisely what Ezra's 'book with the Torah of Moses' contained. Many exegetes think that it comprised the five books of Moses (the Pentateuch) almost complete, in the form familiar to us. Others are more restrained and believe that the Pentateuch as a whole was only completed at the beginning of the Hellenistic era, in the last third of the fourth century before Christ.[6] One thing, at any rate, can be said with certainty: 'by the end of the Persian period the law of Ezra had become what we know as the Penateuch'.[7] These books thus became the first sacred text to be canonical, i.e. to be binding on all; to it two further bodies of texts were added later (the Prophets, Hebrew *nebi'im*, and 'the Writings', Hebrew *ketubim*). These finally formed the Hebrew Bible, the Tenak (Tenak is an artificial word formed of the initial Hebrew consonants of the three bodies of text mentioned, Torah, Nebi'im, Ketubim, with added vowels to make them pronounceable).

With the Pentateuch the book of Genesis also reached its final form, with the completion of the latest source (P = Priestly Writing), which is similarly to be dated after the exile. And with this book the 'patriarchal and matriachal stories' which had originally been handed down orally became part of the canon of the people of Israel. Here everything that was known or was thought to be worth recalling of the prehistory of Israel was fixed once and for all in writing. Here it all now finally emerged from the darkness of history into the light of memory, which will burn as long as there is a people of Israel: Abraham, his father Terah, his brothers Nahor and Haran, his nephew Lot and his wives Hagar and Sarah. Here everything was collected which over the centuries had accumulated into the firm structure of the Abraham narrative and in which people had seen the deep meaning of the story of Abraham for Israel. First of all comes the series of ancestors from the primeval ages of creation, in which the family of humankind is traced back to the sons of Noah who with their father are the only ones to survive the flood: Shem, Ham and Japhet. Then there is the link with the clan of Abraham, since Terah, Abraham's father, is descended from Noah's son Shem (11.20-24). Finally, as far as Abraham himself is concerned, there is the link with the great sanctuaries of Shechem and Bethel which later become so important in the stories of Jacob: the exodus of Abraham from his home in Mesopotamia as an anticipation of the exodus, which will later be depicted at length in the story of Moses; Abraham's migration to Canaan; the settlement, on which much is later concentrated; and finally God's covenant with Abraham, as an anticipation of the revelation of God on Sinai, without which Israel would not have become what it is. So the whole history of the people of Israel transparently leads to Abraham, is as it were anticipated in the personal fate of Abraham. Now this 'composition'[8] had come into being.

3. Everything depends on Abraham: the book of Genesis

We are now prepared for gathering up the threads and evaluating in context the stories of Abraham in the book of Genesis. If here we think not only structurally but genetically, we find ourself in a labyrinth of research, since the more recent source or documentary theory (with the four sources: Yahwist, Elohist, Deuteronomy, Priestly Writing) which was largely accepted for the Pentateuch in the nineteenth century has been completely shaken; indeed some scholars have even brought it crashing down. Furthermore, the trend which first developed in scholarship to date even the earliest tradition in the Pentateuch (the Yahwist) as late as possible[9] has been replaced by the even more radical approach which dispenses with hypotheses about sources altogether and attributes everything to the theological creativity of the exilic and post-exilic period.

I cannot take this highly controversial discussion further here or adopt a particular standpoint on highly controversial questions of detailed exegesis. So instead I shall adopt a systematic structural approach, without completely excluding the historical dimension. For the texts themselves still indicate (for example, through count-less doublets and contradictory details) that they were not written all 'of a piece', however much they demonstrably form units of a later 'composition'. Thus if we note what the texts themselves indicate, the source theory which has been utilized so far provides the best model of explanation.[10] If with a still considerable number of present-day exegetes we presuppose this, then in essentials we can distinguish three stimuli towards creating the Abraham narratives. The earliest texts may still go back to the 'Yahwist', a theologian (or school of theologians) from the period of the monarchy; they need not of course be dated in a static way to the period of the empire of David and Solomon, but could have been active throughout the period of the monarchy until the downfall of the northern kingdom in 722 BCE. Later these and possibly other ('Elohistic') texts underwent a Deuteronomistic revision (the 'Jehovist'); the period of 'Deuteronomy' can extend from the time of King Josiah (620-609 in Judah) far into the time of the exile. The latest texts in the Pentateuch may still be attributed to the 'Priestly Writing' of the exile or the early post-exilic period.[11]

Thus many generations have contributed to the Abraham material that has come down to us. It is clear that this could not give rise to a well-rounded, fully consistent and smoothly polished picture of Abraham. There can be no question of a constructing a biography of Abraham from the existing texts, nor should there be[12] – despite the various pieces of information about places and ages which the text itself discloses to us. We are told of the birth of Abraham in Ur of the Chaldaeans on the lower course of the Euphrates (in southern Mesopotamia) and his move to Haran on the Belihos, a tributary of the Euphrates (in north-western Mesopotamia). From there he emigrated to Canaan at the age of seventy-five (together with his wife Sarah and nephew Lot). His son Ishmael was born when he was eighty-six (Ishmael's mother was the Egyptian slave girl Hagar), he was circumcised at the age of ninety-nine and fathered his son Isaac at the age of one hundred (Isaac's mother was Abraham's own wife Sarah). After Sarah's death he married a second wife, Keturah, and fathered six further sons. Finally he died at the age of one hundred and seventy-five and was buried in the cave of Machpelah near Mamre (present-day Hebron) beside his wife Sarah, who had died at the age of one hundred and twenty-seven, by his two sons Ishmael and Isaac. However, these pieces of information form only the fixed points on the map of a life which lists in a most unsystematic fashion events of very varied importance.

It would take us too far here to go into all the dimensions of the Abraham stories, important though they became for later Judaism: Abraham the resolute general, Abraham the welcoming host or Abraham the stubborn trader. Instead, I shall bring out those high points which have made Abraham theologically so irreplaceable and so indispensable. We need to answer quite briefly and basically the question 'Why is Abraham so central?' What is so important about his figure that even a prophet like Deutero-Isaiah can speak in a quite matter-of-fact way of 'our father Abraham'? Why can there be no people of Israel and subsequently also no Judaism without Abraham?

The remarkable strangeness of Abraham

These questions are all the more urgent when we come to realize that there must already have been something special about Abraham for Israel to have remembered him in particular over the centuries – depite the silence of so many important witnesses. For if we look closely, in many respects Abraham embodies the opposite of the 'pious Israelite', not to mention the orthodox Jew. Indeed we do not find anything at all in Abraham of what later goes to make up 'Jewishness'. Despite all the retouching of the picture of Abraham, despite the way in which he has been commandeered for a later Jewish piety, the Abraham texts of Genesis still show glimmers of the original strangeness of Abraham:

1. Abraham was not an Israelite, but a man from Mesopotamia who migrated into Canaan. Moreover all his life, in this land, too, he felt himself to be a 'stranger and sojourner' (23.4), knowing that he had been an emigrant (24.7) and remained a 'displaced' person, whose 'homeland' (24.7) lay elsewhere. That explains why, for example, Abraham's purchase of a piece of land near Mamre (with the cave which would become his tomb and that of his wife) is told at such striking length (ch.23). For this is the first land that the semi-nomad Abraham acquires in Canaan. And that also explains why Rebecca, the wife for Abraham's son Isaac, has to be got from Abraham's homeland and even from his own family: there must be no mingling with an 'alien people', the Canaanites (24.3). So Abraham never felt 'at home' in Canaan.

2. Yahweh as the God of Israel was unknown to Abraham. According to all that the sources say, Abraham worshipped his own God, who is also always called 'the God of Abraham' (24.27). Certainly our texts, beginning with the 'Yahwist', take great pains to depict Abraham as a Yahweh worshipper who built the altars at Bethel, Shechem and Mamre to none other than Yahweh. But at the same time the Pentateuch has retained an awareness that this is a later theological construction. Abraham was no Yahwist, no worshipper of Yahweh. Moreover Yahweh first appears in the book of Exodus in connection with Moses and his revelation on Mount Sinai. Yahweh is not the god of the hill country and the cultivated land in which the patriarchs lived, but the god of the wilderness. Moreover in the book of Exodus there is a passage which still allows us to follow the theological construction with the help of which the 'gods' of the fathers, the God of Abraham, the God of Isaac and the God of Jacob, were later identified with Yahweh:

> And God said to Moses, 'I am the Lord. I appeared to Abraham, to Isaac, and to Jacob, as God Almighty, but by my name Yahweh I did not make myself known to them' (Ex.6.2f.).

Moreover, since the 1929 study by the Old Testament scholar Albrecht Alt on the 'God of the Fathers', exegetes have concluded that the form of religion represented by Abraham and the other 'patriarchs' was 'polytheistic'[13] and 'monolatric'.[14] In other words, the patriarchs of Israel took for granted the existence of several gods, but in any clan only worshipped their 'own' god. The gods of the 'fathers' are 'not, or at any rate not originally, tied to holy places', but 'to persons and their followers: to the patriarchs whose name they bear'.[15]

3. Abraham's God was not worshipped in a temple. Certainly, we have to be careful about what can reliably be said about Abraham's personal piety. But the sources at least indicate that Abraham was not a priest and had no connection with priests, regardless of what the brief enigmatic episode involving the Canaanite priest-king Melchizedek (Gen.14.18-20) may mean — it falls completely outside the framework of the other stories. Be this as it may, Abraham's worship of his God was quite different in character from the later temple cult which existed from the time of the monachy on. There is no trace of temple practices and priesthood in the earliest stories; no

trace of the practice of a politicized religion organized by the state. Everything that was to characterize the later Yahweh religion is lacking here: there is nothing national or political; no official cult and no national salvation history.

And instead? Instead there is a markedly peaceful religious atmosphere without 'the exclusiveness and intolerance which were later to become so characteristic of Yahweh religion'.[16] The 'polytheistic' type of religion which is mentioned, with the patriarchs as the bearers of revelation and theophanies at cult places, may explain the 'basically peaceful mood of Genesis': 'There are no flashes of lightning, and God deals with human beings almost as though they were his equals.'[17] Moreover all in all, here we have the kind of religious feeling which is characteristic of families, a 'typical family piety'[18] which has 'almost no religious separation and polemic'.[19] And Abraham builds the altar for his God alongside the altars for other gods, in both Shechem and Bethel, which were originally the sites of Canaanite sanctuaries (Gen.12.6-9).

4. Abraham did not yet know the Torah. Whatever the later Jewish texts were to make of Abraham, the sources are clear that it was not Abraham but Moses who received the Torah on Mount Sinai. So Abraham did not practise an archaic Torah piety, nor was he an early Torah scholar or a primal rabbi. Here one of the sources, the exilic/post-exilic 'Priestly Writing', is already interested in a 'legalistic' view of Abraham by emphasizing that Abraham's circumcision is the sign of the covenant (17.24). But according to 'P', no more can be made of Abraham than this. Moreover, nowhere is it said that Abraham fulfilled further commandments. According to Genesis, all that God requires of Abraham is, 'Walk before me and be blameless' (17.1). Abraham is simply to 'keep the way of the Lord by doing righteousness and justice' (18.19). The fact remains that like the revelation of Yahweh's name, so the revelation of Yahweh's will in the form of the Torah is something for later Israel, not for Abraham. So it has rightly been noted that the religion of Abraham consists simply in 'one credal element (the belief in God), one ethical element (righteousness and justice), and one ritual element (circumcision)'.[20]

Thus the question with which we started returns with even greater emphasis: if Abraham was not at all what a pious Jew needed to be, if he was so 'different', why did Israel attach so much importance to him in particular over the centuries? Why did it do so although at the latest in the exile it had moved so far from Abraham in its piety? And why did people refer back to him even after the exile, although all the reformers (and particularly Nehemiah and Ezra) had only one interest:

– The exclusiveness of Yahweh religion: no cultic worship of other gods.
– The purity of the people: no mixing with non-Israelite families.
– Cultic unity in the temple: no worship of Yahweh outside Jerusalem.
– Obedience to the Torah: the subjection of the whole of everyday life to God's commandments.

And there is no trace of any of this with Abraham! What does that mean? Why, despite everything, is there so much interest in this peculiar figure, this 'stranger and sojourner'? Why was there an unwillingness in Israel to let the history of the own people begin without Abraham (and the other 'fathers' and mothers')? There are many answers to the question,[21] of which one seems to me to be particularly important. Too much depended on Abraham for it to be possible to dispense with him. What did? God's promise of a specific land and of the prosperity of a specific people. For without Abraham there would have been no Isaac or Jacob, and without Jacob there would not have been the twelve tribes. Abraham is indispensable because he is the witness and guarantor of indispensable, permanent 'promises', indeed of God's covenant commitment to Israel. We need to look at all of this more closely.

Guarantor of God's promises: people, land, peoples

If we take a cross-section of the Abraham stories, we find that God's promise to Abraham has three dimensions. They do not always appear in a neat systematic way in all the passages at the same time, but they form the nucleus, the permanent principle, of all the Abraham stories and give these stories their unity. They all thus have a surprising theological focus, which shows that here we have a well-thought-out and profound theology of Abraham.

1. God promises Abraham that he will have descendants, and that these descendants will become 'a great people' (12.2). This will prove true of Abraham in particular, an 'individual' with no further family

support, an elderly husband whose wife Sarah, too, has had no children and who would be happy to be in a position to father just one descendant. The tension in the Abraham stories lies precisely at this point, between the promises of God which intensify in the course of the narratives (as numerous 'as the dust of the earth', 13.16; as the 'stars of heaven', 15.5) and the miserable reality of the man Abraham: 'Shall a child be born to a man who is a hundred years old? Shall Sarah, who is ninety years old, bear a child?' (17.17). This is a tension which can seem so comical to Abraham that he even has to laugh at God, as Sarah does later – a laugh of despair at God and his promises: 'Then Abraham fell on his face and laughed' (17.17).

But this is the theological point of this promise. God chooses what is apparently impossible to achieve his goals: the birth of Isaac, from whom Jacob/Israel will descend, will come about. So Abraham and Sarah are real symbols of a dialectic of the divine action: the barren will become fertile; the doubters will be rewarded. God himself allows the laughing doubt of man and woman and transforms it into a shared joy, so that after Isaac's birth Sarah can say: 'God has made laughter for me; everyone who hears will laugh over me' (21.6). Moreover her son is called 'Isaac', which literally means 'God laughs'.[22] And what is the meaning of this story? It has constantly to remind Israel that its existence is not to be taken for granted; Israel does not derive from its own merits but solely from God's grace, since by 'human possibilities' Israel's existence would have been impossible. Israel exists only because God wills it.

It is understandable why Israel did not want to dispense with this particular story, this story of unexpected good fortune and a great future, particularly in times of crisis. For the future generations know what Abraham could not have known: Abraham and Sarah's descendants really did become as numerous as the dust of the earth and the stars of heaven. So especially in the catastrophes of history, this narrative remains an anchor of hope. Just as God had promised Noah not to destroy creation again, so God promised Abraham once and for all that he would make his people great and bless them for all times, come what might. So Israel could trust that in Abraham the people was preserved for all times. As long as it kept to Abraham it would not go under.

2. God promises Abraham and his descendants the land of Canaan. Abraham in particular, the 'stranger', the 'sojourner', the

'Hebrew' (14.13)! He has less right to this land than others, since it is not even his homeland and he personally has never understood it nor claimed it as such. 'Hebrew' here does not yet mean membership of a people but social status, a lesser status, a lowly status. The descriptions of the land which in the course of the narrative are similarly heightened and made more specific – in ways corresponding to the interests of the different sources – are all the more striking:

> To your descendants I will give this land (12.7; cf. 14.7).
> For all the land which you see I will give to you and to your descendants for ever (1.15).
> To your descendants I give this land, from the river of Egypt to the great river, the river Euphrates, the land of the Kenites, the Kenizzites, the Kadmonites, the Hittites, the Perizzites, the Rephaim, the Amorites, the Canaanites, the Girgashites and the Jebusites (15.18-21).

But the more grandiose these descriptions of the land are, the more powerful the theological point they make. God chose the 'stranger', the one without property, who stood outside the social classes, to bestow a homeland on him. Here, too, Abraham is the symbol of a dialectic of the divine action: the one with nothing becomes the landowner; the stranger becomes the one who lives in a homeland which has been given to him. And this land is a gift of God. What is the meaning of this story? Israel is to be reminded once and for all that the 'land of Canaan' is not to be taken for granted; it is not something that has been earned and is legally recoverable, but rests solely on God's free promise; it is pure gift, perfect grace.

It is understandable why particularly in times of crisis Israel did not want to be without the memory of Abraham, in times when the land had been lost and the promises of God seemed to have been revoked. But in Abraham the land remains promised 'for ever'. If the people stand by Abraham, God will not go back on his promise: 'And I will give to you, and to your descendants after you, the land of your sojournings, all the land of Canaan, for an everlasting possession; and I will be their God' (17.8).

3. Through Abraham God promises blessing to all the peoples on earth. Through Abraham in particular! Through a completely unknown local group which, like others, moves with its flocks

through the hill-country and the wilderness in an insignificant area on the map of the world. That makes this promise all the more amazing, a promise which significantly is bound up not only with Abraham but explicitly also with Abraham's wives, with Hagar and Sarah. For the wives, too, receive from God the promise of a vast number of important descendants (16.10; 17.16). The poistioning of the blessing on the peoples right at the beginning of the Abraham stories is also remarkable (12.3). It is remarkable because the reader of the book of Genesis still remembers all the stories of the catastrophes in which the peoples of the world have so far played a fatal role: the fall and thus the expulsion from paradise (Gen.3); Cain's murder of his brother Abel and thus the perversion of a humankind which was originally good (Gen.4); the flood and thus the annihilation by God himself of a creation which was originally good (Gen.6-9); and finally the building of the tower of Babel and thus the arrogant provocation of God (Gen.11). So when the peoples have been talked about so far, it has been only in the context of sin, annihilation, hybris. Certainly, God had already made a first covenant with Noah (Gen.9.8-17), and visibly endorsed it with the sign of the rainbow. But this covenant was about the preservation of creation generally. Only with Abraham, Hagar and Sarah does a history of blessing begin for a new humankind, which no longer stands under the threat of extermination.

But it may not be coincidence that the theme of the blessing of the peoples comes above all from two sources: the earliest, the Yahwist, and the latest, the exilic/post-exilic Priestly Writing. For the 'Yahwist' might well have had in mind the experience of the monarchy and thus the experience that Israel not only became a great people but also came to occupy a special position among the nations of the world. A universal, international perspective had opened up in the time of the monarchy in particular, under the impact of the empire of David and his son Solomon. Since then the peoples of the world had appeared on the horizon, either as conquered peoples or as rival great powers. So there was also a need for theological reflection on their position and function in God's plan for history.

The 'Yahwist' does this by connecting Israel and the peoples, particularism and universalism, in a theologically consistent way. He specifically recalls the man who comes from the 'peoples', Abraham, knowing that this man will be the father of Israel, a blessing for this great people. At the same time he knows that Abraham is destined as a mediator of blessing for the peoples and that Israel, too, thus has a function for the world of the nations, once and for all. Moreover in the key Yahwistic text we have a programme right at the beginning of the Abraham stories:

> And I will make of you a great people, and I will bless you, and make your name great, so that you will be a blessing. I will bless those who bless you, and him who curses you I will curse; and by you all the families of the earth shall bless themselves (12.2f.; cf. 18.17f.).

The mention of Abraham as progenitor which has also been handed down in the Priestly Writing belongs structurally in the same context. There is no longer any explicit mention of a 'blessing for the peoples', and we can understand this if we remember that the 'Priestly Writing' had to come to terms with the experience of the exile. This experience meant that Israel had come under the power of the peoples, was dispersed among the nations, lived abroad under the rule of other empires. God's promise to Abraham had clearly been reversed: instead of being a blessing to the peoples Israel had become a curse; instead of Israel mediating God's blessing to the peoples, the peoples were triumphing over Israel.

Nevertheless the Priestly Writing, too, reactivates God's promise to Abraham, which speaks of his fertility:

> You shall be the father of a multitude of nations. No longer shall your name be Abram, but your name shall be Abraham (father of a multitude); for I have made you the father of a multitude of nations. I will make you exceedingly fruitful; and I will make nations of you, and kings shall come forth from you (17.4-6).

Such a line of thought may have emerged in the first place from the need of the people for comfort and their hope that they would survive the storms of history, since God had promised the father of Israel such potential fertility. But there is also no mistaking the fact that the 'Priestly Writing' still shows an 'amazing generosity towards other people, most of who are hostile to Israel'.[23] And this mention of the peoples possibly served to legitimate a life which was now necessary: if one reflects on Abraham, the peoples must not be obsessively rejected, since Abraham was already destined by God to be the ancestor of a multitude of such peoples.

This universalistic feature of the Abraham stories is further made concrete by the importance which is attached in the texts of the Yahwist and the Priestly Writing, over and above their emphasis on the descendants of Abraham (Jacob/Israel), to the incorporation of Abraham/Israel into the community of neighbouring south-eastern and eastern peoples who are felt to be related. For there is explicit emphasis on the Arabian tribes as descendants of Hagar-Ishmael and Keturah (Gen 25.1-6, 12-18). The Ammonites and Moabites are regarded as descendants of Lot, Abraham's nephew; the Edomites as descendants of Esau, Jacob's brother. This is meant to make it clear that Abraham is the origin of a whole network of peoples at a greater or lesser remove from Israel. So Abraham's presence is also given in these peoples.

Thus the decisive theological point of these texts is:

(a) Israel sees its way among the peoples of the earth anticipated in Abraham. Just as Abraham, on receiving the call to set out, detached himself from all natural ties and went his own way at God's behest, so too Israel as God's people feels itself detached from the community of the peoples and destined to go its own way. Furthermore, the 'Yahwist' already conceived the provocative theology that the blessing and curse of the other peoples depend on their attitude to Abraham (and thus ultimately to Israel). For it is evidently God's will not to communicate himself to the other peoples other than through Abraham/Israel. Abraham/Israel thus becomes the blessing for all the families of the earth if these families 'bless' him, i.e. recognize him and have friendly relations with him; and he becomes a curse if the opposite happens. This creates a relationship of mutual dependence between Abraham/Israel on the one hand and the peoples on the other. The destiny of the peoples is profoundly bound up with the destiny of Israel.[24]

(b) At the same time, in order to avoid misunderstandings, it has to be added that the text of the blessing of the peoples has a universal dimension. God's blessing for Abraham is not an exclusive possession of Israel; it is not a blessing for Israel alone. God's blessing extends beyond Israel, and embraces people who do not stand in the line of Abraham, Isaac and Jacob. The 'Yahwist' already conceived a theological notion which is bold in its magnitude and breadth: the power and scope of the blessing of Abraham is literally universal. Abraham is not a mediator of salvation exclusively for Israel, but the new beginning of a history of blessing for renewed humankind which has been made possible by God (after the fall, the chaos of the flood and the building of the tower of Babel).

Here too we again see the same dialectic of God's action: through God the insignificant becomes significant, a small people becomes the instrument of God's great purpose of salvation with all peoples. Remarkably, enigmatically, enough, God has chosen for himself a people (one of the smallest and most insignificant peoples) to be a mediator of blessing for all peoples, as a way of becoming a God for all peoples, again out of pure grace, in full freedom. The meaning of this story is clear: Israel is to be preserved both from triumphalistic self-isolation (we are better than other peoples) and from despairing feelings of inferiority (we are weaker than all other peoples). Israel is not either to shut itself off in a particularistic way (we are against all the others) or to dissolve itself universalistically (we are like all the others). Rather, it is to live out particularism and universalism at the same time; they are not a contradiction. Why not? Because both are already reconciled in Abraham. Abraham is the ancestor of the people of Israel and at the same time the ancestor of 'a multitude of peoples' on whom God also wills to bestow his blessing. So we can endorse Claus Westermann's comment: 'God's action proclaimed in the promise to Abraham is not limited to him and his posterity, but reaches its goal only when it includes all the families of the earth.'[25]

Partner in God's second covenant

In the course of the process of tradition all these promises made to Abraham are given a theological focus and culminate in the key category of 'covenant'. God does not just give Abraham 'promises'; he formally concludes a covenant with him. We know from critical work on the texts of the First Testament that 'covenant theology' did not come right at the beginning of all of Israel's theology, but arose only later (above all through Deuteronomy). Here the covenant with Abraham may have been conceived on the model of the Sinai covenant – projected backwards – in which Moses endorsed the observance of the covenant document by sprinkling the people with sacrificial blood: 'Behold the blood of the covenant which the Lord has made with you in accordance with all these words' (Ex.24.8). Moreover the background to Genesis 15, a chapter influenced by Deuteronomy and going back to the 'Jehovist', is a sacrifice by

Abraham involving blood and a sacrificial animal, in which God is present in the symbol of fire:

> When the sun had gone down and it was dark, behold a smoking fire pot and a flaming torch passed between these pieces. On that day the Lord made a covenant with Abram, saying, 'To your descendants I give this land, from the river of Egypt to the great river, the river Euphrates' (15.17f.).

But what is the content of the covenant here? It is the promise of the land. So it is not surprising that it is not the 'Yahwist' but only the 'Jehovist', influenced by Deuteronomy, who for the first time uses the category of covenant to interpret the story of Abraham. For he might have had in mind the downfall of the northern kingdom of 'Israel' at the hands of the Assyrians[26] in 722 and that of the southern kingdom of Judah with the capital Jerusalem in 586 at the hands of the Babylonians. And he may well have explained this political failure in good Deuteronomistic style by the breaking of the Sinai covenant and the apostasy of the people from Yahweh. And what about the reference back to the covenant with Abraham? It needed the endorsement of the faithfulness of God, above all in relation to the land which was in danger or lost. Moreover the 'Jehovist' explicitly associates the making of the covenant with the promise of land (15.18-21). For him the whole land of Canaan is the saving gift of Yahweh promised to the patriarchs.

The 'covenant' once again stands right at the centre of the Priestly Writing's theology of Abraham. Here the key text is Genesis 17. Three things are striking in it. First, even statistically, it is remarkable that the key word 'covenant' appears thirteen times in Genesis 17, almost in every sentence, while it does not recur later in other texts of the Abraham narratives. Secondly, the covenant no longer applies just personally to Abraham, as in the 'Jehovist', but explicitly also to Abraham's descendants – 'generation upon generation', as is often emphasized. And thirdly, this covenant is no longer limited in time, but in the Priestly Writing is now designated on several occasions an 'eternal covenant' (17.7, 13, 19). And its content? Alongside the promise of numerous descendants, here too it is a promise of land: 'And I will give to you, and to your descendants after you, the land of your sojournings, all the land of Canaan, for an everlasting possession; and I will be their God' (17.8).

We have to be clear what 'covenant' means here and in the future for Israel and Judaism. Here 'covenant' does not mean some two-sided treaty in the modern sense between two partners with equal rights, each of whom could break it off at any time. Rather, the decisive thing about this 'covenant' is that it is the utterly voluntary, gracious, commitment by God himself to the well-being of the people. To be specific, God commits himself to being the covenant partner of a particular people without any prior action on the human side: 'I will establish my covenant between me and you and your descendants after you' (17.7). So the decisive content of this covenant is its theocentric perspective; it is decisive, because it contains notions which are important for the consolation and survival of the people of Israel, especially in times of crisis and catastrophe. However much the people may have sinned against God's covenant ordinance, as the making of the covenant is not dependent on human achievements, so too the abolition of the covenant is not dependent on human failures. God has freedom over his covenant, no matter what human beings may do with it. He alone determines whether or not there will be this covenant.

But at the same time human beings must meet the obligations of the divine covenant. So that they can do this, the Priestly Writing first of all introduces a sign of the divine covenant on the human side: circumcision of the male foreskin. The 'Priestly Writing' did not invent circumcision; it had been a custom among the Israelites since they settled in Canaan and was originally an initiation into marriage or into the communal life of the tribe. But now – under the conditions of the Babylonian exile – this custom took on a quasi-cultic function, especially as Israel's major neighbours, like the Philistines, the Bablyonians and the Assyrians, did not know circumcision. So with this sign they could set themselves apart from these neighbours all the more clearly, and with it give physical expression to their special position – which was important for survival under the conditions of the exile.

In this way circumcision became a theological symbol and acquired deep historical significance: it is the constant reminder to each individual of his membership of an elect people and at the same time a sign of his duty to God's commandments. Indeed, just how serious the 'Priestly Writing' takes this rite of circumcision emerges not only from the legal precision with which it is ordained (including an exclusion formula if it is not carried out), but also from the speed with which Abraham carries it out. Abraham (at the age of ninety-nine) carries out God's commandment 'the same day' on himself, his son Ishmael (who is thirteen) and all the males who are in his house.

The primal model of faith: being on the way

God's commitment is matched by commitment from the human side – the Abraham narrative leaves no doubt about that. Just as Yahweh, the God of Israel, has continually believed in his people despite everything, so must Israel for its part trust in Yahweh. More than any other figure in the Pentateuch, Abraham stands for this twofold aspect of trust in God and at the same time trust from human beings in return. Indeed, all the Abraham texts seek to give a concrete indication of what faith requires. The Abraham theology of Genesis is fundamentally a narrative anthropology of faith. It relates what human beings do if they really believe. They trust God's word and promise – through all doubt, all scepticism and all hesitation.

Moreover in the course of his story Abraham is required to have faith in this sense:

– Solely at the word of God he abandons all his natural ties (family and homeland) and sets off into the unknown: 'Go' (12.1).
– Despite the manifest physical impossibility, he is to trust in God's promise of descendants: 'Look towards heaven and number the stars' (15.5).
– Despite laughing doubt and manifest anxiety ('O that Ishmael might live in your sight', 17.18), Abraham is to follow God's instructions: 'It shall be done' (17.11).
– Despite the torment of a long wait, despite the fulfilment of a long-desired wish (the birth of his son Isaac), he is to give this son back again, indeed to slaughter him: 'Take your son, your only son, whom you love' (22.2).

If we look closely at Abraham's way we discover that his faith is quite a complex one. There is no trace of blind readiness to follow, of an irrational act of the will, of the obedience of an automaton. Abraham's faith is tested by a long experience of life. And because this is the case, this faith is made up of quite different ingredients: there is a touch of doubt and a touch of cunning, a touch of anxiety and a touch of risk-taking with his God; a touch of wordless obedience and a touch of canny haggling. This faith includes humble sacrifice to this God and bold negotiations to spare innocent human beings. Here is a unique profile: faith as a process of setting out despite everything: despite all reservations, despite all gnashing of the teeth, despite all anxiety. Thomas Mann may have been fundamentally correct in his psychological portrait of Abraham when in his long novel *Joseph and his Brothers* he describes this 'Ur-man' from Chaldaea as 'brooding and troubled', seized by an 'unrest of the spirit', 'unsatisfied and tormented'. It was 'spiritual restlessness' which set him going, 'a need for God' with a view to a new personal experience of God. So Abraham is a man of 'inner dissatisfaction, a traveller', whose 'novel experience of God was destined to shape the future'.[27]

In fact if we look at these original texts it is striking how often, with Abraham, trusting in God is identical with being on the way; it is no coincidence that his story begins with the programmatic word 'Go'. Go 'from your country and your kindred and your father's house to the land that I will show you'. So Abraham goes, as he himself will later say, 'unknowing' (20.13), into the openness of an imponderable future. Here his history contrasts with that of another great wanderer of ancient culture, Odysseus, who in the end is allowed to return to Ithaca, his homeland. Not so with Abraham. As the French Jewish philosopher Emanuel Levinas rightly points out, he leaves his fatherland 'for ever' to 'set out for an unknown land' – with no prospect of return. If Odysseus is the archetype of a movement back to the self and the known, Abraham is the archetype of a movement into the open and the unknown.[28] Moreover the key words of his form of existence are: go forth, wander, travel around, set out, go on. The basic rhythm of this life is one of settling and starting off again, waging war and making peace, fighting battles and concluding treaties.

Indeed, anyone who has even a little sense of the narrative character of the Abraham stories will continue to wonder even now at the drama and dynamic of the narratives. Hardly has Abraham arrived in the land given him by God than he must leave it again for Egypt, because there is a famine. Hardly has he arrived in Egypt than he must disguise his wife from the Pharaoh, because the Pharaoh lusts after her. Hardly has he returned from Egypt than there is a dispute in the 'promised land' over living space with his nephew Lot; wars are waged and the destruction of a city has to be averted. And all this is constantly overshadowed by the threat of definitive childlessness. However, hardly have his sons and heirs been born than there are jealous scenes between his main wife and his concubine, which can only be resolved by a brutal expulsion. And not long after the true son and heir comes into the world, a sacrificial test must be undergone.

Truly, the faith of Abraham and thus the faith of the reader of these stories in God's saving purpose with Israel and humankind must be powerful if God's commitment throughout such events is still to remain credible.[29] The realism of the texts emerges here in particular; however, Abraham is nowhere presented as a morally perfect monument to faith, but rather as a person with strengths and weaknesses.

Moreover, no story in Abraham's life has such depths as the so-called sacrifice of Isaac (Hebrew *akeda*). And it is no consolation that the aim of this story is in fact to narrate how the sacrificial slaughter was prevented (Gen.22). For once again Abraham has to 'arise', once again he has to go 'on his way', once again he must let go of what he 'loves most'. Here there is a parallel to the external exodus from Haran to Canaan symbolized by 'God' in the inner exodus symbolized by the word 'take'. Painters like Rembrandt, Christian thinkers like Søren Kierkegaard and Jewish philosophers like Martin Buber have been moved by this scene in the course of the centuries; they have painted it with words or colours; they have pondered it and become infuriated over it.[30] Here, in the book of Genesis, it has a clearly recognizable function: to show *in extremis* what it means to keep faith and not to stop trusting – despite all the impenetrable things that God requires.

No wonder that Jewish authors of our century like Eli Wiesel have seen this tremendous scene, where annihilation and redemption stand so close together, in particular as a primal image of Jewish faith, especially after the experience of the Shoah. Israel is like Isaac with the knife at its throat, and then has to go on living with the shadow of death behind it. Eli Wiesel understood how very topical this story is.

We have known Jews who like Abraham saw their sons sinking down in the name of the one who has no name. We have known children who like Isaac have suffered sacrifice in their own bodies, and others who went mad when they saw their father on the altar, disappearing with the altar in a cloud of fire reaching to the very height of heaven . . . Isaac survived; he had no choice. He owed it to himself to make something of his memories and his experience so that we would be compelled to hope. So our survival is bound up with his survival . . . Why does Isaac, the primal image of our tragic fate, have such an inappropriate name, a name which means laughter and provokes laughter? The reason is this: as the first survivor he teaches the survivors of future Jewish history that it is possible to suffer and doubt for a lifetime and nevertheless not to lose the art of laughter. Since then Isaac has never forgotten the terror of the scene which destroyed his youth. He will always remember the Holocaust and remain marked to the end of time. Nevertheless he is capable of laughter, and he does laugh. Nevertheless.[31]

4. The politicizing of Abraham between the Testaments

Given all that depends on Abraham for the people of Israel, can it be surprising that in the course of the centuries after the exile the veneration and transfiguration of his figure in Israel continued to increase? The prophet Deutero-Isaiah (41.5) already called Abraham the 'friend of God' (cf. II Chron.20.7). Not only Genesis calls him the 'servant of God', but so do other post-exilic texts, among which Joshua 24 and Psalm 105 in particular stand out.

Judaism as a 'descendant of Abraham': Joshua 24/Psalm 105

To match the exilic/post-exilic theology of history, the book of Joshua, which in other respects is part of the Deuteronomic history work, is given a second conclusion in chapter 24. This chapter was doubtless an independent literary unit and does not correspond to the rest of the 'Deuteronomic history work in the narrower sense'.[32] For in it the Abraham tradition plays a surprisingly independent role,[33] since the worship of Yahweh alone and thus the exclusion of any idolatry is not justified in terms of the Torah of Moses – as elsewhere in Deuteronomy – but in terms of Abraham. For this to be possible Abraham has suddenly to be depicted in his old homeland as the first monotheist and his father Terah as an idolater. Genesis does not say a word about this. But this text derives its authority above all from the fact that here Joshua's testament is given to Israel. And Joshua is no less a figure than Moses' successor, who was allowed to lead Israel definitively into the land of Canaan. That makes the text all the more important for Israel's self-understanding:

> Then Joshua gathered all the tribes of Israel to Shechem, and summoned the elders, the heads, the judges, and the officers of Israel; and they presented themselves before God. And Joshua said to all the people, 'Thus says the Lord, the God of Israel, "Your fathers lived of old beyond the Euphrates, Terah, the father of Abraham and of Nahor; and they served other gods. Then I took your father Abraham from beyond the River and led him through all the land of Canaan, and made his offspring many. I gave him Isaac . . . Now therefore fear the Lord, and serve him in sincerity and in faithfulness; put away the gods which your fathers served beyond the River, and in Egypt, and serve the Lord"' (24.1-4,14).

Indeed, the degree to which the role of Abraham had already taken on stereotyped, hymnic, features, is clear above all from Psalm 105, which depicts the history of Israel in the form of a hymn of thanksgiving:[34]

> Seek the Lord and his strength,
> seek his presence continually!
> Remember the wonderful works that he has done,
> his miracles, and the judgments he uttered.
> O offspring of Abraham his servant,
> sons of Jacob, his chosen ones!
> He is the Lord our God;
> his judgments are in all the earth.
> He is mindful of his covenant for ever,
> of the word that he commanded, for a thousand generations,
> the covenant which he made with Abraham,
> his sworn promise to Isaac,
> which he confirmed to Jacob as a statute,
> to Israel as an everlasting covenant.
> Saying, 'To you I will give the land of Canaan
> as your portion for an inheritance . . .'
> And he gave them the lands of the nations;
> and they took possession of the fruit of the peoples' toil,
> to the end that they should keep his statutes,
> and observe his laws (105.4-11, 44f.)

Here we should note that Joshua 24 and Psalm 105 already show important shifts of emphasis in the post-exilic picture of Abraham which is already emerging in Nehemiah 9, a passage that we have already discussed. The new political interests in Abraham are now as follows:

1. Abraham is once and for all the 'servant of God', an honorific title which is meant to express the special relationship of this one man to God: his submission to God and his unconditional trust in God on the one hand and at the same time his role as the 'instrument' of God's gracious election. Here other aspects tend to get lost.

2. Israel proudly calls itself the 'descendants of Abraham' or the 'people of the God of Abraham' (Ps.47.10).[35] Now Abraham and the line through Isaac and Jacob is the only decisive one. It has become the hallmark of Israel, which gives it its identity in the face of all other peoples. The eternal covenant applies to Israel alone. A tendency towards an exclusivity of salvation is unmistakable.

3. This tendency can be seen above all in the relationship between Israel and the peoples, which reveals itself in these texts. For in Joshua 24 Abraham is clearly celebrated as the model of a monotheistic champion of the faith who is to legitimate the fight against the idols of the time ('Put away the gods'). Nothing is left here of Abraham's readiness for peace which is shown in Genesis, or of the blessing for the world of the peoples. According to Psalm 105, God has rather given the people of Israel the 'lands of the peoples' for a possession. Israel does not bless but rules. And the picture of Abraham in post-exilic Judaism will now develop further in this direction.

A self-portrait with Abraham: Ben Sirach

Beyond doubt this Abraham theology reaches its climax in the middle of the second century BCE. In the meantime the historical, political and spiritual cultural situation in Judaea had been exposed to extreme tensions. For more than a century (from 304) this land had been able to undergo a relatively peaceful development. But now (finally after 200), in their great-power politics, the Hellenistic ruling dynasty of the Seleucids, which originally came from Babylon, also had the land of Judaea under totalitarian control, with the result that – above all under King Antiochus IV Epiphanes (175-164) – it increasingly suffered cultural and religious oppression. The tensions among the people between adaptation to Hellenistic culture and the preservation of their own Jewish traditions began to increase in a threatening way.

This is the situation in which the Jewish scribe Ben Sira produced a book (Jesus Sirach, composed between 190 and 175 BCE) that gives unique expression to the tension between the Jewish heritage and the Hellenistic-pagan culture of the time. For motivated by a 'deep antipathy to the Seleucid oppression and its Jewish supporters', Ben Sira now resolutely decides for loyalty to the Jewish heritage, for pride in the 'Jewish fathers'.[36] With the utmost self-confidence he therefore makes it clear to his environment 'that Judaism was no obscure religion in a distant enclave of the civilized word but was on the same level as the religious and philosophical trends of this world'. As a matter of course this theologian wants to emphasize 'to the educated world that reason, the wisdom which everyone seeks in order to get the utmost from life, was to be found among the Jews; the God of the Jews had already set it in the word in creation, indeed divine wisdom had itself shared in the work of creation (thus Sirach 24.1-11)'.[37]

Ben Sira derives his pride above all from looking at the history of Israel, the history of an 'honoured people', as he puts it. So his theology of history in particular is at the service of a self-portrait of Jewish culture to rival the now dominant world culture of Hellenism.[38] Nor does Ben Sira hesitate to praise the 'famous men' of Jewish history, 'our fathers in their generations' (44.1). The great are summoned to testify: Moses and Aaron, the judges and the prophets, and – of course – Abraham, too. He is now spoken of in the style of a wisdom hymn:

Abraham was the great father of a multitude of nations,
and no one has been found like him in glory;
he kept the law of the Most High,
and was taken into covenant with him;
he established the covenant in his flesh,
and when he was tested he was found faithful.
Therefore the Lord assured him by an oath
that the nations would be blessed through his posterity;
that he would multiply him like the dust of the earth,
and exalt his posterity like the stars,

and cause them to inherit from sea to sea
and from the river to the ends of the earth (44.19-21).

What is striking about this text is not only the retouching of the portrait of Abraham, the reduction of his complex and problematical features to the portrait to a perfect, pure man. It is also the high status that the Torah of Moses now has in an Abraham text. For the fact that Abraham observed 'the commandment of the Most High' is not only mentioned in second place but is also the presupposition of the covenant, of the free commitment on God's part. Moreover the mention of circumcision in third place – at God's command – fits into this 'legalistic' picture of Abraham.

These, too, are remarkable shifts of accent. They could be described as a moralizing of Abraham. In post-exilic Judaism Abraham has become a morally immaculate man. Why? Because he is exemplary in his fulfilment of the Torah (as can be seen, for example, from his circumcision), and in this way in his well-tried loyalty to faith. The fulfilment of the Torah on the human side is matched by the covenant promise on God's side. The presupposition of God's keeping of his oath is the obedience of faith. This already foreshadows a feature of the Jewish picture of Abraham: Abraham's faith is in fact identical with obedience to the Torah. Abraham becomes a figure with whom Judaism loyal to the law can identify.

Radical separation: the spirit of Qumran

The historical and political situation in Palestine in the three centuries around the beginning of the Christian era (second/first century BCE to the first century CE) was generally very unstable. The reason for that was doubtless the brutally aggressive expansionist policy of the Seleucids. They sought not only military and political but also cultural and religious domination of their subject peoples. In Judaea this took the form of an unprecedented 'forcible Hellenization': the temple was plundered, Jerusalem was devastated, and pagan cults were imposed, including the worship of the imperial god Zeus Olympios and even worship of the ruler in the temple of Yahweh. This was unheard-of blasphemy.

The people itself was polarized. The upper class largely adapted to the new conditions and joined in the game of Hellenization. Cultural assimilation was the fascination of the time. Indeed the reform party of the time in Jerusalem, well disposed towards Hellenism, did not hesitate even to construct their links with Greece by genealogies, in so doing going back to Abraham. At this time the legend of the affinity of the Jews with the Spartans, which was presumably already an old one, was revived; it could now serve the interests of foreign policy. The Spartans were 'brothers of the Jews' since 'both were descended from Abraham' (I Macc.12.21). It is no coincidence that the author of the Hellenistic reform in Jerusalem, the shadowy high priest Jason, then decided to flee from Palestine to Sparta via Egypt (II Macc.5.9). What was the starting point for this fictitious kinship? It may have been the account of the descendants of Keturah (Gen.25.1-6) which was now elaborated further. The Tübingen New Testament scholar Martin Hengel has made further conjectures: 'Speculations of this kind were helped on by the fact that there was a certain analogy between the Jews and the Spartans with their strict laws, their lawgivers Moses and Lycurgus and the divine authorization on Sinai or through Delphian Apollo. Just as the Jews, even according to the first Greek account of Hecataeus of Abdera, led a "xenophobic life", so according to Herodotus the Lacedaimonians were regarded as xenophobic, and while Lycurgus, the Spartan lawgiver, was designated "friend of Zeus" by the oracle at Delphi, so, according to Exod.33.11, God talked with Moses "as with a friend".'[39]

By contrast, other parts of the populace reacted to the Hellenistic cultural shock with radical repudiation, either political or religious. For many people the perspective was revolt or systematic withdrawal, rebellion or emigration. The way of open political rebellion was taken by the Maccabee brothers – Judas (166-160), Jonathan (160-142) and Simeon (143-134) – and the circles close to them when they achieved rule. They fulfilled the testament of their father Mattathias, a passionate champion of the Torah. It is no coincidence that in this connection, at a difficult time, Mattathias had evoked Abraham's loyalty to faith. Here, too, is a variant of the theme that I have already mentioned: righteousness in faith before God is the result of loyalty to the Torah. This is what Mattathias says to his sons on his death-bed:

Remember the deeds of the fathers, which they did in their generations; and receive great honour and an everlasting name. Was not Abraham found faithful when tested, and it was reckoned to him as righteousness? . . . My children, be courageous and grow strong in the law, for by it you will gain honour. Now behold, I know that Simeon your brother is wise in counsel; always listen to him: he shall be your father. Judas Maccabaeus has been a mighty warrior from his youth; he shall command the army for you and fight the battle against the peoples . . . Avenge the wrong done to your people. Pay back the Gentiles in full, and heed what the law commands (I Macc.2.51-52, 64-68).

And indeed Judas the Maccabean continues the battle against the wicked aliens utterly in the spirit of his father. There are countless battles, attacks and political manoeuvres, the political consequences of which could not be seen at the time, when Judas summoned the rising world power of Rome for help against the Selecuids (I Macc.8.1-32). After that, Rome's influence over Palestine could not be removed again.

People who were similarly antagonized by the assimilation policy of the priestly establishment in Jerusalem but drew other consequences from it took a second course. They retreated and formed separate communities (the Essene movement), for example in the Judaean wilderness, where, not far from Jerusalem, down by the Dead Sea, Qumran was founded around the year 150 BCE. They were called 'Hasidim', 'the pious', people who with a radical observance of the law turned away from their sinful environment. They regarded the wilderness as a place of salvation, because here God was no longer worshipped by impure priests but by people who were prepared to live consistently by the letter of the law. They were people who in rigorous segregation and with a consistent theology of cleanness rejected all compromises and expected an imminent judgment on the sinful world. After all that we have heard, it will hardly be thought surprising that Abraham was also used to endorse their views.[40]

A decisive piece of evidence for us here is the book of Jubilees, written in the spirit of Qumran. It was probably composed at the time of the military campaigns of the Maccabees between 145 and 140 BCE.[41] This writing shares with Qumran an interest in the calendar (it calculates time by 'jubilees', weeks of years and years), seeking precision for cultic regulations, priestly tithes, the dates of festivals and above all the scrupulous observance of the Torah. In short, it shares with Qumran the priestly concept of life: the hallowing of all the life of all the people throughout the year.

Another decisive factor is that the self-understanding of the Jewish group which stands behind this book is legitimated by the 'fathers' of Israel, in other words by antiquity. This is meant to give the impression that things had been like this in Israel from the beginning and that everything would only become good when the old had been recognized to be true and had been restored. So Jubilees is a book which 'on the basis of the authority of the fathers and Moses seeks once again to communicate to all the different groups of the people a common self-understanding with a historical basis' in order to 'restore the identity of the people threatened by Hellenism by referring to the patriarchal traditions. In particular the numerous blessings on Israel uttered by the fathers which attract the reader serve this aim. Behind the book we therefore have an anti-Hellenistic priestly restoration reform movement closely connected with the Qumran group which came into being soon afterwards.'[42]

Twelve chapters of this work (chs.12-23) are devoted to Abraham; these elaborate the Genesis narrative with fantasy and in a tendentious way. Individual aspects of the post-exilic picture of Abraham are taken up again and now fused into a synthesis. Moreover a particular Jewish picture of Abraham has been given historical form here. It has three dimensions.

1. In line with Joshua 24, Abraham is now depicted completely as the first monotheistic champion of the faith who himself burns the idols in his father's house and has departed from pagan idolatrous astrology.[43] In keeping with this, in Jubilees from the beginning Abraham speaks only 'Hebrew' with God, here designated 'the language of creation'. A rapid course in the study of the Torah then follows:

And he took his father's books — and they were written in Hebrew — and he copied them. And he began studying them thereafter. And I caused him to know everything which he was unable (to understand). And he studied them (in) the six months of rain.[44]

2. In line with Sirach 44 the moralizing of Abraham is considerably stronger: Abraham offers the sacrifice correctly, gives the priestly tithe for the first time and performs circumcision correctly. All these actions are described at length.

3. Very much in line with Psalm 105, Abraham is claimed for the belief of Israel in election. At the same time Abraham's significance for the peoples is visibly played down, as has been mentioned in passing.[45] By contrast there is excessive stress on Israel's special position: Israel alone has been chosen from among the peoples. All the blessings of the 'fathers', all the promises of God, are exclusively transferred to Jacob by Abraham. Indeed the whole of the patriarchal tradition is focussed solely on Jacob, whereas Ishmael, Abraham's son, and Esau, his grandson, no longer count:

> For the Lord did not draw Ishmael and his sons and his brothers and Esau near to himself, and he did not elect them because they are the sons of Abraham, for he knew them. But he chose Israel that they might be a people for himself. And he sanctified them and gathered them from all the sons of man.[46]

Abraham cannot be claimed more clearly as the possession of Israel – for manifest religious and political interests. The politicizing of Abraham here means that he is claimed exclusively for Israel. And this exclusivity with regard to Abraham beyond doubt attains dramatic power in those scenes in the book in which the dying Abraham takes leave of his son Jacob and charges him with building the 'house of Abraham', for which he has already laid the foundations.[47] This is presumably an allusion to the Jerusalem temple, which may go back to II Chronicles, where it is reported of Solomon that he built the temple on 'Mount Moriah' (II Chron. 3.1), i.e. on the place where according to tradition Abraham was to sacrifice his son Isaac (Gen.22.2: Genesis only knows a tradition about a 'land' of Moriah generally). The temple at Jerusalem has thus become the 'house of Abraham'.[48]

Abraham as a militant figure: 'The Apocalypse of Abraham'

The battle of the Maccabees against the Seleucid rulers by no means brought peace to the land. On the contrary, the political situation in Palestine would continue to be complex over the next few decades. Soon Rome, summoned by the Maccabees, not only had influence over Palestine but was its real ruler. Moreover the Roman soldiers had no inhibitions about plundering the temple, for the first time in 54 BCE under their general Crassus. The Romans still did not exercise direct rule but ruled through puppet governments, headed by people like Hyrcanus and above all Herod, an upstart who between 40 BCE and 4 CE became a key figure in local politics. But even they could not bring peace to the turbulent land. Countless disturbances and rebellions compelled Rome finally to intervene directly with an army; this intervention reached its terrible peak in the destruction of the Second Temple in 70 CE under the Roman general Titus (son of the Flavian emperor Vespasian).

At a spiritual level, the cultural struggle between Hellenism and Judaism was fought out with a specific theology. We know it under the name of apocalyptic.[49] This was a radically different theology of history based on the conviction that the previous concept of history had failed. Political events only confirmed this. History could now no longer be understood as an ongoing continuum, but only as a battlefield of good and evil, as an eschatological drama moving towards an imminent end in which God himself would intervene to judge. Moreover this judgment was awaited impatiently. In the face of the misery the question of the apocalyptists was not so much 'Why?' but 'How long?': 'How long will the abomination of desolation remain . . .?' (Dan.8.13).

However, the apocalyptists did not utter this tormented 'How long?' in complete ignorance. On the contrary, in view of the failure they attempted to find concrete disclosures about the mysteries of nature, the supernatural heavenly origin of and background to the natural events on earth, in short about the last act of the cosmic and historical drama. How? Through visions and dreams! So the apocalyptists often give their disclosures a 'mysterious enigmatic form':[50] similitudes, dream visions, parables, allegories, numerical ciphers and animal symbols are frequent in apocalyptic. Moreover the narratives of apocalyptic to a large degree also contain visions, auditions, heavenly journeys and, in connection with these, extensive dialogues with heavenly figures, with angels and demons.

We can easily see how this development would also inevitably have some effect on the picture of Abraham, on the significance which Abraham had now attained for post-exilic Judaism. Here we can only concentrate on the most important work about Abraham in this genre. Its name, The Apocalypse of Abraham,[51] is already a sign of the time. It is a relatively late work which was presumably composed after 70 CE, since it quite manifestly alludes to the destruction of the Jerusalem temple under Titus.[52] It is typically apocalyptic in the way in which it reports visions of Abraham on a heavenly journey which depict the secrets of the future of the people of Israel. This is no more original than is the dualism of good and evil, the doctrine of the princes of light and princes of darkness, which are widespread here.

More decisive is the role of Abraham in this apocalyptic view of heaven. This role goes far beyond that of a visionary. In these texts for the first time Abraham becomes a direct propaganda figure, a figure militating against the evil, atrocious conditions of the time. Moreover the present embattled situation of the group behind this work, fighting against idolatry, the desecration of the temple and the triumph of the Gentiles, is then either projected back into the time of Abraham or attributed to Abraham in visions. As a start, in the first nine chapters Abraham is depicted as an iconoclast of idols, one who destroys the images of gods, and thus as a militant monotheist, now even more strongly than in the book of Jubilees. The allusions of Josh.24 ('Put away the gods whom your fathers served') are developed in narrative form from an apocalyptic perspective and concentrated in dramatic scenes: Abraham works in his father's workshop making statues of gods, but gets the idea that God cannot be identical with these human fabrications, since they can be destroyed or burned. However, he only becomes completely clear about this as a result of a heavenly voice which not only presents itself as 'God of the fathers' but also destroys his idolatrous parents' home. Abraham has no difficulties over this.

> And it came to pass as I went out − I was not yet outside the entrance of the court − that the sound of a great thunder came and burned him and his house and everything in his house, down to the ground, forty cubits.[53]

The motif of Abraham as an instrument of polemic against idols, as a figure in the apocalyptic rivalry with other religions, continues in other scenes of the book. But the many dramatic details of the visions are not decisive for us here; what is important is the overall religious and political tendency of this work. And there can be no doubt that this book faces the political triumph of the Gentiles over the people of Israel. But this political triumph is turned in a religious direction and interpreted as punishment for the pollution of the temple which had already taken place in Israel a long time before. At the same time the certainty is conveyed that the wickedness will not last much longer, but will soon be overcome by a small group of righteous known only to God, by God's true elect. They alone are now God's people, they alone are now Abraham's 'seed':

> And then from your seed will be left the righteous men in their number, protected by me, who strive in the glory of my name toward the place prepared beforehand for them.[54]

In other words, in the new circumstances of the time, in the apocalyptic circles of Palestinian Judaism, Abraham becomes a political figure fighting for the preservation of the 'true Israel', the remnant of Israel. The tendency to make Abraham exclusive is radicalized even further here. While the Abraham of Genesis was the father of Israel and the ancestor and mediator of blessing for a multitude of peoples, and the Abraham of Jubilees was at least still a possession of the whole people of Israel, here he is now only the possession of a group of elect, a remnant of the pure and true believers who seek to legitimate their will to survive in the cultural and religious battle in the light of Abraham. But in all the texts we have a spirit of anti-Hellenistic self-assertion, typical of particular groups of the Palestinian Judaism of the time. Abraham has become a key figure in the religious and political struggle over assimilation or segregation, against the background of a Palestine which is being torn apart in the cultural battle between Hellenism and Judaism.

5. The idealization of Abraham: the spirit of Hellenism

Completely different conceptions are put forward by men who do not seek the segregation of Judaism but rather spiritual links between Jewish and Hellenistic culture. One of these men was born in the cultural capital of the then world, Alexandria: his name is Philo. The other, two generations later, would spend large parts of his life in the political capital of the then world, Rome: his name is Josephus. For both, Abraham plays an essentialy different role from the role he plays for the circles in Palestine of which we have heard so far.

Abraham as the primal model for knowledge of God: Philo

Philo was born around 25 BCE in Alexandria and died there in 40 CE. A contemporary of the Galilean Jew Jesus of Nazareth, he grew up in an educated and politically influential family which had good relations with the Roman imperial house. He was soon to become a significant philosopher, theologian and exegete, author of an imposing series of academic works, and was to rise to be the spiritual leader of Alexandrian Judaism. Indeed in the days of Hellenism, Alexandria was not just anywhere. Founded by Alexander the Great in 332/31 BCE, it had developed not only into one of the most important ports and trading cities in the then world but above all into a unique centre of science and art. The most visible expression of this was the most important library in the ancient world, built here, in which the knowledge of whole eras had been documented and made available on hundreds of thousands of scrolls. Damaged in 30 BCE at the time of the Roman siege (in the civil war between Caesar and Anthony), it gradually disintegrated during the third century and was finally destroyed at the end of the fourth century, when an inestimable cultural heritage was lost for ever.

It is no wonder that a by no means inconsiderable Jewish community had settled in this city of culture. Nor that the Jews of Alexandria had become assimilated to Hellenism; already in the first half of the third century BCE it was a matter of course that Greek was spoken in Jewish worship in Alexandria. Moreover in this city there was a unique combination of Greek and Jewish thought (as later there was of Jewish and Arab thought in Cordoba, Jewish and German thought in Berlin, and Jewish and American thought in New York). Not only Jewish scholars like Aristobulus and Philo were active here; programmatic works like the book of Wisdom, which is part of the biblical canon for Christians, were also written in Alexandria.

We cannot go into Philo's complex philosophical and exegetical work here,[55] nor into his remarkable scriptural hermeneutics, which largely rests on an excessive use of typology and allegory. But it is by no means a secondary issue for us to concentrate on Philo's picture of Abraham, since through Abraham Philo's basic attitude to one of the most important problems becomes clear: how does a Jew live in a thoroughly non-Jewish culture? How does one explain one's own tradition to non-Jews? How is the relationship between 'the' people and 'the peoples' to be defined against the new horizon of the time? Is polemical demarcation the solution? For Philo in this context Abraham takes on a key role, so it is no coincidence that Philo deals with Abraham not only in his commentaries on scripture but also in two separate books. They are called *On Abraham* and *On the*

Migration of Abraham. We cannot interpret these complex works in detail here either. We have to limit ourselves to essential features of Philo's picture of Abraham.

We can best see the interest with which Philo pursues Abraham by means of a text from his work *On the Virtues*. For here he summed up his picture of Abraham with a concentration which he did not achieve elsewhere:

> The most ancient member of the Jewish nation was a Chaldaean by birth, the son of an astrologer, one of those who study the lore of that science and think that the stars and the whole heaven and universe are gods, the authors, they say, of the events which befall each man for good or for ill, and hold that there is no originating cause outside the things we perceive with our senses. What could be more grievous or more capable of proving the total absence of nobility in the soul than this, that its knowledge of the many, the secondary, the created, only leads it to ignore the One, the Primal, the Uncreated and Maker of all, whose supreme excellence is established by these and countless other attributes of such magnitude that no human reason can contain them?
>
> Perception of these truths and divine inspiration induced him to leave his native country, his race and paternal home, knowing that if he stayed, the delusions of the polytheistic creed would stay with him and render it impossible for him to discover the One who alone is eternal and the Father of all things, conceptual and sensible, whereas if he removed, the delusion would also remove from his mind and its false creed be replaced by the truth. At the same time, also, the fire of yearning, which possessed him to know the Existent, was fanned by the divine warnings vouchsafed to him . . .
>
> Would you not say that this lone wanderer without relatives or friends was of the highest nobility, he who craved for kinship with God and strove by every means to live in familiarity with him, he who while ranked among the prophets, a post of such high excellence, put his trust in nothing created rather than in the Uncreated and Father of all, he who as I have said was regarded as a king by those in whose midst he settled, a sovereignty gained not with weapons, nor with mighty armies, as is the way of some, but by the election of God, the friend of virtue, who rewards the lovers of piety with imperial powers to benefit those around them? He is

the standard of nobility for all proselytes, who, abandoning the ignobility of strange laws and monstrous customs which assigned divine honours to stocks and stones and soulless things in general, have come to settle in a better land, in a commonwealth full of true life and vitality, with truth as its director and president.[56]

If we interpret this text, too, in the light of Philo's great works on Abraham, mentioned above, the following characteristic outlines emerge.

1. Philo deliberately portrays Abraham as a foreigner. It is not by chance that he emphasizes that Abraham was a 'Chaldaean', a 'lone wanderer'. These statements may have been directed against circles within Judaism in the spirit of Qumran which gave their consciousness of God and their pride in religion to some degree a genealogical foundation, and saw it guaranteed by descent. By contrast, Philo points out that a Gentile stands at the beginning of Jewish history. The principle of natural descent and thus of natural rights and privileges has been broken through by God – right from the beginning. Before God, something else is important. But what?

2. Philo presents Abraham as the model of true faith. He seeks to demonstrate by him that what counts before God is not nobility of descent but nobility of spirit, nobility of faith. The allusion to astrology underlines this. For Philo, the knowledge of astrology is neither a cultural good to be striven for nor the expression of reprehensible idolatry. Rather, for him astrology stands symbolically for a lack of nobility of the spirit, i.e. for a lower form of knowledge (it is objects that are being worshipped). But Abraham was different. He is the primal model of someone who overcame such false views – though at the cost of having to leave the sphere of the false and the deceptive to live in solitude in accordance with the truth. Moreover this very thought is developed at length allegorically in the major works about Abraham: Abraham's migration is – at a 'deeper' level, i.e. understood allegorically and spiritually – at the same time a migration from false ideas of God and the attainment of a correct knowledge of God.

3. Philo portrays Abraham as the primal model of a reconciliation of reason and revelation, nature and Torah. Interpreters have even said that 'for the first time' in the history of ideas Philo sought to reconcile 'two radically different claims to be the truth, namely reason and revelation'.[57] Be this as it may, the phrases quoted above,

'the fire of yearning, which possessed him to know the Existent, was fanned by the divine warnings vouchsafed to him' beyond doubt express the basic intention of his thought. Philosophy and theology, true knowledge and true faith, are not opposites; rather, faith completes knowledge. For both microcosm and macrocosm are permeated by one and the same spirit of God, one and the same reason (Logos). The task of human beings here is to perfect themselves through insight into the basic spiritual structure of the world, the regularity of the natural order. God's revelations and commandments are simply aids, ways, instruments. The laws of nature are related to the Torah as originals to copies, as principles to commentaries on them.

So we can understand why Philo does not see any alienation of human reason in God's commandments. Abraham is the best example of this. For although Abraham lived before the Torah of Moses, he already observed the law. What law? The law of nature! Thus Philo need not commandeer Abraham for the written law of Moses, but he does not play him off against it either. Abraham already lived out 'the unwritten legislation', following only his 'own voice', 'his own conscience', teaching himself. So Abraham 'kept to the order of nature, in the conviction that nature itself was the oldest principle'.[58] So for Philo Abraham is the archetype of the pursuit of the law of nature, the natural law which then becomes concrete in the Torah of Moses.

4. Philo portrays Abraham as the primal model of all converts. If it is not physical, ethnic descent that is decisive before God, but only faith in the creator of the world; if Abraham knew and observed the Torah in the form of the natural law, is he then not also the model for all those who, while not yet Jews, are spiritually close to Judaism? Indeed, in the text that I have quoted Philo does not hesitate to speak of Abraham as the 'standard of nobility for all proselytes'. In other words, if people give up all immoral actions, believe in God as the creator of all things and thus open themselves to the spirit and truth, then they are like Abraham; then they are Abraham's descendants.

Abraham as the great bearer of culture: Josephus

The second great exponent of Jewish openness to the world of that time, Josephus, also wrote in this spirit of universalism. Born in 37 CE in Jerusalem of an old priestly family, like Philo, Josephus received a high degree of education, but initially he followed the way of strict asceticism in the spirit of Essenism. However, then he started a political career in Jerusalem as a priest, which in 64 CE came to a first climax with a journey to Rome, the then capital of the world.

On his return to Palestine this promising and highly skilled man found himself caught up in the deadly clashes between the Roman occupying forces and Jewish rebels. He began to manoeuvre between the fronts, but this did not prevent him ending up as a Roman prisoner in 67 CE. He was set free after prophesying (in circumstances which still remain mysterious) that the Roman general Vespasian, from the family of the Flavians, who was operating in Palestine at the time, would soon become emperor. The prophecy came true two years later. Josephus was rewarded with freedom, went on to become a favourite of the emperor and from then on added the name of his patron, Flavius, to his own.

A year later in 70 CE, this Roman Jew was then torn in two directions by witnessing by the destruction of the temple and the city of Jerusalem by Roman troops. For much as Josephus suffered at the destruction of the capital of his people, he had regarded the militant resistance policy carried on above all by the Zealots as a catastrophe. And catastrophe it indeed was when in 73 the Romans also captured the fortress of Masada on a hill overlooking the Dead Sea and in despair hundreds of Zealots, including wives and children, killed themselves. In Josephus' view this was a senseless sacrifice.

The emperor's favourite then left Palestine and went to Rome, where he became one of the most significant historians of his time and his people. His work on the *Jewish War* was written between 75 and 79. It depicts the origin, course and consequences of this war in the period from Antiochus IV to the fall of Massada; Josephus also gives his political evaluation of events. The climax of his literary achievements is the *Jewish Antiquities*, which appeared in 93/4; in these books Josephus gives a great panoramic account of the whole history of his people from the creation of the world to the outbreak of the war against Rome. In this work Josephus also grapples with Abraham in the framework of the patriarchal traditions.

It should not surprise us that for a man who is so open to the world and to culture Abraham cannot be the exponent of Jewish segregation, the strictest observance of the Torah and militant anti-Hellenistic propaganda. However, it is surprising how consistently Josephus has eliminated exclusively Jewish features from his picture of Abraham. In his eleven chapters on Abraham (I, 1-7), there is not a word about God's 'eternal covenant' with Abraham with a view to later Israel, and not a word about the Torah. Circumcision is mentioned briefly. By contrast, it is striking what great value Josephus attaches to Abraham's involvement with the world of nations; this only underlines his tendency to prevent any segregation of the Jewish people and emphasize how Judaism is interwoven with the nations of the world. Indeed Josephus does everything possible to deprive Abraham of any key theological status and put him on the same level as any other biblical figure. Instead of this, at decisive points the pride of the Jew in his great history flashes out. This happens in connection with the scene of the binding of Isaac:

> He (God) moreover foretold that their race would swell into a multitude of nations, with increasing wealth, nations whose founders would be had in everlasting remembrance, that they would subdue Canaan by their arms and be envied of all men.[59]

Like Philo, Josephus wants to bring out programmatically that a non-Jew stands at the beginning of the history of Israel. This man comes from Chaldaea, and later has connections with the Nabataeans (through Ishmael), the Ptolemies and the Egyptians. The ancestor of Israel is at the same time the father of great peoples and kingdoms. And the ancestor of Israel is a man of great culture. Indeed, Philo does precisely what the circles round the books of Jubilees and the Apocalypse of Abraham wanted to avoid – here as with Philo Abraham is inculturated as the bearer of the great cultures of humankind. It is also decisive for Josephus' picture of Abraham that:

1. Abraham was the first monotheist. However, this did not make him a militant iconoclast; rather, he was a 'wise man' through and through.[60] For his monotheism Abraham simply needed to be 'of ready intelligence, persuasive with his hearers, and not mistaken in his inferences'.[61] Why? So that he could be 'determined to reform and change the ideas universally current concerning God'.[62] But what is the right view of God? This: that there is only one God, the creator of all things. And Abraham arrives at this view like a philosopher through 'observations' of land and sea, of sun, moon and stars. The intent is to demonstrate that Abraham is the first 'physico-theologian', i.e. one who infers God's existence from nature. Abraham is the beginning of all natural theology.

2. Abraham was a great bearer of culture. After his persuasiveness evidently failed to have any effect on his fellow countrymen (there is no talk of militant iconoclasm), Abraham decided to migrate, arrived in Canaan and from there went on to Egypt. He came like the head of a Greek philosophical school. For he wanted – thoughtfully and self-critically – also to hear the 'opinion' (!) of the Egyptian priests about their gods in case there was something that he could 'learn' from them. However, there was no occasion for that. On the contrary, Abraham himself became the teacher of the Egyptians. What did he teach?

> He introduced them to arithmetic and transmitted to them the laws of astronomy. For before the coming of Abraham the Egyptians were ignorant of these sciences, which thus travelled from the Chaldaeans into Egypt, whence they passed on to the Greeks.[63]

Abraham the inventor, the great astrologer – that is how other sources of the time also portray him.[64] But in Josephus the political intent is quite different from that in Jubilees and indeed in Philo. There astronomy is regarded as an indication of reprehensible idolatry or as a lowly form of knowledge, whereas for Josephus astrology is a highly prestigious science. That Abraham has a command of it is meant simply to underline the advanced knowledge of the progenitor of the Jews compared with all other peoples – and in a sphere like astrology, which 'in the Hellenistic period was regarded as the root and crown of all knowledge', as a 'real manifestation of wisdom and the most certain way to the divine'.[65] In other words, in Josephus Abraham does not become a weapon for religious and cultural segregation but the model for a cultural profile of the Jews over against other nations. Even such great nations of culture as Egypt and Greece are not the givers but the receivers: 'The way taken by culture runs from Abraham through Canaan and Egypt to Greece.'[66]

3. Abraham was the ideal embodiment of all the virtues. For Josephus the purity of his marriage is part of this, as is his hospitality; his readiness to engage in battle (including a 'wise', moderate settlement with his opponents), and also the parental love and piety which puts Abraham to the test in the scene of the binding of Isaac. In short, for Josephus Abraham is 'a man in every virtue supreme, who

received from God the due meed of honour for his zeal in his service'.[67]

One might be critical about Josephus' picture of Abraham. A Jewish scholar like Samuel Sandmel not without justification says that Josephus' Abraham appeared 'in the garb of a Greek philosopher', without Josephus giving deeper insights into 'what kind of a philosopher' Abraham really was.[68] The Hellenistic colours are, he says, present, but at the same time a little 'faint'.[69] That may be the case, but this is doubtless part of Josephus' literary and religious political strategy. For we should not forget that Josephus is writing about Judaism in a non-Jewish city like Rome for a non-Jewish public. So his picture of Abraham seems 'coherent'.[70] Why? Because in this city Josephus must be concerned to demonstrate self-awareness as a Jew without succumbing to religious arrogance. As a member of a defeated and conquered people he had to seek a delicate balance: between levelling down his own history and giving it privileges, between dissolving it and detaching it. His picture of Abraham was intended to show a non-Jewish audience, readers trained in Stoic philosophy, that Judaism was a completely reasonable religion (with its monotheism) at a high cultural level (arithmetic, astrology, religion) and with lofty ethics (virtues), on a par with the Stoic doctrine of virtues. And it had this character from the beginning! Abraham is already 'the ideal statesman who has powers of persuasion and the force of logical thinking and scientific knowledge'.[71]

The 'attractiveness' of Judaism for Gentiles

Not national or religious segregation of Judaism but cultural openness: that was the basic principle of Philo and Josephus. Openness without any dissolution of the religious substance, with pride in the spiritual achievements and great ethical demands of one's own religion. The interest was not in reclaiming Abraham as a possession for Judaism alone, but in presenting Abraham as a universal figure from whom all could learn: learn what it means to recognize God and live appropriately before God. Thus Abraham did not become the exclusive progenitor of the Jews but a 'religious cosmopolitan'.[72] Abraham is the possibility contained within the Jewish tradition of a way to God which is also offered to non-Jews.

Moreover many non-Jews in antiquity took up this offer. For the remarkable combination of monotheism and ethics made Judaism an attractive religion for many people of the time, and moreover won more converts, so-called 'proselytes' (literally, those who come over, a Greek translation of the Hebrew word *ger* = 'sojourner') than other religions. Abraham, the original Gentile, was of decisive significance here: he was the figure which legitimated Jewish mission, a figure of integration for non-Jews. A proselyte? He simply 'repeated in his own way the existential decision of Abraham',[73] in other words leaving behind a wrong way of thinking and being open to true faith. At the same time Abraham could be understood as an 'example' for the situation of many Jews of the time, since the problems of Jewish existence in a pagan environment could be depicted by the model of this 'primeval wanderer'. The Protestant exegete Dieter Georgi has brought out this twofold aspect precisely: 'He (Abraham) was seen as the ancestor of the Jewish people, but at the same time there was an awareness of his involvment in paganism. People liked to stress his origin from the land of the Chaldaeans and his later links with the Phoenicians and Egyptians. His departure from his father's house was not understood as a way into isolation and into a corner in Palestine but as a departure for the wide world.'[74]

Indeed many Jews saw an opportunity given with Abraham, the original Gentile, for Judaism to assert itself as a universal religion, the 'light of the nations', as the prophet Isaiah had already exclaimed to his people in the exile: 'I will give you as a light to the nations, that my salvation may reach to the end of the earth' (49.6). Moreover, particularly at the time of Philo and Josephus, Jewish missionary work was chalking up great successes. Even a whole royal house like that of Adiabene, on the frontier between the Roman empire and the Parthian empire, had gone over to Judaism, as Josephus, too notes with pride in his *Antiquities* (XX,4). Indeed we can say that in the first century, at the beginning of the common era, Judaism was well on the way to becoming a world religion.

6. Abraham observes the halakhah: the rabbis

We have come across two basic options for overcoming the cultural conflict between Hellenism and Judaism: segregation on the one hand and openness on the other; retreat behind the limits of the

Torah bound up with a selectiveness and exclusiveness on the one hand, and an offensive on the other demonstrating the reasonableness and natural character of Jewish faith, combined with integration into the world of the nations. When Philo of Alexandria died in 40 CE it may not yet have become clear to whom the future in Judaism would belong. Further development along the lines of Philo and Josephus – who could have ruled this out a priori? And in 40 even the death of the 'rabbi' from Nazareth was barely ten years in the past. A Pharisaic pupil named Paul from Tarsus had just confessed him Messiah of Israel and the Gentiles with an appeal to Abraham, and some Jews who believed in Jesus as the Messiah even before Paul had just left Jerusalem and begun to settle in Syrian Antioch, where for the first time they called themselves 'Christians' (Acts 11.26).

A new 'paradigm' of Judaism

However, as we know, things turned out differently for Judaism. The destruction of the temple and the devastation of Jerusalem in 70, which had been witnessed by Flavius Josephus, had epoch-making consequences – for Judaism as a whole. At any rate with the execution of Jesus as a false Messiah the chance had been lost to achieve a reform in keeping with the message of the rabbi from Nazareth and bring the Gentile Christian into God's history of covenant and blessing with his people through belief in him as the Messiah – truly universal belief. The only religious political group to have survived the catastrophe of 70 intact was that of the Pharisees, after the upper-class Sadducees had ceased to have any religious function with the loss of the temple, and the Zealots had been entangled in a fatal fight with the Romans. This ended in 135 with a final defeat: the crushing of the rebellion under the military leadership of Simeon Ben Koseba, who had also been proclaimed Messiah by one of the leading rabbis of the time, Rabbi Akiba, and since then had borne the honorific title Bar Kochba ('Son of the star', according to Num.24.17).

So only the Pharisees were left, and they now attempted to re-establish themselves as orthodoxy in the city of Jabneh (on the Mediterranean coast near Jaffa). The school in Jabneh (Bet Midrash') – first under the leadership of Rabbi Johanan ben Zakkai and then under that of Rabbi Gamaliel – became the new centre of

Judaism, and the Pharisaic rabbinate began to ensure that no one departed from the predetermined line on pain of excommunication. We shall hear more of this policy in connection with the Christian community which stands behind the Gospel of John.

The march into the long Jewish Middle Ages had now begun. Judaism was now completely stamped by what Hans Küng has called the paradigm of the rabbis, the synagogue and the Talmud,[75] which had to secure the survival of the people who were now living almost totally in the 'Diaspora', i.e. the 'Dispersion'. This survival was to be behind the barricade of the Torah.

– The rabbis: instead of the priesthood, the 'rabbis', the 'scribes', were the dominant authority, and now exclusively those of the Pharisaic trend. The rabbi became *the* model and norm of Jewish existence – after the model of Moses, whom the rabbis primarily regarded as a teacher of the law: as teacher of the written and oral Torah. Moreover among the rabbis Moses bore one of the highest titles of honour: our master, our teacher, in Hebrew *Moshe Rabbenu*.

– The synagogue: the temple had now been completely replaced by the synagogue, which was a place of assembly, of prayer and of study of the Torah. Here the typical rabbinic view became fully established that intensive study, regular worship and good works are a substitute for temple worship and sacrifice. Indeed studying the Torah and thus study generally became the ideal of the pious Jew, a lifelong process which began in childhood. Now Jewish life was definitively life under the Torah, interpreted and made concrete with the help of a comprehensive law of religion (halakhah). Everyday life was governed by this religious law, and bowing under the 'yoke of the Torah' was a consequence of the previous two great catastrophes of Judaism, one which the Jews chose for themselves.

– The Talmud: it had already been important for the Pharisees that alongside the written Torah there always had been and was an 'oral Torah' which represented the interpretation of the written Torah – along with all the different rabbinic views down the centuries about the individual commandments and prohibitions. These 'traditions of the fathers' were initially not set down in writing, but handed on orally. However, later they were written down, at first privately and then officially.

This process of commenting on the Torah, which had existed since the Babylonian exile and had now grown to a tremendous degree, becoming increasingly complex, reaches a climax and a conclusion in two phases. The first is the codification of the Mishnah (Hebrew 'repetition', 'learning'), which in sixty-three tractates on six orders embraces the whole religious law of the 'oral tradition' (it was completed under Patriarch Jehuda ha-Nasi around 200 CE). The second is the Talmud (Hebrew 'study', 'teaching'), which contains the material handed down after the codification of the Mishnah. There are two strands of tradition in the Talmud: the Palestinian or Jerusalem Talmud (completed towards 425 CE). which comments on .thirty-nine Mishnah tractates, and the Babylonian Talmud, which comments on thirty-seven, and may first have been completed in the seventh or eighth century CE. The most important distinction from the Mishnah is that the Talmud contains not only religious, halakhic passages but also edifying, haggadic passages (from *haggada* = narrative, proclamation) and all kinds of material can be contained in these parts: legends and parables; astronomical, anatomical and medical information; and ethical and moral instructions.

The decisive thing here theologically is that according to the orthodox view this oral Torah is of equal value to the originally written, biblical Torah. Why? Because it, too, was already revealed to Moses on Mount Sinai. Thus the rabbis accorded the halakhic tradition the same divine authority as the Bible itself. And to the present day, Mishnah and Talmud are the normative basis for all the decisions of rabbinic Judaism on the religious law, and for the religious teaching and religious law of Jewish orthodoxy. Normative Judaism is the Judaism of the rabbis, the synagogue and the Talmud.[76]

We can understand how in the new historical circumstances in which Jews – dispersed all over the world – literally had to fight for their survival as Jews they no longer had, nor could have, any perspective for an Abraham theology along the lines of Josephus and Philo, open to the world and culture. Moreover neither Jewish thinker found acceptance in normative Judaism down the centuries. We owe the survival of their writings largely to Christian church fathers. So what the Jewish theologian Samuel Sandmel said in the case of Philo also applies, *mutatis mutandis*, to Josephus: 'As contrastable with normative, rabbinic Judaism, Philo and his associates reflect a marginal, aberrative version of Judaism which existed at a time when there were many versions of Judaism, of which ultimately only Rabbinism and Christianity have survived to our day.'[77] Indeed the stimuli towards a Jewish theology thinking in universalistic terms were taken up by a Jew like Paul: we shall be hearing about this in due course. However, rabbinic Judaism in principle took another course, the course which had been marked out in respect of Abraham by texts like Nehemiah 9, Joshua 24, Psalm 105, I Macc.2 and the book of Jubilees.

It would take us too far here to reconstruct all the aspects of the rabbinic picture of Abraham.[78] At all events we have to be aware that on no question can one quote 'the' opinion of 'the' rabbis. At no point do either the Talmud or the additional rabbinic interpretations of the Bible, the Midrashim (= interpretations, explanations) contain systematic and ordered accounts of Abraham such as we know, say, from Philo and Josephus. The Talmud and the Midrashim are a polyphonic choir of hundreds of rabbis from the most varied times and places and thus represent an open process of discussion of all kinds of questions of faith and life. Moreover, apart from the biblical commentaries, Abraham often appears only as it were 'by chance' in most rabbinic sources, by way of association or as an example. That in itself does not allow systematization or even generalized statements, especially as all the remarks are to be found in the haggadic parts and thus have no binding halakhic quality, in other words are not religious law.

On the other hand, the voices documented in the rabbinic works are not simply the random private views of random people. The rabbis have authority, and not all questions remain open. So pragmatic talk of the 'rabbis', as here, seems quite justified. It is not meant either to systematize the polyphonic choir or to trivialize the sayings of the rabbis. It is meant to cover two dimensions: there is always only the individual rabbi in his century with his specific meaning, but in the context of the Talmud and the Midrashim he has an authority which at least every orthodox Jew has to take seriously.

As far as Abraham is concerned, over the centuries countless rabbis in countless places have kept talking about him, taking up and transforming the various traditions, some of which are already known to us: from the iconoclasm and monotheism of Abraham, through his obedience in faith despite severe testing, to his hospitality and love of God. All that has been taken up and confirmed by the rabbis. They leave no doubt about the significance of Abraham for Israel, as a text from the Babylonian Talmud impressively emphasizes:

On the day when Abraham our father passed away from the world all the great ones of the nations stood in line and said: 'Woe to the world that has lost its leader and woe to the ship that has lost its pilot' (bBaba Bathra 91a/91b).

Abraham as arch-priest and primal rabbi

It should come as no surprise that in a religious environment in which the written and oral Torah has normative significance, in which indeed there are even theories of the pre-existence and mediation of the Torah at creation,[79] Abraham the tribal ancestor could not be excluded from the Torah. After all, was Abraham, God's 'friend' and 'servant', any less pious and loyal to the law than the rabbis themselves? Didn't 'our father Abraham' in particular observe the law, which is of divine origin? If for Jews the will of God is codified in the Torah of Moses, how can Abraham and the other 'fathers of Israel' have lived before God without the Torah? On the other hand, Abraham indisputably lived at a time before the Torah. What does that mean? How can this dilemma be avoided?

What is already hinted at in post-exilic texts about Abraham is now fully confirmed by the rabbis. Abraham is now declared to be a loyal follower of the Torah of Moses. To be specific, for the rabbis Abraham already observed the commandments and festivals of later Judaism: he celebrated the Passover (GenR 42), he observed the laws of purity (BM 87a), knew all the sacrificial practices (GenR 44), was the first to offer a tithe (NumR XII), initiated the morning prayer (NumR II) and was the first to prescribe tassels and beads for daily prayer (Mid.Hag Gen.14.23). Indeed in all this Abraham in fact acted like a priest, and this dignity is explicitly attributed to him (GenR 55).[80] Abraham the archpriest!

This transformation of Abraham into a priest finds its strongest support in the discussion of circumcision in rabbinic commentaries. If we follow one of the sources, this great act of circumcision, the realization of the sign of the covenant, took place on the day of the forgiveness of sins and atonement (Yom Kippur) and since then has benefited future generations. How? Because God looks 'each year at the blood which Abraham shed at his circumcision' in order to 'forgive the sins of Israel'.[81] Furthermore, according to one of the finest passages in the Midrashim, God would have abolished the existence of the world again had Abraham rejected his circumcision (and thus the Torah):

> The Holy One said to him: When I had created my world, I was patient with you for twenty generations until you would come and receive circumcision. So now, if you do not accept circumcision, it is enough for me that the world has existed until now; and I am returning it to being void and without form. It is unnecessary for me that the world exist any longer. He therefore said (in Gen.17.1): I AM GOD ALMIGHTY. I have had enough, O world. But if you accept circumcision for yourself, we are enough for the world, just I and you.[82]

God and Abraham: they are enough for the world. And here of course Abraham is a symbol for Israel loyal to the law. Indeed Abraham's loyalty to the law as the model of all pious Jews goes so far for the rabbis that they declare that Abraham observed not only the written Torah but also the oral Torah.[83] Thus Abraham has completely become the primal rabbi of Judaism, who then like a rabbi can preside over a rabbinic school, as we are told in the tractate Yoma of the Babylonian Talmud. And at the same point one can then find the following discussion among the rabbis (the allusion to the 'seven commandments' is to the seven commandments of Noah, which all human beings have to observe, and 'erub of the dishes' refers to legislation for preparing foods on fast days before the sabbath):

> Rab said: Our father Abraham kept the whole Torah, as it is said: *Because that Abraham hearkened to my voice.* R.Shimi b.Hiyyi said to Rab: Say, perhaps, that this refers to the seven laws? – Surely there was also that of circumcision! Then say that it refers to the seven laws and circumcision [and not to the whole Torah]? – If that were so, why does Scripture say: '*My commandments and My law*'? Raba or R.Ashi said: Abraham, our father, kept even the '*erub* of the dishes', as it is said: '*My Torahs*', one being the written Torah, the other the oral Torah (b.Yoma 28b).

Abraham: the beginning and end of all things

If Abraham is so indispensable for the existence of the world, then another thought springs to mind: the world and all human beings were

created solely for Abraham/Israel. The world owes not only its
ongoing existence, but even its origin in the first place, to Abraham:

> R.Levi said: It is written, *The greatest man among the Anakim*:
> '*man*' means Abraham, and why is he called the greatest man?
> Because he was worthy of being created before Adam, but the
> Holy One, blessed be He, reasoned: 'He may sin and there will be
> none to set it right. Hence I will create Adam first so that if he sins,
> Abraham may come and set things right.' R.Abba b.Kahana said:
> In general practice, when a man joins a pair of beams [so that they
> meet] at a slope, where does he place them? Surely in the middle of
> the chamber, so that they may support the beams in front and
> behind. Even so, why did the Lord create Abraham in the middle
> of generations? In order that he might bear the generations before
> and after him.[84]

So Abraham is the 'beam' between the generations, the beam which
holds everything together. No wonder that in one of the most valued
rabbinic source works, the 'Sayings of the Fathers' (Pirke Aboth), we
also find the notion of the pre-existence of Abraham in God's
thoughts before the creation of the world. Abraham – the divine
logic of God, for whom the whole world was conceived.[85]

The world began under the aegis of Abraham. And as in God
beginning and end correspond, it is no wonder that Abraham also
plays a decisive role at each human being's end. In the last judgment
he prevents the pious Jew from sinking into the world of shadows,
the underworld (Gehinnom).

> [God said to him]: 'Thou has opened a good door for travellers;
> thou hast opened a good door to proselytes, for if not for thee I had
> not created heaven and earth . . . Again, but for thee I had not
> created the orb of the sun . . . But for thee I had not created the
> moon . . .' R.Levi said: In the Hereafter Abraham will sit at the
> entrance to Gehenna, and permit no circumcised Israelite to
> descend therein. What then will he do to those who have sinned
> very much? He will remove the foreskin from babes who died
> before circumcision and set it upon them [the sinners] and then let
> them descend into Gehenna.[86]

This is matched by the notion that the merits which Abraham
obtained before God are so great that they can be put in the balance

in favour of poor, humble Israel not only in temporal forgiveness of sins but also at the last judgment. In one of the great rabbinic sources Israel is compared with an 'orphan' who grew up in a palace and at the time of her marriage, when asked about her dowry, could only refer to the merits of 'father' and 'grandfather'. Thus the merits of ancestors count from generation to generation, and these merits can finally also be reckoned in the last judgment of Israel.[87]

Indeed some rabbis even go so far as to emphasize the significance of Abraham for God himself. In the Midrash on the Psalms there is a unique passage, the theological focus of which is surely not to be read without the humour which is always a characteristic of the rabbis. In interpreting Psalm 18.36, various rabbis are discussing what is said here about the relationship between God and human beings: 'and your help made me great'. They are agreed on two things. This verse speaks of a God who behaves in a surprisingly different way from what one would expect of a human being. And this verse is about Abraham. So Rabbi Judan in the name of Rabbi Chamas tells the following little story, which is unique in theology, by way of illustration:

> In the time-to-come, when the Holy One, blessed be He, seats the Lord Messiah at His right hand, as is said, *The Lord saith unto my Lord: 'Sit thou at My right hand'* (Ps.110.1), and seats Abraham at His left, Abraham's face will pale, and he will say to the Lord: 'My son's son sits at the right, and I at the left!' Whereupon the Holy One, blessed be He, will comfort Abraham, saying: 'Thy son's son is at My right, but I, in a manner of speaking, am at thy right.'[88]

We should be clear that in Israel to sit 'at the right hand' is an expression of unique dignity and power. So the one who sits at God's right hand participates in God's divinity. In addition, this Midrash passage probably reflects a change of meaning in the interpretation of Psalm 110, which the earlier synagogue evidently applied to Abraham (cf. bSanh 108b), while later generations applied it to the Messiah.[89] However, the 'jealousy' of 'grandfather' Abraham over his 'grandson' which necessarily emerges as a result is settled by God himself, who condescends to put Abraham at the centre (in his own place) and says that he is on Abraham's right hand. One could hardly exalt Abraham higher than this in Judaism.

The first monotheist and missionary

It is very much in keeping with the post-exilic theology of Abraham (above all Joshua 24 and Jubilees) that individual rabbinic scholars also express the conviction that Abraham freed himself from the idolatry of his family and of his own accord discovered the existence of the true God with the help of reason. The only dispute is over the age at which Abraham came to believe in the true God, whether at one, three, ten or forty-eight years of age.[90] Indeed the great Midrash on the book of Genesis contains an entertaining story in which Abraham's fight with the idolators is depicted in a more colourful way and at greater length than had previously been the case in tradition. This is one of the finest pieces of haggadic tradition. For in the corresponding legend, which is meant to explain Gen. 11.28 ('Haran died before his father Terah in the land of his birth, in Ur of the Chaldeans'), now not only Abraham's father Terah and brother Haran play a role, but also the ruler of Ur, the mighty Nimrod, of whom we have already heard in the prelude, in connection with Nelly Sachs' poetic drama.

Let us listen to this dramatic story, which is similarly told with humour and was to have unusual influence (extending even to the Qur'an). In it many aspects come together: Abraham's wit and cunning towards the false gods, whose emptiness and nothingness he unmasks; Abraham as a destroyer of idols, who is himself saved from the fire in a miraculous way with the help of the true God – in contrast to his brother Haran, who was still undecided:

> Terah was a manufacturer of idols. He once went away somewhere and left Abraham to sell them in his place. A man came and wished to buy one. 'How old are you?' Abraham asked him. 'Fifty years,' was the reply. 'Woe to such a man!' he exclaimed, 'you are fifty years old and would worship a day-old object!' At this he became ashamed and departed. On another occasion a woman came with a plateful of flour and requested him, 'Take this and offer it to them.' So he took a stick, broke them, and put the stick in the hand of the largest. When his father returned he demanded, 'What have you done to them?' 'I cannot conceal it from you,' he rejoined. 'A woman came with a plateful of fine meal and requested me to offer it to them. One claimed, "I must eat first," while another claimed, "I must eat first." Thereupon the largest arose, took the stick and broke them.' 'Why do you make sport of

me,' he cried out; 'have they then any knowledge?' 'Should not your ears listen to what your mouth is saying,' he retorted. Thereupon he seized him and delivered him to Nimrod. 'Let us worship the fire!' he [Nimrod] proposed. 'Let us rather worship water, which extinguishes the fire,' replied he. 'Then let us worship water!' 'Let us rather worship the clouds which bear the water.' 'Then let us worship the clouds!' 'Let us rather worship the winds which disperse the clouds.' 'Then let us worship the wind!' 'Let us rather worship human beings, who withstand the wind.' 'You are just bandying words,' he exclaimed; 'we will worship nought but the fire. Behold, I will cast you into it, and let your God whom you adore come and save you from it.' Now Haran was standing there undecided. If Abram is victorious [thought he], I will say that I am of Abram's belief, while if Nimrod is victorious I will say that I am on Nimrod's side. When Abram descended into the fiery furnace and was saved, he [Nimrod] asked him, 'Of whose belief are you?' 'Of Abram's,' he replied. Thereupon he seized and cast him into the fire; his inwards were scorched and he died in his father's presence. Hence it is written, 'And Haran died in the presence of his father Terah'.[91]

This rabbinic story achieves its moral point by the contrast between Abraham and two false ways of believing: idolatry, represented by his father Terah and king Nimrod, which is unmasked as self-deception (the transitory has been confused with the eternal), and despair and indecision, represented by his brother Haran, who has to pay for it with his life. But the true believer in God is the one who cannot be conquered, since – as is demonstrated in the case of Nimrod – fire is one of the transitory things which can be annihilated by the representatives of the 'eternal'.

This motif finds a focus in other texts in which Abraham is seen as the first monotheistic missionary. For according to this same great midrash, Abraham 'brought Gentiles to the knowledge of God' even in his homeland: Abraham 'converted the men and Sarah the women to Judaism'.[92] Indeed for some rabbis Abraham's wandering is like opening a flask of balsam from which the savour streams forth and spreads everywhere:

What did Abraham resemble? A phial of myrrh closed with a tight-fitting lid and lying in a corner, so that its fragrance was not disseminated; as soon as it was taken up, however, its fragrance was disseminated. Similarly, the Holy One, blessed be He, said to Abraham: 'Travel from place to place, and thy name will become great in the world.'[93]

7. The paradox: the non-Jew Abraham is made a Jew

It is not surprising that there is a price to pay for this process in which Abraham becomes a priest and a rabbi. And the price which the rabbis were prepared to pay in their special situation was that of a far-reaching restriction of the biblical narrative about Abraham to Abraham's role for Israel alone. Here, too, the rabbis reinforce a particular post-exilic picture of Abraham.

Israel alone is the child of Abraham

There is no mistaking the fact that among the rabbis God's blessing for the nations of the world has largely been replaced by the exclusive line of blessing which runs through Abraham, Isaac and Jacob, loyal to the rabbinic programme of the deliberate segregation and self-preservation of Israel among the nations of the world. For this theological logic the rabbis could resort to biblical texts. According to the Torah God in fact elected only one son of Abraham in a special way and made him partner in the third covenant, namely Isaac. The other descendants of Abraham, Ishmael and the sons of Keturah, are only sons of the flesh, sons of human will and not divine promise. So it is no coincidence that these sons were rejected or paid off by Abraham himself. However much may have grown out of the root of Abraham, even though Ishmael shares a grandfather and Esau a mother (Rebecca) with Jacob-Israel, they do not now belong in Israel's line of covenant and blessing and are therefore not part of God's uniquely elect people.[94]

In other words, in the view of many rabbis Israel can claim for itself the exclusive right to be a child of Abraham. According to the tractate Sanhedrin in the Babylonian Talmud:

An alternative answer to this: Circumcision was from the very first commanded to Abraham only: *Thou shalt keep my covenant, therefore, thou and thy seed after thee in their generations*, meaning, thou and thy seed are to keep it, but no others. If so, should it not be incumbent upon the children of Ishmael? – *For in* Isaac *shall thy seed be called*. Then should not the children of Esau be bound to practise it? *In* Isaac, but not all Isaac. R.Oshaia objected: If so, the children of Keturah should have been exempt! Did not R.Jose b.Abin, or as others say, R.Jose b.Hanina, state: he hath broken my covenant – this extends the precept [of circumcision] to the children of Keturah (bSanh 59b).

Other texts move in the same direction, above all when they depict rivalry between Ishmael and Isaac as to who is Abraham's favourite son. Here the possibility of the sacrifice of Isaac became the criterion for the rabbis as to who was the authentic child of Abraham. According to the great midrash on Genesis:

Isaac and Ishmael were engaged in a controversy: the latter argued, 'I am more beloved than thou, because I was circumcised at the age of thirteen'; while the other retorted, 'I am more beloved than thou, because I was circumcised at eight days.' Said Ishmael unto him: 'I am more beloved, because I could have protested, yet did not.' At that moment Isaac exclaimed: 'O that God would appear to me and bid me cut off one of my limbs! then I would not refuse.' Said God: 'Even if I bid thee sacrifice thyself, thou wilt not refuse.' (Another version: Said Ishmael to him: 'I am more beloved than thou, since I was circumcised at the age of thirteen, but thou wast circumcised as a baby and couldst not refuse.' Isaac retorted: 'All that thou didst lend to the Holy One, blessed be He, was three drops of blood. But lo, I am now thirty-seven years old, yet if God desired of me that I be slaughtered, I would not refuse.' Said the Holy One, blessed be He: 'This is the moment!' Straightway, God did prove Abraham.)[95]

We should not deceive ourselves: behind this apparently playful children's dispute lies a serious theological problem: that of the exclusive election of Isaac (and thus of Jacob/Israel) as the only legitimate son of Abraham. So the claim of rabbinic Judaism is clear: the other sons of Abraham or Isaac (Ishmael or Esau) are the primal ancestors of alien peoples. Only the descendants of Jacob/Israel, the third patriarch, are 'perfect':

From Abraham sprang Ishmael and all the sons of Keturah; from Isaac sprang Esau and all the chiefs of Edom; but Jacob's bed was perfect, all his sons being righteous.[96]

Abraham as the primal father of all converts

And yet even the rabbis still left the 'door' of their Judaism very slightly ajar. For they, too, could not overlook the fact that scripture knows a phase of Abraham's life in which he was not yet the pious Jew who was faithful to the law, as the rabbis were fond of seeing him. For some of his life Abraham had been a Gentile; he was still in search of the true God, and did not yet practise the Torah. This fact must also have had some significance. What was it?

In short, Abraham's 'non-Jewish' phase of life helped to solve a theological problem with which the rabbis, too, were constantly confronted, for all their efforts to segregate themselves: the problem of non-Jews who wanted to convert. Didn't Abraham provide something like a primal model for dealing with the proselytism of the time, with people who were eager to convert to Judaism? Philo and Josephus had also reflected on this problem. Certainly at different times the rabbis had different attitudes to proselytism, sometimes friendly and open, sometimes dismissive and reserved.[97] Yet they, too, could not overlook the fact that here Abraham showed another way. A complete separation of Judaism from the world was therefore impossible. For even the rabbis could not deny that God evidently loved the proselytes: not least because of Abraham. Moreover in the Bablyonian Talmud and in other rabbinic collections Abraham is called 'the first of the proselytes' (bHagigah 3a), indeed the 'father of proselytes'.[98] To explain this the rabbis did not cite the 'unwritten' Torah of nature, as Philo of Alexandria did. Another structure of argument was needed. And here the late circumcision of Abraham played a decisive role.

'Why was Abraham only circumcised at the age of ninety-nine?', many rabbis asked. They explained it by saying that this indicated that no candidate for conversion need regard himself as being too old. The door was not to be closed on the proselytes.[99] And there was a second argument: Abraham had been an alien, a 'sojourner' in the promised land. The rabbis also took up this important feature of the biblical stories about Abraham. Its meaning, too, could now be transferred – transferred to the way in which strangers were dealt with in the Judaism of their day. Moreover, in a midrash on the book of Exodus (Mekhilta) there is a vivid illustration of how certain rabbis thought about this process:

Beloved are the sojourners, for Abraham, our father, first circumcised himself as a son of ninety-nine years; for had he
circumcised himself as a son of twenty or as a son of thirty years, a
sojourner could only have become a proselyte with less than thirty
years. Therefore God pondered about him (postponed making a
covenant with him) until he reached ninety-nine years, so as not to
close the doors against sojourners who should come.[100]

So Abraham is the door through which even 'sojourners', non-Jews,
find access to Judaism. What is left of the blessing of the nations is at
least that individual people from the nations are blessed if they
convert to the true God. The blessing to the nations has become a
blessing for the proselytes.

However, we should not minimize this. For there is a theological
basis here for a relationship between normative Judaism and other
forms of faith, 'godfearing' people. For the rabbis, too, through
Abraham, Judaism in principle remained capable of such a relationship, capable of choosing, of being open to others, as is also the case
with the great patriarchal figure of Noah. It is enough for non-Jews
to observe the seven 'Noachide' commandments in order to gain a
'portion in the world to come'.[101] In the second part of this book we
shall be returning to this decisive theological model – the foundation
of the capacity for Judaism to have inter-religious relationships even
today.

Moreover one of the finest texts on the significance of Abraham
and Sarah (!) appears in the rabbinic work Pesikta Rabbati, a writing
presumably compiled as early as the ninth century CE, which
contains conversations about festivals, fast days and special celebra-
tions of the sabbath. Here we have a model explanation of almost
erotic attraction as to why proselytes and godfearers are welcome in
Judaism. At the centre of this story stands Abraham's wife Sarah,
who here is regarded as the mother of all non-Jewish peoples and
nations:

At the time that Sarah gave birth to Isaac, the nations of the earth
said, 'He is really the son of her maidservant, and she makes
believe that she is suckling him.' In instant reply to them Abraham
said to Sarah: 'Sarah, don't just stand there! This is not a time for
modesty. For the hallowing of the Name arise and uncover
yourself.' Sarah arose and uncovered herself, and her two nipples
were pouring out milk like two jets of water, as it is written: *and*

she said: 'Who would have said unto Abraham that Sarah would give children suck?' (Gen.21.7) . . .

At the sight of Sarah's milk the nations of the earth brought their children to Sarah to give them suck, thus confirming the truth of the statement that Sarah would give children suck. Now some of them in all sincerity brought their children for Sarah to give them suck, some brought their children only to check up on her. Neither the former nor the latter suffered any loss. According to R.Levi, those who were brought in sincerity became proselytes. In regard to these scripture says, *Sarah would give children suck.* How is the expression *give children suck* to be interpreted? That these children of the nations of the earth became children of Israel. And according to our Masters, those children who were brought to check up on Sarah achieved promotion to great office. Accordingly, all Gentiles throughout the world who accept conversion and all Gentiles throughout the world who fear God spring from the children who drank of the milk of Sarah. Hence Sarah is alluded to as a *joyful mother of children.*[102]

Thus it is clear that for certain rabbis Abraham is the primal model of all proselytes, the ancestor of all non-Jewish nations who are in search of the true God. Moreover, to the present day non-Jews who confess Judaism are called 'sons of Abraham'. If for example a convert went over to Judaism, he would be invited to read the Torah at worship with the call 'son of our father Abraham'.[103]

What does it mean to be a spiritual child of Abraham?

So we face an ambiguous result in the way in which the figure of Abraham is deal with within Judaism.

First, from the beginning Abraham was a theological-political figure with the help of whom creative theological attempts were made to react to ever-new challenges of history. Down to the Hellenistic period reception of him oscillated between particularism and universalism, between strict religious segregation and openness to religious culture. Only in Jewish orthodoxy – reinforcing certain post-exilic tendencies – does a process begin in which Abraham becomes a priest and rabbi, in short, a process in which Abraham becomes linked with the halakhah. There is thus something quite paradoxical about the evidence: in Jewish orthodoxy the non-Jew Abraham, living before the halakhah, becomes a pious Jew who has already observed the whole Torah (both written and oral) and thus seems almost like a rabbi and a priest. And the spiritual interpretations of Abraham in later Jewish mysticism, in Hasidism and Kabbalism, which have been impressively described by the American Jewish reform theologian Arthur Green, do not change this basic tendency.[104] For it is also clear to the mystics that Abraham belongs only to Judaism; only from the descendants of Isaac and Jacob do the true children of Abraham stem. Of the blessing for the people communicated through Abraham, only the blessing on the people Israel is left.

Secondly, orthodoxy left open just one crack in the system of halakhah. For it, too, could not deny that while Abraham belongs to Judaism, at the same time he also transcends it. So even for the rabbis Abraham remained a connecting link between Israel and the nations, between Judaism and paganism: a man of two worlds, who moreover can lead from one world to the other. In the end the rabbis, too, leave no doubt that Abraham is not only the physical ancestor of Israel but also the spiritual ancestor of all those who come from non-Jewish nations, in so far as they seek the true God. Certainly the peoples are not blessed for their own sake, but only in so far as they already seek the God of Israel. But Abraham can thus at least be the primal ancestor of all converts, of all those from the peoples and nations who want to attain true knowledge of God.

Thus we also find in the rabbis that notion which will become so important for the 'New Testament' of the Christians: being a child of Abraham is not measured only by external descent but also by moral criteria, and of itself is not as yet a guarantee of salvation. One of the finest texts on this again appears in the 'Sayings of the Fathers', the Pirqe Aboth. Here the disciples of Abraham and the disciples of Balaam are contrasted, i.e. the disciples of the man who is presented in the Bible as a malicious seducer to idolatry (Num.31.8,16; Josh. 13.22) or as a false teacher (II Peter 2.13f.):

He in whom are these three things is of the disciples of Abraham our father; but [he in whom are] three other things is of the disciples of Balaam the wicked. A good eye and a humble spirit and a lowly soul – [they in whom are these] are of the disciples of Abraham our father. An evil eye, a haughty spirit, and a proud soul – [they in whom are these] are of the disciple of Balaam the wicked. How do the disciples of Abraham our father differ from the disciples of Balaam the wicked? The disciples of Abraham our father enjoy this world and inherit the world to come, as it is written, 'That I may cause those that love me to inherit substance and that I may fill their treasuries. The disciples of Balaam the wicked inherit Gehenna and go down into the pit of destruction; bloodthirsty and deceitful men shall not live out half their days.'[105]

So someone who has a good eye, a humble spirit and a lowly soul is part of the family of Abraham. And someone who belongs to the family of Abraham is accepted into God's history of covenant and blessing with his elect people. So to be a child of Abraham in normative Judaism can be more than a matter of genealogy. It can become a moral term – in accordance with the saying from a tractate of the Talmud:

> Whoever is merciful to his fellow-men is certainly of the children of our father Abraham, and whosoever is not merciful to his fellow-men is certainly not of the children of our father Abraham.[106]

Maimonides and the case of a convert

No Jewish theologian more impressively embodies the greatness and limitations of orthodox Judaism than Moses Maimonides (1135-1203). He was born in Cordoba and died in Cairo, and is regarded as one of the greatest orthodox theologians of mediaeval Judaism. His greatness emerges in particular in his interpretation of Abraham, as has recently been shown by the Jerusalem Jewish theologian David Hartman in his book on Maimonides. For in Maimonides Abraham is not the model of the halakhic man but according to the haggadic tradition a man of reason, a God-seeker who repudiates idolatry and the natural knowledge of God. Philo's and Josephus' pictures of Abraham are akin to this thought.

Thus Maimonides, too, stressed the philosophical tradition more strongly in the case of Abraham. And the Midrashim in particular gave Maimonides the possibility of showing through Abraham 'how the tradition understood the way of reason to God. By reflecting on nature, people became aware that the universe cannot be known without the recognition of God as the source of Existence. It is equally central that haggadic man feels challenged to put the world of idolatry in question.'[107]

In this context we can also have a better understanding of the treatment of a 'case' by Moses Maimonides. When a Crusader, Obadiah, who became a Jew, put a question to Moses Maimonides as to whether although he was not biologically descended from Abraham he could still worship God as the 'God of *our* father Abraham, Isaac and Jacob', Maimonides replied to this question quite decisively in an 'opinion'.

> Therefore anyone who turns to Judaism and confesses the oneness of the divine name as it is written in the Torah, will be counted to the end of all times among the disciples of Abraham, our father, peace be upon him. These people are of the household of Abraham, and he it is who has converted them too to the good. Just as he converted his contemporaries by his discourse and his instruction, so he converts all those in the future through the Testament which he has presented to his sons and his house after him. So Abraham our father, peace be upon him, is the father of his pious descendants who walk in his ways and the father of his disciples and all proselytes who turn to Judaism. Therefore you shall pray, 'Our God and God of our fathers', for Abraham, peace be upon him, is *your* father.[108]

Maimonides and many rabbis in his spirit indicate impressively the greatness and the limitation of the world of orthodox Judaism. Its limitation beyond doubt lies in the exclusive claim to Abraham for Israel and the denial of God's blessing for all peoples which is communicated through Abraham. Its greatness consists in the confession that in principle Judaism is also open to non-Jews, that one can also be the descendant of Abraham if one does good works in a good spirit. So with the Jewish theologian Jacob Petuchowski it can be said: 'In Judaism the term "son of Abraham" is not limited to people of a certain descent, as one can also be a son of Abraham in the spiritual sense.'[109]

Particularism and universalism: this tension governs the thought of Jews from the time of the Yahwist. Israel as the people elected by God and God's purpose with the peoples — how does that go together? This tension was now taken up and sustained by a religious movement which came from Jewish roots and which was to transfer the blessing of Abraham to the world of the peoples: Christianity.

II. Abraham and Christianity

As we have seen, anyone in Israel who wanted to demonstrate that they belonged to the elect people and the true God could, indeed had to, refer to Abraham. 'Our father Abraham' – that was the proud formula. To be the 'seed' of Abraham, the 'child' of Abraham: that was the all-important thing. Abraham our father, Moses, our teacher; around these poles, like an ellipse, life revolved for any pious Jew. And Abraham in particular was the idealized figure with which Jews faithful to the law identified. That was also the case at the time when a Jew was growing up in the Galilean town of Nazareth – far away from Alexandria, Rome and Jerusalem – who was to develop into an authoritative preacher of repentance, pointing to the imminent 'kingdom of God': Jesus of Nazareth.[1]

1. Jesus of Nazareth: renews, does not displace, Israel

A tremendous amount has been written about him down to most recent times. The portraits of the Nazarene range from uncritical adulation to the commandeering of him for a political ideology. Some regard him as the 'founder of Christianity', others as the 'first new man' or even as a 'marginal Jew'.[2] And it has to be conceded that countless individual features of his person, his message, his conduct and his fate are still disputed – not only their authenticity but their significance and meaning.

However, there is a widespread consensus over one thing: the carpenter's son from Nazareth was out to convert Israel, not to found a new religion. On his wanderings, from Galilee in the north to Judaea in the south, from Nazareth and the area round the Sea of Galilee to Jerusalem, he attached supreme importance to one thing: to a renewal and purification of the spirit, a change of heart, not to a new religious institution. 'The time is fulfilled, and the kingdom of God is at hand; repent, and believe in the gospel' (Mark 1.15). That may have been the basic challenge of his message, and not the replacement of Israel with something else.

What Israel has to relearn

In principle Jesus lived as a Jew faithful to the law. And yet the form of religion which he encountered everywhere led him to object, indeed occasionally to burst out with angry polemic:
— What about the externalized practice of religion which he found, for example, in the temple in Jerusalem? He abhorred it, and in a moment of enthusiastic divine wrath could exclaim: 'My house shall be called a house of prayer for all the nations? But you have made it a den of robbers' (Mark 11.17);
— What about the pious practice of separating to become an elite so that there are those who please God and sinners, those knowledgable in the law and those who have no clue about religion? He broke through this, where it seemed right to him to do so, for the sake of God and human beings: 'Why does he eat with publicans and sinners?' (Mark 2.16).
— What about the pious moralism which consisted in an inflated system of religious accomplishments? Jesus could set himself above this in a sovereign way, or, more precisely, in a spirit of untroubled joy in God and creation could break through traditional social barriers and limits: 'Can the wedding guests fast while the bridegroom is with them?' (Mark 2.19). The principle had to apply everywhere that 'the sabbath was made for man, not man for the sabbath' (Mark 2.27).

With none of this did the man from Nazareth want to declare sweepingly that the old and venerable Torah was invalid or to abolish it completely. It would never have occurred to him to put himself in the place of Abraham. As a matter of course the Galilean Jew Jesus shared the faith in the God of Israel, who for him was also the God of Abraham, Isaac and Jacob. At all events, the evangelist Mark does not hesitate to put a saying to this effect on the lips of Jesus (Mark 12.26). So once again: with his message Jesus did not want to 'displace' Israel, but to renew Israel in the spirit of repentance. To be blunt, Israel was 'his "church"; it was the people, who had once again definitively to be summoned to the kingdom of God'.[3] And Jesus emphasized this kingdom, this kingly rule of God, in such a way that it seemed to be concentrated in his own conduct and the law seemed to be interpreted in terms of the unconditional and boundless humanity of God.

In the light of this rule of God, Israel was above all to learn to remove the artificial separations, limits and demarcations – they were not in accord with God's will. Away with pious hypocrisy, religious conformity and casuistic morality – this did not accord with God's boundless mercy. Away, too, with the hierarchies of achievement, the pious desires for comparison: 'If anyone would be first, he must be last of all and servant of all' (Mark 9.35). An end, above all, to thought in terms of descent and legitimation, an end to the notion that it was enough simply to refer to one's membership of the chosen people, to descent from the 'fathers', to be well pleasing to God, i.e. justified in God's eyes. No, before God something else was important: to fulfil his will rather than engage in human calculations, seek human privileges and inherited rights.

So already among the disciples of Jesus other relationships, other families, form, different from physical families, which are a matter of inheritance and can be demonstrated with genealogies. Moreover, the three earliest evangelists, Mark, Matthew and Luke, have handed down a saying of Jesus to this effect, which may exactly express his basic attitude:

And his mother and his brothers came; and standing outside they sent to him and called him. And a crowd was sitting about him; and they said to him, 'Your mother and your brothers are outside, asking for you.' And he replied, 'Who are my mother and my brothers?' And looking around at those who sat about him, he said, "Here are my mother and my brothers. Whoever does the will of God is my brother, and sister, and mother"' (Mark 3.31– 35; Matt.12.46–50; Luke 18.19–21).

Many of Jesus' Jewish brothers and sisters followed him and thus formed the first new Jesus community. Discipleship was indeed the decisive word, and initially this consisted quite specifically in travelling around with Jesus, giving up one's homeland, parting from one's original family, leaving one's work. The old homeland was to be replaced 'in the Spirit', the old family transcended in the new, work relegated to a matter of secondary importance by the calling: 'Truly, I say to you, there is no one who has left house or brothers or sisters or mother or father or children or lands, for my sake and for the gospel, who will not receive them a hundredfold' (Mark 10.29f.).

But the religious authorities of the time saw this itinerant preacher from Galilee above all as a religious provocation. The guardians of the temple (the Sadducees) and the guardians of the written and oral Torah (Pharisees) did not see the liberating, purifying impulse in the message of Jesus, but only what was irritating and scandalous. There was anxiety over matters of principle, especially as 'many people' flocked to the man from Nazareth or began to listen to him (cf. John 11.47–50). As we heard, unrest was a sign of the times. Shortly beforehand, Rome had sent a governor for the first time, after the death of King Herod. His name was Pontius Pilate and he was regarded as a brutal man. Unrest with religious motivation was therefore now anything but opportune. So it did not take much more to do away with this figure, so highly praised by his followers and celebrated with neo-messianic enthusiasm, in the interplay of Jewish and Roman authorities.

The failure of Israel to convert

Jesus of Nazareth died in 30, shamefully executed on the cross like a common criminal. But the calculations of those responsible for his death did not work out. The messianic fire among his followers, rather than being quenched, turned into a conflagration. For, taking up a belief in the resurrection of the dead which had been widespread since the time of apocalyptic, Jesus' followers could not give up their conviction that the crucified Jesus was alive. He had not remained dead. God himself had not left this just man in the lurch but had raised him to new life. Indeed God had by his authority made the risen Christ Messiah of Israel and Lord of the whole world (Acts 2.36). He was now appointed – through the resurrection – 'Son of God in power' (Rom.1.3f.). Now he was sitting 'on the right hand of God'[4] – thus the first Christians, taking up the image of the throne from Psalm 110.

But that meant that from then on the Jewish followers of Jesus – initially in Jerusalem and later also in Palestine and Syria – formed first communities. To begin with, these differed from their Jewish environment in only one thing: they believed in Jesus as the Messiah of Israel confirmed by God, who would soon appear again as Son of Man in judgment. And they believed that the renewal of Israel in the spirit, which had already been practised by Jesus, had to go on. The first Christians, too, had not thought of abandoning Israel, of superseding it, replacing it or over-trumping it. As pious Jews, of course they too maintained Israel's unique position before God. The New Testament sources themselves report that the first Jewish followers of Jesus practised circumcision, observed the sabbath and the festivals, and submitted to the legal demands for ritual cleanness. Down to the destruction of the temple they will have taken part in temple worship and prayed in the synagogues (cf. Acts 2.46; 5.42). The 'shema Israel', 'Hear O Israel', the primal confession of the one and only God, resounded among them; so did the Shemoneh esre, the Eighteen Benedictions, in the first petition of which God is invoked as the God of 'Abraham, Isaac and Jacob', indeed as the 'shield of Abraham'. There is no doubt that, like Jesus of Nazareth, his Jewish followers believed in this God who revealed himself to Abraham, Isaac and Jacob, and in the promises for the people which this God had never revoked.

So the conversion of Israel was to go on. But since the man from Nazareth had suffered this shameful death and had been unmasked as a false Messiah in the eyes of all, all attempts in this direction met with even more bitter resistance than before – resistance above all among certain parts of the populace and among the leaders. Indeed the repudiation of the followers of Jesus may have been heightened further by the fact that with its eschatological proclamation the earliest community was caught 'between the fronts in the situation of growing political crisis in Palestine': 'It was branded a traitor by the zealot movement because of its call for non-violence and peacemaking. By contrast, because of its eschatological message it could be lumped with the rebels by moderate Jewish groups prepared to collaborate with the Romans.'[5]

No wonder that the Jewish-Christian itinerant missionaries seemed to have been sent like 'sheep among wolves' (Matt.10.16). Being a disciple of Christ now often literally meant taking up the cross, and was associated with humiliation and persecution. That is explained above all by the fact that the more time went on, the clearer it was that the mission was failing. A conversion of 'all Israel'? In the course of time this proved increasingly illusory. All experiences in this direction were negative. The consequence was words of judgment against a people which was so manifestly blinded.[6] And these words of judgment already appear in the earliest collection of New Testament sayings, known to scholars as Q (for Quelle, German for 'source' – a sayings source). It may have been composed in Palestine-Syria in the 60s. It represents a collection of usually brief, pregnant, sayings of Jesus which the evangelists Mathew and Luke later worked into their Gospels.

So here already we have first polemic – possibly going back to Jesus himself – against the Israel of the present which is unready to repent and incapable of being converted, against what is explicitly called the 'evil generation' (Luke 11.29), and not against Israel as a whole. This generation is threatened with judgment:

> The queen of the South will arise at the judgment with the men of this generation and condemn them; for she came from the ends of the earth to hear the wisdom of Solomon, and behold, something greater than Solomon is here. The men of Nineveh will arise at the judgment with this generation and condemn it; for they repented at the preaching of Jonah, and behold, something greater than Jonah is here' (Luke 11.31f.).

The theological point of this and other threats is abundantly clear and arises from the contrast between the 'men of Israel' on the one hand and the 'Gentiles' on the other. Gentiles like the Queen of Sheba or the men of Nineveh did something that would have been expected of members of the people of Israel: they listened to the true wisdom and turned from the wrong way. If this did not happen, so much the worse for this generation! For this gospel surpassed any 'wisdom' (Solomon) or prophecy (Jonah) hitherto known in Israel. But the result was indifference, a failure to pay attention. And that would have consequences in the last judgment. The pagans would rise up against the Israel of 'this generation'.

The other table-fellowship with Abraham

Against this background we can now have a better understanding of the New Testament text in which Abraham first appears. This may be the earliest primitive Christian allusion to Abraham, as the text also comes from the Sayings Source. Nor would it be wholly wrong to conjecture that this saying, too, goes back to Jesus himself. In the version that Matthew has preserved, which may be the more original, it runs:

> 'Many will come from east and west and sit at table with Abraham, Isaac, and Jacob in the kingdom of heaven, while the

sons of the kingdom will be thrown into the outer darkness; there men will weep and gnash their teeth' (Matt.8.11f.; Luke 13.28f.).

After all that we have heard of Abraham and the 'fathers of Israel', we can see that the provocation in this saying of Jesus for the Israel of his time could not be greater. Here he touches on a sore point and means to do so. In their boundless disappointment at the attitude of large parts of the people, Jewish followers of Jesus rise to making an unprecedented claim. The 'many from east and west' – who else can they be than the Gentiles? The 'sons of the kingdom' – who else are these than the originally elect people of Israel, who have been promised 'salvation' and not disaster by God? But in the new conditions everything has changed. Everything has been turned upside down: non-Jews will sit at table with the 'patriarchs of Israel', with Abraham, Isaac and Jacob (there is an allusion to Isa.25.6). By contrast Israel sees itself rejected, banished into a cruel darkness.

The nations will come: this saying of Jesus takes up the old prophetic idea of the pilgrimage of nations to Mount Zion in Jerusalem, but with a significant 'Christian' shift of meaning.[7] For according to the visionary statements of the prophets Zechariah and Isaiah, one day the people will stream to Mount Zion to receive from Israel's God 'instruction about his ways' (Isa.2.2f.; Zech.2.15). Now this announcement presupposes that Israel itself serves its God without reservations. However, for the Jewish followers of Jesus, precisely that is not the case at present. Therefore now everything is different. Now the nations are coming – despite Israel. Now the nations are participating in the blessing for Israel – without Israel. So the original meaning of the pilgrimage of the nations, in the light of Israel's attitude to Jesus, is being stood on its head. Instead of the Gentile nations receiving blessing through Israel, they alone are blessed. Israel is rejected, banished into 'outer darkness'. This is a tremendous statement – but is it an anti-Jewish statement? Is this one of the earliest examples of Christian anti-Judaism in the New Testament?

Scholars are not agreed about this. For some, such a saying presupposes not only a friendliness towards the Gentiles but already a break with Israel and a Gentile mission which has been set in motion, and at the same time the presence of Gentile Christians in the communities which stand behind the Sayings Source.[8] Others can see here only a controversy between Jews and Jewish Christians.[9]

Whatever the case may be, the decisive thing seems to me that even this word of judgment on Israel is not a definitive, damning farewell; it is not a disinheritance of Israel but an act of final hope for Israel. For there is no doubt about it here: 'the kingdom' really belongs to Israel. The Jews are really the elect 'sons'. The pilgrimage, the great feast of the nations announced by the prophet Isaiah (25.6): none of this is taken back, but on the contrary is once again confirmed by the saying about Abraham.

In other words, the allusion to Abraham and the threat about the Israel of the day do not go so far as to dispute in principle that Israel is the child of Abraham and now to claim the 'patriarchs of Israel' exclusively for the Gentiles. In the context of judgment it has a quite limited function: to warn and shake Israel, so that it may truly repent. The Gentiles who recline at table with the 'patriarchs' instead of Israel are meant to present Israel with an extreme possibility, to make it think. The saying of Jesus to be reflected on here is thus 'not a promise of Jesus for the nations but a warning for the "sons of the kingdom" – they alone are addressed, and the whole saying is intended for them'.[10] In short, the saying about different company for Abraham at table, in the form of a threat and a judgment, is an act of final trust in Israel.

And yet, if the Jewish Christians, too, who interpreted their own difficult situation by means of this saying, did not yet want anything to do with a deliberate mission to the Gentiles, the possibility indicated here did seem one for the future – in a terrifying way. What the earliest Christians, whose collection of sayings was probably completed as early as the 60s, could not know but probably suspected, then actually took place: the temple was destroyed and Israel was again driven out of the promised land. The journey into the 'darkness' had in fact begun. And what about the saying about the other company at table for Abraham? It should probably be understood as storm clouds,[11] as the sign of a great catastrophe in Israel which then actually took place and did not spare even the Jewish Christian communities.

For these communities, too, were severely affected by the fall of Jerusalem. The earliest Jerusalem community had in any case perished in the confusions of the Jewish war. According to the first church historian, Eusebius, it had left Jerusalem even before the beginning of the war and as a result of a revelation moved to Pella, a Hellenistic city in Transjordan. We do not know whether this account is reliable. Presumably after the destruction of Jerusalem Jewish Christians again settled in the ruins of the city, but the Jewish Christian community of Jerusalem now no longer had any significance for the church as a whole – compared, say, to the time of the apostle Paul. The church of Jesus Christ, which was originally made up of Jewish Christians, then of Jewish and Gentile Christians, increasingly developed into a church purely made up of Gentile Christians. Indeed, at a later date this Gentile church did not hesitate to make its own development the criterion for Christian orthodoxy and to brand the Jewish Christians as heretics, thus forcing them right to the periphery of the church.

The Jewish Christians have left behind an enigmatic saying, a paradox by means of which they attempted to express the dark mystery of their theology. It identifies a problem which must have tormented them without their finding a solution. This problem was: why has God closed up Israel against the promise? Why has the message of Jesus as the Messiah not been accepted? They attempted to fathom this riddle theologically. Evidently they saw no other possibility than to refer back to a paradoxical saying of the prophet Isaiah, who had already rebuked Israel for its hardness, indeed had even interpreted this hardness as an act of divine judgment (Isa.6.9f.); God himself was the author of the hardening of Israel. At any rate the evangelist Mark has handed down this offensive, 'horrendous saying'[12] of the Jewish Christians without further commentary:

> And when he was alone, those who were about him with the twelve asked him concerning the parables. And he said to them, 'To you has been given the secret of the kingdom of God, but for those outside everything is in parables; so that they may indeed see but not perceive, and may indeed hear but not understand; lest they should turn again, and be forgiven' (Mark 4.10–12).

Indeed this is a 'horrendous saying', which cannot be grasped with categories of the 'healthy human understanding', but can only be seen as an attempt on the part of a group of Jewish Christians to use the Isaiah saying as a heuristic tool and with its help clarify an oppressive problem of their day. 'How is the sovereignty of Yahweh to be thought of in view of the (apparent) failure of his prophet, the refusal of the people to think? That was the point from which Isaiah started. How is the sovereignty of God to be thought of in view of the (apparent) failure of his Messiah, the rejection of the Messiah by his own people? That is what the Christians asked. The Isaiah saying proved helpful for the analogous problem, in overcoming it both intellectually and also linguistically. Because the original situation of the Isaiah saying recurred in new co-ordinates, the original wording of Isaiah also proved fruitful.'[13]

2. Abraham, 'the father of us all – in the presence of God': Paul

However, in the long run it is impossible to do theology with riddles and paradoxes. And the age-old problem of the relationship between Jews and Gentiles had to be thought through again, in principle, at the latest at the time when both began to live together in one and the same Christian communities. That was now the case above all outside Palestine, in Greece and Asia Minor, and the main person behind this development had once been a pupil of the Pharisees and a Diaspora Jew: Paul from Tarsus, a city in Asia Minor. It is to him that we owe the first great theological scheme about Abraham, Israel and the nations – in view of the fact that many of the Gentiles had recognized Jesus as the Messiah of Israel for the world.[14]

The tension: Jew and Christian at the same time

As far as we can infer from his authentic correspondence, at the time of his activity as an apostle Paul left no doubt about two facts which at the same time formed the poles of his life and led to his being sharply repudiated by many fellow-Jews:

1. Paul was a Jew and even as a Christian did not deny his Jewishness. In his letters he attaches the utmost importance to this, above all when his Jewishness is put in question by his opponents. He was circumcised on the eighth day; he came from the 'people of Israel', or more precisely from the 'tribe of Benjamin'; he was a 'Hebrew of the Hebrews' and as a 'Pharisee' lived 'after the law' (Phil.3.5). Furthermore, he concedes that as a Jew he was particularly faithful to the law, i.e. surpassed most of his contemporaries in his loyalty to the Jewish law and devoted himself 'with the utmost zeal' to the traditions of the fathers (Gal.1.13f.). Indeed Paul himself concedes that on the basis of his earlier conviction he had persecuted the young Christian community 'zealously' (Phil.3.6), even 'violently' (Gal.1.13).[15]

2. The Jew Paul believed in Jesus as the Messiah of God for Israel and for the world. In this if in nothing else he differed from large parts of his people, above all from the Sadducean and Pharisaic establishment. He had experienced a 'new calling' through God, a revelation of Christ (Gal.1.10–16) which had led to a decisive change in his life. Instead of being a persecutor of Christians he had become a missionary to Christians who, in his unresting work, found himself exposed to infinite difficulties, harassments, trials and tribulations, even from the Jewish authorities in particular places. One only has to read the gripping autobiographical sketches in II Corinthians (4.7–12; 6.3–10; 11.22–33) to understand the kind of life this man led for the sake of Christ.

But weren't becoming a Christian and remaining a Jew mutually exclusive? For most Jews, yes, but for Paul certainly not. As a Christian he did not think of denouncing Judaism. Moreover even after he turned to Christ, Paul remained convinced that God had not rejected the people of Israel. If we follow his last letter, that to the Romans (9.1–5), Israel still has:

– the 'sonship': Israel remains God's 'firstborn son' (Exod.4.22).

– the 'glory', the 'Shekinah': it still dwells in the midst of the people, in the temple at Jerusalem (Ex.25.8).

– the 'covenants': all three covenants of God with Noah, Abraham and Moses remain in force.

– the 'Torah': it, too, has not simply been abolished after Christ, but is a permanent expression of God's will.

– the 'worship': the cultic ordinances of the temple have not been put out of action.

– the 'promises': the promises to Abraham and Isaac (a great people, land) and the expectation of a comprehensive consummation by the Messiah of Israel (II Sam.7.1) have not been revoked.

– the 'patriarchs': Abraham, Isaac and Jacob remain the formative figures for faith and life and serve to provide identity.

But it is precisely this which produced the tension: despite all the repudiation of Jesus as the Messiah, Israel might continue to feel that it was 'loved by God'. Why? Paul gives an unmistakable answer in good Jewish fashion: 'for the sake of the fathers' (Rom.11.28). So it is only consistent that at decisive points in his correspondence Paul continues to confess that he himself is a child of Abraham, above all when there is a dispute over this, i.e. when it is put in question by opponents in his communities. He can then passionately defend his own descent from Abraham: 'Are they Hebrews? So am I. Are they descendants of Abraham? So am I' (II Cor.11.22). But he will fight just as passionately for all those who believe in Jesus as the Christ to be able to be called children of Abraham, whether they are Jews or Gentiles. Why? What experiences underlie this? Wasn't being a child of Abraham an exclusive hallmark of Israel, indicating its election and salvation?

Certainly. But it was one of Paul's bitterest experiences, too, that large parts of Israel had refused to believe in Jesus as the Messiah, although God himself had appointed the crucified Nazarene 'Son of God in power' through the resurrection (Rom.1.4). That must have been deeply disturbing to a Jew like Paul: that the majority of the people chosen by God rejected the new message of salvation sent by God. But it was part of the same experience that the Gentiles who had not been specially thought of by God had seized this offer. Paul had drawn his own conclusions from this and since then had worked as an apostle for the Gentiles. Not to part company with Israel, but to make the members of his own people 'jealous', 'jealous of the new riches of the Gentiles', as he was to write later (Rom.11.11–15). At least this good thing had come out of the 'failure' of Israel by God's grace: now salvation really could come universally 'to the Gentiles' (Rom.11.1). But this presupposed that Gentiles did not have to do the works of the law, were free from Jewish ceremonial and ritual law, in other words free from the halakhah. Moreover Paul had argued passionately for precisely this.

The climax came at the so-called 'apostolic council' in Jerusalem in 48. Here Paul had gained the assent of the other apostles that Gentile Christians should be free in matters of the law. Belief in Christ and obedience to the Torah were in principle uncoupled – in principle, as far as the question of salvation was concerned. 'In Christ' there is freedom from the works of the law, even if in some circumstances – with inner freedom, like Paul himself – one can observe the law. But under the rule of Christ, who had been exalted by God and was present in the spirit, the halakhah had lost its absolute significance for salvation once and for all. Gentiles did not need first to become Jews in order to share in God's salvation: their faith in God's action in Jesus Christ was enough. That was the all-important thing for Paul.

But how could this be justified in theological terms? Paul derives his justification for his own personal life-style and missionary task from the most important figure with whom his people identified: no less a man than Abraham. That was also necessary if he was to be able to withstand the struggle which had now broken out. We first become witnesses of this passionate conflict over legitimation in the letter to the Galatians. It is a dispute over the correct interpretation of the story of Abraham, in which Paul is utterly convinced that he has scripture on his side.

The battle over the inclusion of the Gentiles

Chronologically, the letter to the community in Galatia, in Asia Minor, is Paul's second.[16] The first letter had gone to Thessaloniki, in Greece, written in a peaceful, friendly, sometimes admonitory tone. Now, in the letter to the Galatians, Paul is certainly in militant mood; he is disturbed at what has evidently taken place there in the community. Judaizing agitators (probably Jewish-Christian missionaries) had required that Gentile Christians should not only believe in Christ but also observe the Jewish command to be circumcised and thus the halakhah.

That necessarily disturbed Paul. Why? Because this demand (implying that faith in Christ was not enough for salvation, that the halakhah was necessary to complete it) went against everything that he had been working for over a long period. Above all it went against the consensus at the 'apostolic council' only a few years before. With good reason Paul had even 'opposed Peter to his face' (Gal.2.11). In short, it went against the spirit of Christian freedom. And because there was a threat that this freedom would be lost again in the Galatian community, Paul was furious and at the same time resolved to make a theological example of the question of freedom from the works of the law. He did so by referring to Abraham, the father of the Jews and the father of many peoples.

Why Abraham? Because Abraham in particular had presumably been used by Paul's rivals in the mission to make the incorporation of Gentile Christians, too, into the chosen people dependent on obedience to the Torah. All this was in accordance with the Jewish view that Abraham was the father of the proselytes. As we have heard, for a long time Abraham had been a model of observance of the law in the Jewish tradition. Indeed, the spirit of post-exilic theology reigned even in the time of Paul: to believe like Abraham meant loyal fulfilment of the commandments of the Torah; the righteousness of faith meant being rewarded by God for obedience to the faith. And even the blessing for the nations mediated through Abraham no longer had any unlimited, universal dimension but in fact had been reduced to a blessing for Israel and the proselytes. Abraham had become the property of Israel. God's blessing for the peoples had been condensed to a blessing for Israel as a people.

This may explain why Paul now comes to speak at length about Abraham, and does so in a way which breaks open the framework of the picture of Abraham in the post-exilic tradition. How does he do this? There are three important points here.

1. Anyone who reads Paul will immediately note that for him, as for any Jew, Abraham is not a memorial to faith from distant, past times, but a living reality. Moreover Paul makes direct associations with him: his own situation corresponds to that of the ancestor of his people. Parallels should be recognized. Of what kind? With a sure sense, Paul puts at the centre as his first key statement the biblical narrative about Abraham: 'Abraham believed in the Lord and the Lord imputed it to him as righteousness' (Gen.15.6). What is special about this statement? Here Paul had a lever with which he could upset any attempt to take a theological stand on the 'works of the law'. The recollection of Genesis 15.6 can only be understood as a polemical thrust, since between Abraham and Paul there lies the Torah, the halakhic system. And what about Abraham's 'faith'? For Paul, it is originally the opposite of loyal fulfilment of the commandments of the Torah, the opposite of a 'work of the law' that has to be performed.

2. So what does Abraham's faith consist in, as already depicted by Genesis? For Paul in none other than unconditional trust in God's promises – despite all appearances, contrary to all human calculations, through all temptations. Abraham had stood before God with empty hands: an impotent old man who will nevertheless have offspring; a homeless alien who is nevertheless promised a land; an individual in a marginal zone of the earth who will become the father of many nations. Abraham's trust in God alone is enough for him to be given by God things which he himself would never have thought possible, in order in this way to stand before God, justified by God. And what about the law?

3. By contrast, the law (or, better, the 'works of the law')[17] has lost its key significance for salvation and damnation. Jews may have to observe them, but they have forfeited their saving power. Abraham already shows this is an impressive way. For Abraham

could not have known anything of the 'works of the law', and yet he had a faith which was recognized by God. He was justified before God without any religious or moral achievement. He had become the partner of God's promise (a 'great people', a 'blessing for the nations', an 'eternal covenant') without his own efforts, without any moral distinction – out of the pure grace of God. Conversely, for Paul that means that before God the 'works of the law' are manifestly not important. The law, Paul thinks, was not there at the beginning, but only came '430 years later' (3.17). In any case it had not been decreed by God but by an 'angel' or a 'mediator' (3.19). One cannot be any clearer in wanting to relativize the law 'before God'. In short, for Paul Abraham shows the one and only thing which is important for the person before God: trust, not religious and moral achievements.

4. From this it follows for Paul that 'those who believe are children of Abraham' (3.7). Who is meant? In keeping with the whole thrust of Galatians, these will be non-Jews, people from the nations. The blessing on the nation which the biblical narrative about Abraham already envisages is to be related to them. And it is no coincidence that the apostle emphasizes the saying about this blessing as his second key statement from Genesis: 'by you all the families of the earth shall bless themselves' (Gal.3.8).

Who are Abraham's children?

With his 'Christian midrash' the Jew Paul had put *the* authority within Judaism, Abraham, on his side. Abraham in particular had demonstrated for Paul that the decisive thing was not descent, physical descent, privileges of salvation, but this genuine faith as trust in the future of the mysterious God whose actions are surprising. And this made a second thing clear: if Gentiles demonstrate such an understanding of faith in the case of the Christ event – can Jews be said to have any advantage over them? Do Gentiles still have to go over to Judaism in order to become Abraham's children? No, if such a faith was enough in the case of the 'Gentile' Abraham, then it is enough for all Gentiles in the future. Abraham can no longer remain the exclusive property of the Jewish people; Israel must once again take seriously Abraham's universal significance for salvation, for the world of the nations as well.

This is the motive behind a quite central distinction which Paul now makes: someone who is the 'seed' (Greek *sperma*) of Abraham need not automatically be one of the 'children' (Greek *tekna*) of Abraham. Fleshly descent does not yet convey much about real, spiritual belonging to Abraham. Indeed one can more genuinely be a child of Abraham in the spiritual sense than through descent, however pure (cf. Gal. 4.21–31; Rom. 9.7). What is important here is that Paul is not speaking of the faith of Gentiles in the abstract, but quite concretely of the faith of Gentiles who have become Christians. The Christ-event is the key to this Abraham theology. It is not the Gentile as such who is already justified before God (like any Jew, he too is a sinner), but the Gentile who has confessed God in Jesus Christ. It is the Christ event which has made it possible for Paul to rediscover the depth of the structure of faith. And for Paul 'Christ event' always means trust in God who has raised the crucified Jesus of Nazareth, rejected by his people and therefore 'godless', and thus has identified him as his Son. The Christ-event means that God has put to rights the one who hung helplessly 'on the tree', incapable of doing anything. Out of pure grace he showed solidarity with the one who was completely under the 'curse of the law'. In short, the Christ-event in particular had made Paul aware that he was dealing with a God who justifies the 'godless', those outside the law, and not the guardians of the 'works of the law'.

This event opens Paul's eyes to the depths of history, and above all to Abraham. Wasn't he equally to begin with one of the 'godless', outside the law? Didn't God once justify Abraham out of free grace, as he had now justified the crucified Jesus of Nazareth in the act of the resurrection? And since then, wasn't every Christian free from the law, as Abraham already was? Wasn't this the paradoxical 'meaning' of the cross, with which Christ had redeemed Christians from the curse of the law? That helps us to understand a bold analogy which Paul uses in Galatians:

– Anyone who like Abraham unconditionally trusts the mysterious God, whose promises and actions are incalculable, who in his grace is truly incomprehensible to human beings, is a 'son of Abraham'(3.7).
– Anyone who believes unconditionally in the mysterious God who has shown his incomprehensibility and unpredictability once again in the act of raising the crucified Jesus from the dead is also a 'son of God in Jesus Christ' (3.26). For Paul, being a son of Christ and being a descendant of Abraham have now become interchangeable. This is what he actually says:

For in Christ Jesus you are all sons of God, through faith. For as many of you as were baptized into Christ have put on Christ. There is neither Jew nor Greek, there is neither slave nor free, there is neither male nor female, for you are all one in Christ Jesus. And if you are Christ's, then you are Abraham's offspring, heirs according to promise (3.26–29).

Thus Paul has made it clear that all those who believe in God's action in Jesus Christ may call themselves children of Abraham and even as non-Jews participate in God's blessing through Abraham for the peoples. Indeed through faith in Christ this divine blessing becomes really universal. It no longer remains limited to Israel but becomes truly comprehensive. God's promise of the blessing of the nations to Abraham has achieved a dimension which really spans the world with Christ and those from among the Gentiles who believe in him. Abraham ceases to be the saving possession of Israel and is freed again really to become the 'father of many nations'. So Paul can say:

Jesus Christ has redeemed us . . . that in Christ Jesus the blessing of Abraham might come upon the Gentiles, that we might receive the promise of the spirit through faith (3.14).

Is Israel disinherited?

Christians are spiritual descendants of Abraham: that is a thoroughly positive statement. But doesn't this positive statement also have another, polemical, side in Paul, especially in Galatians? In this letter in particular didn't Paul allow himself to be drawn into a fatal anti-Jewish polemic? Doesn't his formula 'those who believe are sons of Abraham' sound Christian in an unpleasantly exclusivist way? Even worse, with the statement which immediately follows, that scripture speaks only of one descendant of Abraham, Christ (3.16), hasn't Paul completely lost sight of Israel? And worst of all, with the 'bizarre interweaving of allegory and typology'[18] in which Paul engages very soon afterwards, speaking of Hagar the slave girl (who embodies the slave law of Mount Sinai and thus the 'present Jerusalem') and Sarah, the free woman (who embodies the 'heavenly Jerusalem', the mother of Christians) doesn't he reach the depths of 'anti-Judaism'? This is literally what Paul says:

Tell me, you who desire to be under law, do you not hear the law? For it is written that Abraham had two sons, one by a slave and one by a free woman. But the son of the slave was born according to the flesh, the son of the free woman through promise. Now this is an allegory: these women are two covenants. One is from Mount Sinai, bearing children for slavery; she is Hagar. Now Hagar is Mount Sinai in Arabia; she corresponds to the present Jerusalem, for she is in slavery with her children. But the Jerusalem above is free, and she is our mother (4.21–26).

Can one write more anti-Jewish polemic than that? Paul seems sweepingly to make Jewish existence in faith existence in slavery, and in fact to deny that Jews are the children of Abraham. Anyone who continues to be orientated on the law is evidently no longer a son of Abraham and Sarah but a son of Hagar, a slave. So everything seems to culminate in a 'disinheriting of the Jews who persevere under the law'.[19] Moreover anti-Jewish Christian exegesis has made abundant use of these passages in Galatians.[20] Nor is it a coincidence that Jewish theologians in their turn have objected to this Pauline interpretation: 'In order to eliminate radically any sense of inferiority among the Galatians, here Paul descends to an exegesis which reads more into the text of Genesis than it reads out of it.'[21] What is the answer to this?

Both Jewish and anti-Jewish readings of these texts in Galatians fail to see that here Paul does not have Jews generally in view as his opponents, but Jewish Christians. There is no mention whatsoever of Jews in this context. As I have already indicated, in this letter Paul is concerned with rival Jewish Christian missionaries who had evidently been hawking the slogan 'We are the true sons of Abraham, because in addition to believing in Christ we also observe the law and adopt the sign of the covenant with Abraham, circumcision.' So Franz Mussner, a Catholic New Testament theologian who has done much to bring about a new relationship between Jewish and Christian theology, has rightly emphasized: 'Contrary to this claim to exclusivity on the part of his opponents, which in his eyes is completely unjustified, Paul rightly states who (among Christians) are "sons of Abraham": they are those who are sons "by faith". It is not Jews, but his opponents, whose claim to be true sons of Abraham he denies. Interpreters of Galatians often fail to see that Paul is arguing throughout with the preaching of his opponents, their false gospel, and not with the Jews . . . Nowhere in Galatians or Romans does Paul say that the Jews are excluded from the promise of blessing through Abraham.'[22]

That being so, we may not take the statement about Christ being the sole descendant of Abraham (3.16) to denote a disinheritance of Israel. Granted, to put it mildly, it sounds like a 'Christian appropriation' (H.D.Betz); at all events it is 'very high-handed' (F.Mussner), or, less politely, like a 'conjuring trick' (G.Ebeling), but such exegesis was not unusual within the Judaism of the time. And in content too, the aim is not a sweeping disinheritance of Israel. Why not? Because here Paul simply wants to indicate a criterion, a criterion of distinction within Israel, between those who before God insist on the 'works of the law' and those who, in the Spirit of Christ and Abraham, insist on faith. That is provocation of Israel by differentiation within Israel, but not the negation of Israel. Paul will later sum up this basic idea in the statement 'not all who are descended from Israel belong to Israel' (Rom.9.6). So we can agree with what Hans-Dieter Betz says in his commentary on Galatians: 'The evidence must be considered on two levels: as a whole it is meant to show that "those from faith" who are blessed with Abraham and identical with those who belive in Christ (3.6–14) are also the heirs of the covenant and the promises. However, this simply serves as a preparation for the discussion which follows later. Here Paul uses the singular, "descendant", in order to refute the traditional Jewish interpertation and reserve the role of heir for Christ. Of course this is a Christian appropriation, but it was made possible by the text of the Septuagint and perhaps by Jewish thought.'[23]

Jews – Christians: the universal perspective

But however Galatians is to be interpreted, it is certainly not the apostle's last word on Jews, Christians and Abraham. His last letter, that to the Romans, written around 55, once again has a fundamental discussion of this question and arrives at a universal theological conception which embraces Israel and the church equally, and which is still Paul's legacy.[24] Here in this letter Paul has no forced apology, no questionable allegory and typology, nor any christological formulations which might provoke misunderstandings.

This last letter is addressed to a community in the world capital which Paul does not know personally, and which he therefore has to imagine. Here he concentrates utterly on 'his' case, which he wants to make clear by means of Abraham. And his case is a distinction between 'seed' of Abraham and children of Abraham by the criterion of the Spirit of God, by the criterion of 'promise' (9.7). This case is that God is free to make people who have no claim to it children of Abraham by sheer grace. It is about the right relationship of human beings to God in confident faith in the free, gracious mercy of God.

In Romans (ch.4), Paul once again emphasizes these decisive elements, which give us the opportunity to gather together his Abraham theology.

1. What is decisive for human beings before God is trusting faith, not the fulfilment of works of the law. That applies equally to Jews and Christians. For Paul, the 'physical ancestor Abraham' demonstrates two things right from the beginning: a quite concrete expression of God's divinity and a human faith which corresponds to this expression. This is common to both Christians and Jews, for God as he has already shown himself to Abraham has also shown himself in Jesus Christ in the same way. The divinity of this God is made concrete in the way in which he enables the barren couple Abraham and Sarah to have descendants and in the way in which he has raised the crucified 'Lord' from 'the dead' (4.24). Here too there is a bold analogy: just as God made the barren bodies of Abraham and Sarah fertile again and thus created life from death, so God acted in Jesus of Nazareth by calling him to new life from the dead. God himself thus showed himself as the one who he wills to be: the sovereign creator who makes 'the godless righteous', brings the dead to life and 'calls into existence what is not' (4.5,17). Thus for Paul, too, Abraham is the archetypal figure of a radical hope; he is the man who believed 'full of hope against all hope that he would become the father of many nations' (4.18).

2. So for both Jews and Christians, authentic faith means hoping against all hope, not doubting in the promise of God, being convinced that 'God has the power to do what he has promised' (4.18–21). Thus structurally Christians and Jews have to perform one and the same act of faith, in that Abraham's faith directed forwards (the promises of God have still to be fulfilled) corresponds to the faith of Christians directed backwards: Christians are expected to believe in what God has already done, in the resurrection

of Jesus Christ, their 'Lord'. The Christ-event thus does not found a
new or different faith, but requires of Christians the faith that
Abraham had already shown: faith that human beings can entrust
their life to God in unconditional confidence (Hebrew *emunah*).
Where this is believed, where *emunah* is really lived out, there men
and women are true children of Abraham, and there too they are true
brothers and sisters of Christ (cf. Rom.8.29). Thus Abraham's faith
proves to be an anticipation of that faith which Christians show
when they trust the gospel of Jesus Christ.

3. Paul makes this priority of faith clear once again in connection
with the problem of circumcision. For the rabbis, too, as we heard,
circumcision had become a theological symbol. They explained the
fact that Abraham could have been uncircumcised for a long time as
a kind of compromise on God's part, to give converts as long an
opportunity as possible to submit to Jewish ritual law. By contrast,
for Paul, the fact that Abraham was for a long time uncircumcised
shows that it is not circumcision that is important before God, since
Abraham was justified by God in a state of uncircumcision, i.e. as a
Gentile. Accordingly circumcision, and thus the law generally, is not
a condition of the righteousness of faith but at best its ratification, its
subsequent symbolic confirmation. And that means (if we read with
traditional Jewish eyes) that the 'sign of God's covenant'
(Gen.17.11), without which participation in the blessing promised
to Abraham is inconceivable, is no longer important in the future for
those who come from the nations. According to Paul they already
participate in the blessing of Abraham on the basis of their belief in
Christ, and are members of the elect people without having to bear
the required divine symbol of circumcision any longer. What follows
from this?

4. It follows that Abraham can no longer remain merely the
'father of proselytes', i.e. the father of the uncircumcised who seek
circumcision and thus submission to the yoke of the Torah. For Paul,
Abraham is, rather, the father of all Gentiles who, if they believe in
Christ, are already justified before Christ without having to submit
to the halakhah. For Gentiles this is an occasion for gratitude, not
arrogance. They have always to remain consciously Gentile Christians: they are like the branches of the 'wild olive tree' which have
been grafted on to the 'noble olive tree' in order to have a share in the
'power of its roots' (Rom.11.17). A warning follows from this (and
how much blood and tears would the Jewish people have been

spared in the coming centuries had Christians taken this statement to heart): 'Do not boast over the branches'. For 'it is not you that support the root, but the root that supports you' (Rom.11.18).

But here, too, we must ask: didn't the apostle also engage in passionate polemic against his people? Didn't he emphasize, here in particular, that in holding fast to the 'works of the law' his own people had taken a false, disastrous way? Didn't he speak here in particular in an unmistakable way of 'failure, of the hardening', of the fault of Israel? Certainly. And there can be no doubt that since his Damascus experience it had been his unresting concern to convince as many Jews as possible of God's new offer of salvation in Jesus Christ. Israel is the first one to whom the gospel is addressed. Indeed, according to Paul, this gospel is 'the power of God for salvation to everyone who has faith, to the Jew first and also to the Greek' (Rom.1.16).

All this is indisputable. But Paul does not go so far in his disappointment at great parts of Israel as to deny that Jews are children of Abraham and thus deny that they have God's blessing and love. It is wrong to interpret Romans in anti-Israel terms. As we already heard at the beginning of this chapter, for Paul Israel remains 'loved by God, for the sake of the fathers' (Rom.11.28). Paul would not think of claiming that to be a child of Abraham was the exclusive prerogative of Christians; he would not deny this in principle to Jews and thus make Jewishness a matter of indifference. He only rejects a Jewish exclusivism, without promoting a new Christian exclusivism. For according to Paul Abraham continues to remain father of the Jews – but of course in accordance with a particular criterion, the criterion of faith. As Paul puts it, Abraham remains the father 'of the circumcised who are not merely circumcised but also follow the example of the faith which our father Abraham had before he was circumcised' (4.12). Thus for Paul Abraham is 'the father of us all before God' (4.17). So we can reduce his Abraham theology to the following formula: Gentiles who believe in Christ become children of Abraham in the spiritual sense. Children of Abraham after the flesh, the Jews, remain children of Abraham by following the faith of Abraham, which is not trust in the 'works of the law' but trust in a God who calls into being that which is not and thus breaks through and surpasses all earthly, human, criteria and expectations.

This Abraham theology had literally historic consequences. For with reference to Abraham Paul could make his own fruitful use of the universal dimension of Jewish theology which had been lost as

Abraham increasingly became associated with the halakhah. Here Paul's thought structurally comes closest to that of Philo, his contemporary. Both demonstrate a cosmopolitan perspective in their Abraham theology, though without being identical in their understanding of faith (justification of the godless). Paul is firmly of the view that the movement of God's salvation for humankind began with the election of Abraham; however, it has not yet found its final goal in Israel, but only in Christ, through whom the blessing mediated through Abraham could really establish itself as a blessing for the nations (and not merely as a blessing for the people). And if Westermann's interpretation of the Yahwistic blessing on the nations, according to which the effective blessing of God announced to Abraham achieves its aim only when all the families of the earth are included, is correct, then the apostle Paul may have Genesis on his side here.

In other words, the Jew Paul is opposing a Jewish particularism in favour of a Jewish universalism. Through the proclamation of Christ, Abraham's blessing can now extend to all peoples, even if Israel itself fails to confess Jesus as the Christ. For with Christ, Israel is deprived of its exclusiveness in mediating salvation, without being excluded from salvation and without thus being able to boost Gentile-Christian arrogance. In positive terms, this means that only with Christ has the originally universal promise of God to Abraham as the father of the nations and mediator of their blessing really been achieved, since only through belief in Christ has the message of the God of Abraham, Isaac and Jacob been carried literally to the ends of the earth in quite a different way from the Jewish proselytism practised previously,

In short, in Paul's view, what happened to Abraham happened 'for our sake', i.e. for the sake of all those who believe in Christ. So we can follow the Berlin Protestant theologian Friedrich Wilhelm Marquardt, who sums up his view like this: 'The promise to Abraham and trust in Abraham, but also the miracle of childbearing through dead bodies – these have "happened for our sake", these are "imputed" to us; in other words, they are the basis of the community to which we too (we Christians) belong, in so far as we too have experience of the God who raises the dead and who raised Jesus from the dead. And to the degree that we too, like our father Abraham, believe and trust in this God, we too – who were born a milllennium, two millennia, later, even if we were not born of the family of Abraham, live among the descendants of the faith of Abraham.'[25]

3. From Abraham to Jesus – the line of God's blessing

None of the New Testament authors was again to reflect on the significance of Abraham for Jews and Christians more basically and comprehensively than the apostle Paul. What follow in the other writings are individual important references, indispensable clues which must be taken seriously but should not be overestimated. And part of the overall picture is that important writings of the New Testament like the Deutero-Pauline letters to the Ephesians and Colossians, and also the Pastorals (the two letters to Timothy and the letter to Titus) do not mention Abraham at all. In others that do mention him, the passionate theological fire of Paul has long since been quenched. The Letter of James is manifestly already writing polemic against a crude Paulinism which has simply played off faith against works and with reference to Abraham's readiness to sacrifice his son once again emphasizes works as an expression of faith (James 2.21), very much along traditional Jewish lines (Sirach 44.19–21; I Macc.2.52).

In I Peter, by contrast, Abraham is marginalized even more. His wife Sarah has here sunk to being a moralizing model for wives, who are to be subject to their husbands and obey them (3.6). All in all, I Peter seems to be one of the New Testament writings in which the 'Old Testament' is no longer a book of Israel but solely a book of the church, since here the notion of a history of revelation leading from Israel to the church is totally absent. Paul's passionate concern – Why must there be a 'church', although 'Israel' received everything from God? Why isn't Israel open to Jesus Christ? – no longer has a role here. So the Regensburg patristic scholar Norbert Brox may be right in his analysis: 'The topic of Israel has to be put on the debit side of Pauline legacies in I Peter. There is no longer a sense here that Israel is the root of the church. I Peter is on the way to a theological forgetfulness of Israel in Christianity, without polemic and without interest.'[26]

And yet the theological discussion over Israel and thus over Abraham did not cease in other Christian communities of the second and third generations. It went on in a way which still betrays sharp conflict within the Christian communities. For the writings which mention Abraham fall clearly into two groups. Such heterogeneous texts as the Gospels of Matthew and Luke along with Hebrews see Jesus Christ in a line with Abraham, without being completely negative about Israel. By contrast, the Gospel of John claims Abraham exclusively for Christians. Let's look at this more closely.

Jesus Christ — the 'son of Abraham': Matthew

As a Christian can one begin a history of Jesus more programmatically with a reference to Abraham than this?

> The book of the genealogy of Jesus Christ,
> the son of David, the son of Abraham.
> Abraham was the father of Isaac,
> and Isaac the father of Jacob,
> and Jacob the father of Judah and his brothers . . .
> So all the generations from Abraham to David were
> fourteen generations,
> and from David to the deportation to Babylon
> fourteen generations,
> and from the deportation to Babylon to the Christ
> fourteen generations (Matt.1.1f.,17).

One can hardly begin an account of the good news more programmatically than this if as an author one is concerned with two things:
– The man to be spoken of here is not someone from the 'forty-two generations since Abraham' but the Messiah of Israel. So his Davidic sonship must be put before his descent from Abraham, and there must be a role for Bethlehem, the city of David, the city from which the coming of the Messiah had been announced by the prophet Micah (5.1; cf. Matt.2.6). It must be emphasized that the promise of the prophet Isaiah has now been fulfilled: 'Behold, the virgin will conceive a child, she will bear a son, and his name shall be called Immanuel' (Isa.7.14; Matt.1.23). But at the same time:
– Jesus the Messiah of Israel is a son of Abraham. In other words, he comes from the depths of the history of his people. Behind him, in one and the same series, he has all the ancestors: Abraham, Isaac and Jacob; Solomon and all the kings down to the Babylonian exile; and all his kin from the exile to Joseph, his physical father and husband of Mary. For the stylization into three times fourteen generations is meant to bring out right from the start a basic theological notion in a

symbolic way: with Jesus of Nazareth there is no break in God's history with Israel; rather, the great history of God with his people which began with Abraham goes further, indeed enters a new phase. Jesus Christ does not stand against Abraham, in place of Abraham, but in a line with Abraham, as a new climax of a great history.

But does Matthew maintain this basic line, even in bitter earnestness? Doesn't his Gospel constantly portray the resistance above all of the leaders of the people of Israel to Jesus, in which the Pharisees stand in the foreground as Jesus' bitterest opponents (23.13–33). Doesn't Matthew presuppose that in 70 CE Judaism suffered its greatest defeat – in punishment for shedding the blood of the innocent Jesus? The climax is the statement which had such disastrous consequences: 'Then the whole people answered, "His blood be on us and on our children"' (27.25). So isn't Matthew in particular concerned that Israel should be disinherited and replaced by the church?

Evidently such an assumption is confirmed by the dispute over who Abraham's children are, which he too depicts. He already puts a polemic saying about this on the lips of John the Baptist. For to the Pharisees and Sadducees who come to his baptism of repentance, the Matthaean John retorts:

> You brood of vipers! Who warned you to flee from the wrath to come? Bear fruit that befits repentance, and do not presume to say to yourselves, 'We have Abraham as our father': for I tell you, God is able from these stones to raise up children to Abraham. Even now the axe is laid to the root of the trees; every tree therefore that does not bear good fruit is cut down and thrown into the fire (3.7–10).

In other words (and we have already come across this 'Christian' theme, which can also be found here and there among the rabbis), a purely formal appeal to Abraham means nothing before God. Before God, repentance and 'good fruit' are decisive. Anyone who shows this is Abraham's child. So being a child of Abraham does not depend solely on mere membership of the chosen people, and is not automatically guaranteed by descent from Israel. The same theological passion which drove Paul, the apostle to the Gentiles, can also be felt here: God is free to make Abraham's children out of people who are completely outside any kind of legitimation, whether through descent or through observance of the law. Being a child of Abraham is a matter for God alone!

How important this notion evidently is to Matthew emerges from the way in which a short time later he even attributes it to Jesus himself. And we now understand even better why Matthew could make good use for his Gospel of a text from the Sayings Source which I quoted at the beginning of this book:

> I tell you, many will come from east and west and sit at table with Abraham, Isaac and Jacob in the kingdom of heaven (Matt.8.11).

Matthew now puts this saying in his context and makes it concrete with a healing miracle which he similarly takes from the Sayings Source:

> As he entered Capernaum, a centurion came forward to him, beseeching him and saying, 'Lord, my servant is lying paralysed at home, in terrible distress.' And he said to him, 'I will come and heal him.' But the centurion answered him, 'Lord, I am not worthy to have you come under my roof; but only say the word, and my servant will be healed. For I am a man under authority, with soldiers under me; and I say to one "Go," and he goes, and to another, "Come," and he comes, and to my slave, "Do this," and he does it.' When Jesus heard him, he marvelled, and said to those who followed him, 'Truly, I say to you, not even in Israel have I found such faith. I tell you, many will come from east and west and sit at table with Abraham, Isaac and Jacob in the kingdom of heaven' (Matt.8.11).

It becomes clear that Matthew further reinforces the theological point of this early saying about Jesus by using as a specific comparison a member of the Roman army, a despised Gentile *par excellence*. He is meant not only to illustrate Jesus' messianic authority (command-result), but also to serve as a provocative contrast for any traditional Jewish hearers. The faith of a Gentile in Jesus as the Messiah is meant to differ in an unprecedented way from the faith which Jesus has found in Israel. Furthermore, this individual centurion is only the anticipatory symbol of the 'many from east and west' who are still to come and whom Matthew – in contrast to the Sayings Source – already envisages, ten to twenty years after the destruction of the temple.

So is this the disinheriting of Israel, to be replaced by the church? For doesn't the parable of the wicked husbandmen (21.33–46) also say that the kingdom of God will be 'taken away' from Israel and given to another 'people' which will bring forth its 'fruits'? Doesn't the parable of the king's banquet (22.1–14) say that those who were first invited have not proved themselves worthy, so that the banqueting hall must now be filled with quite different guests 'from outside'? And didn't the risen Christ in Matthew give his disciples the commission to go 'to all nations' (28.19) and no longer merely 'to the lost sheep of the house of Israel' (10.6)? So once again, what are we to conclude?

However, we must note carefully not only what Matthew says but also what he does not say. For strikingly, in the parable of the wicked husband in particular Matthew avoids any characterization of the 'people' which brings forth its fruits. There is no mention, for example, of a new Israel to replace the old. The same is the case with the guests who were invited to the wedding first. If this parable is meant to reflect the situation of the Christian community and the synagogue, here the judgment is clearly directed at the present generation in Israel, but not in principle at Israel as a whole. And what about the mission command of the risen Christ? It does not say anything about the definitive fate of Israel. The disciples are sent to the nations, without anything being said about Israel's future (as it is, say in Paul). And the Gentiles sitting down at table with Abraham? They, too, are not meant to exclude Israel from salvation once and for all. The point of this scene is quite the opposite, and here corresponds to the point made by the apostle to the Gentiles: God acts for the salvation of the nations even if Israel fails. The salvation of the nations is no longer bound up with the mediating role of Israel but is now made possible by faith in Jesus Christ. But here Israel is not completely excluded. For the 'many' receive salvation, not in place of unbelieving Israel but despite it. Moroever the Erlangen Protestant New Testament scholar Jürgen Roloff has made a decisive point here: 'The many who have come no longer gather round the eschatologically redeemed Israel as a centre. The centre remains empty. God's historical saving action reaches its goal with the peoples of the world, even if Israel drops out of it.'[27]

In fact Matthew does not narrate the history of Jesus and his disciples as a history of the total rejection and complete failure of Israel, but ultimately as a history of hope for Israel, embodied in the community of the disciples. These are and remain part of Israel, since they represent the group of those Jews who recognize Jesus as the Messiah of Israel (16.16), among whom the word falls on good ground and has borne its 'fruits'. Indeed through their abiding links with Israel the disciples are the ones who bear witness to the abiding faithfulness of God to his promises to his people. The Gentiles, too, are enabled to rely on this faithfulness without the relationship of Jews and Gentiles in the new church of Jesus Christ being given clearer contours or even structures in Matthew. But the decisive thing is that for Matthew, too, despite all conflicts between Jews and Christians there is not a total discontinuity between Israel and the church. Jesus Christ is and remains the son of David, but he also is and remains the son of Abraham.

God's mercy on Jews and Gentiles: Luke

If in Matthew the precise relationship between Jews and Gentile Christians remains indefinite, Luke the evangelist and first historian of the church has a clear conception: a new community of Jews and Gentiles in the one church of Jesus Christ. Certainly in his Gospel the Gentile Christian Luke also shows the tension between the Christian community and the traditional synagogue, and then goes on in Acts to report the new message to the Gentiles. But at the same time he puts even more emphasis than Matthew on the continuity of the history of God with his elect people, to which the non-Jewish Gentile peoples have now recently been added.

Luke, too, has put what is theologically decisive here at the beginning of his Gospel, since the birth of Jesus in Bethlehem, the city of David, is set in the framework of the history of blessing within Judaism. For before Jesus is born he is deliberately announced by or reflected in representatives of the Judaism of the time: by Zechariah, the father of John the Baptist, the representative of the penitential movement within Judaism, and Mary, the representative of the ordinary people, who is chosen by God for great things – out of pure grace, without any merit of her own; nor should we forget the wise Simeon. Luke has left it for him to pronounce what he feels to be the decisive double dimension of the Jesus event, right at the beginning of the Gospel: Jesus' significance for Israel and for the peoples. Luke makes Simeon exclaim:

> Lord, now let your servant depart in peace,
> according to your word;
> for my eyes have seen your salvation,
> which you have prepared in the presence of all peoples,
> a light for revelation to the Gentiles,
> and for glory to your people Israel (2.29–32)

In sending the Messiah to Israel and the peoples God is acting anew in a surprising way which was no longer thought possible: this is the theological point of all Luke's stories surrounding the birth of Jesus. And one would have to be theologically blind not to see immediate parallels to the story of Abraham. For didn't God act just as surprisingly towards Abraham? The wanderer without a homeland who is promised a 'land'? The insignificant foreigner who becomes the instrument of God's plan for the peoples? The childless old man who will nevertheless bring forth a great people? Moreover there are obvious parallels between Abraham's aged wife Sarah and Zechariah's aged wife Elizabeth. Analogies should be evident between Mary's surprise at the announcement of the angel and Abraham's and Sarah's surprise at the appearing of the three angels in Mamre. Moreover all the narratives which are a prelude to the birth of Jesus have been conceived by Luke with abundant allusions to the story of Abraham and Sarah. The parallels should strike any hearer or reader. So it cannot be surprising that at the end of Mary's song of praise at the dialectic of God's action, later to become so famous, Abraham is mentioned explicitly:

> He has helped his servant Israel,
> in remembrance of his mercy,
> as he spoke to our fathers,
> to Abraham and his posterity for ever (1.54).

Nor can it surprise us that the priest Zechariah, the father of John the Baptist, sees the faithfulness of God which had been established in the covenant with Abraham confirmed in the unexpected birth of his son. Here Luke unmistakably makes Zechariah recall Psalm 105, which now refers even more strongly to Abraham (but here God's oath refers to Abraham and not to Isaac, as in Psalm 105.9):

> He has performed the mercy promised to our fathers,
> and remembered his holy covenant,

the oath which he swore to our father Abraham, to grant us,
that we being delivered from the hand of our enemies,
might serve him without fear (1.72f.).

Both texts have one and the same theological focus: in Jesus, the
Messiah of Israel, God does not produce anything completely new.
What emerges afresh is what God has already given through
Abraham: grace and mercy for Israel, which in the existing political
situation must specifically mean the messianic liberation of the
Jewish people from foreign rule. God's promise to Abraham, his
covenant, the oath which he swore to Abraham; none of this is
superseded by the appearance of Jesus of Nazareth; it is not dead or
withered but is given new life, confirmed, made fruitful. God has
now *completed* his mercy towards the patriarchs.

So from Abraham to Jesus there is a great line of God's blessing for
his people. Now the people – in Zechariah's words – can be
redeemed and saved from their enemies. Now the people shares in
the 'salvation' and the 'forgiveness of sins' which it has long desired –
in the light of the 'merciful love of our God' (1.78). Now, in Mary's
words, the proud are dispersed, the mighty cast down from their
thrones, the lowly exalted, the hungry given gifts and the rich sent
away empty. Why? Because God has not forgotten his 'mercy'. He
has not forgotten anything of what he once promised to the
patriarchs of Israel. 'Abraham', the source of blessing, is still active:
the energy of mercy which had already accumulated with the
patriarchs can now be detected again, since Jesus, the Messiah, has
come – as the culmination of Jewish history, as the fulfilment of
God's promise to Abraham.

This social criticism in the preaching of the gospel which is already
expressed in the *Magnificat* then finds parallels later in the text. For it
is striking that Luke's Jesus addresses ordinary men and women
from the people directly as 'daughter of Abraham' or 'son of
Abraham'. Moreover, on the sabbath, to the fury of the leader of a
synagogue, Jesus heals a woman who has had to live for eighteen
years with a bent back, incapable of walking upright. This is what he
is told by Jesus:

You hypocrite! Does not each of you on the sabbath untie his ox or
his ass from the manger, and lead it away to water it? And ought
not this woman, a daughter of Abraham whom Satan bound for

eighteen years, be loosed from this bond on the sabbath day? (13.15f.).

Luke even singles out the publican Zacchaeus, generally despised because of his profession, by indicating that he is a 'son of Abraham', and thus promises him salvation:

Today salvation has come to this house, since he also is a son of Abraham. For the Son of man came to seek and to save the lost (19.9f.)

Thus Luke shows that for his Jesus no social status is incompatible with salvation. Being a daughter or a son of Abraham is not a privilege of the respectable and the well-to-do, but simply depends on God's gracious concern for all men and women, particularly for the crippled and the despised, to whom 'the Son of Man' turns in a unique way, the one who is himself the embodiment of God's love for humankind.

However, this social criticism in Luke is combined with something far greater: the controversy over Jesus' acceptance among his people. The key text here is the parable of the poor man and the rich Lazarus (16.19–31). Here Abraham plays an even more decisive theological role. The parable is about a rich man who has enjoyed his prosperity during his lifetime heedlessly and without concern. He dies, and now leads a life of torment in the underworld, whereas Lazarus, who was formerly wretched, can rest after his death in 'Abraham's bosom'. The rich man now attempts to get Abraham to plead on his behalf for some relief from his torment. But what happens? Abraham rejects the role of intercessor here, indeed even refuses to accede to a further wish of the rich man: to warn those who are still alive, so that they do not suffer the same fate. Here is the decisive passage.

And the rich man said, 'Then I beg you, father, to send him to my father's house, for I have five brothers, so that he may warn them, lest they also come into this place of torment.' But Abraham said, 'They have Moses and the prophets; let them hear them.' And he said, 'No, father Abraham; but if some one goes to them from the dead, they will repent.' And he said to him, 'If they do not hear Moses and the prophets, neither will they be convinced if some one should rise from the dead' (Luke 16.27–31).

This parable, too, initially focuses on social criticism in an unmistakable way. The Catholic exegete Peter Dschulnigg has drawn attention to this in his important study on rabbinic parables and the New Testament: 'The fact of belonging to Abraham, which lasts beyond death . . . is solely decided in life before death, and in particular is measured by the practice of those who have been harmed and disadvantaged, the sick and poor who are dependent on the merciful goodness of the rich. After death a lifelong decision against the poor can no longer be revised. But anyone who belongs to the covenant people knows what the issue is and by what the blessing of belonging to Abraham is measured.'[28]

But the decisive theological point of this text goes far beyond that. For with this story Luke's community is making clear to itself the failure of the belief of Israel in Jesus as the crucified and risen Messiah – with an appeal to the authority of Abraham, who, as we heard, within Judaism had been given the role of intercessor for Israel before God in the last judgment. But something happens here which is shocking for a Jew: Abraham refuses to intercede for the rich man. And the rich man here is doubtless also a model of Israel, which is 'really' rich before God, whereas the 'poor Lazarus' reflects the rejected and marginalized Christian community. Every Jewish person addressed is meant to hear that those who reject Jesus as Messiah also draw down upon themselves the rejection of Abraham. They cannot count on Abraham's intercession in the last judgment. On the contrary, Abraham is on the side of the rejected, the despised and the marginalized. And from Luke's perspective that applies not only to social groups in Israel who are forced to the margin but also to whole peoples outside Israel who belong to the despised. Luke, the Gentile Christian, now quite resolutely argues for them to be valued and integrated into God's history with his people, since the Christian proclamation to Israel has largely failed. In Luke, Jesus increasingly becomes the light that lightens the Gentiles. And in Acts we are witnesses to this process of being a light to the Gentiles, or more precisely this plea for the theological legitimacy of Gentile Christianity.

The key text in Acts for our purpose is Paul's speech in the synagogue of Perga (Acts 13.13–52). The apostle – as Luke depicts him – has followed his custom of first going to the synagogue of the city, out of the conviction that the word of God, which for him is the word of Jesus Christ, must first be preached to the Jews (13.46).

When, as is the custom, the leader of the synagogue invites him to speak 'a word of consolation for the people', Paul takes the opportunity to explain his gospel by integrating it into the great history of God with his people. So Paul explicitly addresses those who are in the synagogue as 'sons of the family of Abraham'. He explicitly emphasizes that Jesus was 'not recognized', condemned though innocent, and crucified by the inhabitants and leaders of Jerusalem – of Jerusalem, not all Israel. But God raised Jesus from the dead. So the God of Israel has fulfilled for us, their children, the promise which was given to the fathers. Thus through Jesus Christ the forgiveness of sins is now proclaimed. For in all in which the law of Moses could not make righteous, 'everyone who believes is made righteous by him'.

But this sermon in the synagogue did not have the effect that Paul hoped for. Instead of integrating, it polarized. Certainly 'many Jews and pious proselytes' came to believe in Jesus as the Christ, but others became 'jealous, contradicted the words of Paul and uttered blasphemies'. So Paul makes his Paul perform an act of deep symbolism: he ceases to preach to the Jews and turns to the Gentiles. This is what he says to the Jews – and again the prophet Isaiah's picture of light and illumination is deliberately introduced into the argument:

> It was necessary that the word of God should be spoken first to you. Since you thrust it from you, and judge yourselves unworthy of eternal life, behold, we turn to the Gentiles. For so the Lord has commanded us, saying, 'I have set you to be a light for the Gentiles, that you may bring salvation to the uttermost parts of the earth.' And when the Gentiles heard this, they were glad and glorified the word of God: and as many as were ordained to eternal life believed. And the word of the Lord spread throughout all the region. But the Jews incited the devout women of high standing and the leading men of the city, and stirred up persecution against Paul and Barnabas, and drove them out of their district (13.46–50).

This is meant to demonstrate two things:

1. The Gentile Christian Luke in particular cannot ignore the fact that both the preaching of Jesus himself (depicted in his Gospel) and the preaching of Jesus as the Christ (depicted in Acts) began a process of division in Israel, as the Christian message now had a polarizing

effect amongst the people of God. Indeed in this Gospel it is already prophesied to the newborn Jesus that he is 'destined to the fall and rising of many in Israel', that he will become a 'sign that is spoken against' (Luke 2.34). And because the resistance was so great, above all among the leaders and authorities of the Jewish people (not among the ordinary people themselves), the new proclamation of salvation has to go over to the Gentile peoples, the foundations for which are in Luke's view already laid in the promises to the fathers. But that means, conversely:

2. For Luke, too, the promises of God to the fathers have not become obsolete with the Christ event but are still valid. Israel maintains its precedence in salvation history. The Gentile Christians are added to the people of God, are the beneficiaries of the original promises to Israel. In a very similar way to Paul, Luke uses Abraham here, not to exclude the Jews from the people of God but rather 'to qualify Jewish inclusiveness. He qualifies it by parting company with the traditional basis of such inclusiveness: physical descent.'[29]

Thus Luke proves to be the writer among the third generation of New Testament writers who shows the strongest interest in Israel. A forgetfulness of Israel which is widespread, especially in the Gentile Christianity of the third generation (as in I Peter), is not his view. For he still understands the church as 'Israel', albeit as Israel gathered, renewed and perfected by God in the end time. It is perfected, because through Jesus Christ the salvation mediated through Israel now achieves truly global universality. Here, too, Jürgen Roloff has made the decisive point: 'In the church, Jewish Christians and Gentile Christians do not stand side by side as two peoples of God; the church is the one people of God in whose existence God's promises for Israel have been fulfilled, and in which God's history with Israel is continued and completed.'[30]

Abraham – a model for faith: the Letter to the Hebrews

Whereas Luke had already struggled to give an impressive narrative foundation to the great continuity of the Christ event in the history of Israel, this is no kind of theological brilliance compared with a New Testament author whose name is unknown to us but who has left behind the 'Letter to the Hebrews'.[31] No one surpasses him in his mastery at assimilating the Jewish theological heritage. Even if we do not know him as an individual, his skilfully arranged collage of quotations from the First Testament nevertheless suggests that he is a highly-educated Hellenistic Jewish Christian. He has sovereign command of the art of midrashic exegesis (2.7–4, 11), cites the Septuagint as a matter of course, takes a wealth of examples from the Hebrew Bible, and in many details suggests contacts with the thought of Philo of Alexandria.

Moreover it is important for assessing the letter that the author is evidently one of the second or third generation of Christians who can now already look back on the 'apostolic period'. It is a look back in anger, or at least in concern and anxiety. For throughout the letter the author shows himself deeply disturbed by the declining faith of the Christians of his time. Moreover his work is full of appeals, invocations, admonitions and indeed threats.

If I reconstruct it rightly, the situation in many local churches of the time may have been something like this. For many people the Christ-event, which for Gentile Christians was the basis of freedom from the 'works of the law', seems already to have become an excuse for a decline in zeal for God. Moreover commentators have not unjustly seen Hebrews as a 'letter against the laxity of the post-apostolic period', since a certain 'loss of knowledge' threatens the community, a loss which our author seeks to remove by a kind of 'revision course'.[32] The key words 'loss of knowledge' and 'revision course' will be of help to us here.

For how does the author attempt to counter the laxity of the post-apostolic period? On the one hand by announcing a fearful judgment (the key sentence here is 'It is dreadful to fall into the hands of the living God', 10.31), and on the other by remembering. He recalls the great examples of faith from Jewish history, who had to struggle with similar difficulties and despite everything held fast to the faith. The decisive thing here is that the whole letter is provided with a great christological prelude, since Jesus Christ here is to be praised as the presupposition and culmination of Jewish history – to the Hebrews, i.e. to those who are most familiar with Jewish history.[33] So the very first sentence is already programmatic:

In many and various ways God spoke of old to our fathers by the prophets; but in these last days he has spoken to us by a Son, whom he appointed the heir of all things, through whom also he created the world (1.1f.).

The author now goes on to read the whole of Jewish history with this christological hermeneutic, and here Abraham is given an important role. For like Luke and Paul, the author leaves no doubt that with the incarnation of Jesus Christ God has again accepted 'the descendants of Abraham'. So here, too, the appearing of Jesus Christ does not aim at the extinction of Israel but at its renewal, at an Israel to whom God's promise applies unbroken. On this christological and salvation-historical basis, in the letter Abraham is now claimed for three central themes.

I. Endurance and loyalty in faith. In view of the flagging zeal among Christians, the author reactivates a picture of Abraham which had become classic in post-exilic Israel: Abraham as an example of the perseverance of faith and loyalty to the promise, the source of which was God himself. Furthermore Christians could trust in a second irrevocable act of God: Jesus Christ. That was all the less reason for flagging in commitment to the faith. This is what he says:

> For when God made a promise to Abraham, since he had no one greater by whom to swear, he swore by himself, saying, 'Surely I will bless you and multiply you.' And thus Abraham, having patiently endured, obtained the promise. Men indeed swear by a greater than themselves, and in all their disputes an oath is final for confirmation. So when God desired to show more convincingly to the heirs of the promise the unchangeable character of his purpose, he interposed with an oath, so that through unchangeable things, in which it is impossible that God should prove false, we who have fled for refuge might have strong encouragement to seize the hope set before us (6.13–18).

II. Jesus Christ as the true high priest: more than any other book or any other letter of the New Testament, Hebrews contains a specific christology of sacrifice and priests. We need not concern ourselves with the details here. We can concentrate on the basic notion in which Abraham plays a key role, through his relation to the priest Melchizedek. As we heard, he is mentioned in the book of Genesis as 'king of Jerusalem' and priest of 'God Most High' (not Yahweh, but the supreme Canaanite god). I have already indicated that Melchizedek appears in Genesis as suddenly as he disappears again. He blesses Abraham, and Abraham gives him 'a tithe of all things' (Gen.14.18–20). Melchizedek is an enigmatic figure; we do not know where he comes from, and he retreats into silence again without our knowing where he is going. So already in Genesis this figure stands out from the framework of the other Abraham naratives: a man without a genealogy, whose beginning is not known and whose end remains unknown.

But the author of Hebrews derives a theological and christological point from precisely this figure, and does so against the legitimate Jewish priestly family: the Levites with their ancestor Aaron, the brother of Moses (cf. Exod.4.14). Let's first listen to this theologically complicated text:

> For this Melchizedek, king of Salem, priest of the Most High God, met Abraham returning from the slaughter of the kings and blessed him; and to him Abraham apportioned a tenth part of everything. He is first, by translation of his name, king of righteousness, and then he is also king of Salem, that is, king of peace. He is without father or mother or genealogy, and has neither beginning of days nor end of life, but resembling the Son of God he continues a priest for ever. See how great he is. Abraham the patriarch gave him a tithe of the spoils. And those descendants of Levi who receive the priestly office have a commandment in the law to take tithes from the people, that is, from their brethren, though these also are descended from Abraham. But this man who has not their genealogy received tithes from Abraham and blessed him who had the promises. It is beyond dispute that the inferior is blessed by the superior. Here tithes are received by mortal men; there, by one of whom it is testified that he lives. One might even say that Levi himself, who receives tithes, paid tithes through Abraham, for he was still in the loins of his ancestor when Melchizedek met him (7.1–10).

The lines drawn here are at first confusing and can only be understood if we separate them. I shall try to do that.
– There is the Melchizedek-Christ line. The author thinks it important to make the priest Melchizedek the man 'without a beginning of his days or an end of his life', the image of the pre-existent and post-existent Son of God, Jesus Christ, and thus the counterpart to the established Jewish priesthood from the tribe of Levi 'after the order of Aaron'. This means that this Melchizedek is 'priest for ever', whose priesthood is more important than the

levitical priesthood because it is earlier, and will be surpassed only
by the last high priest – Jesus Christ. After him, sacrificial priesthood and temple cult are unnecessary.
– There is the line from Melchizedek to Abraham. Melchizedek is
enhanced since Abraham gave him 'the tithe' and he could bless
Abraham, although he stood completely outside any usual priestly
chain of legitimation. On the other hand, Melchizedek is a mortal
man. So he is surpassed only by the one of whom it is attested that
he lives, and this is the risen Jesus Christ. Thus the focal point of the
argument is that the progenitor Abraham already shows that the
traditional priesthood is not important before God, otherwise
Melchizedek would not have been able to behave like this. So
Abraham has already broken though any later priestly notion of
legitimation. This is now definitively overcome by Jesus Christ,
who is the eternal, immortal high priest.
– There is the line from Abraham to Levi. Levi's significance is
relativized by the fact that Abraham lived before Levi. Simply by
virtue of that Abraham has precedence over Levi. And by giving a
tithe to the priest Melchizedek (and not, say Levi), Abraham makes
it quite clear that priestly genealogy is not important before God.
The Levitical is to some degree already contained in Abraham, so
that Levi's role can fundamentally be dispensed with.

So in this chapter everything focusses on the legitimation of belief
in Christ as the true link to God. Here, as in Paul, Abraham has a
key role within Judaism. For just as Paul wanted to abolish the
exclusiveness of observing the Torah for salvation, so the author of
Hebrews attempts to upset the Jewish priesthood's claim to salvation with Abraham. As a lever he uses the axis Melchizedek –
Abraham – Christ. The aim of the argument is to prove that Christ
is the only, the last, high priest, whose sacrifice on the cross has
reconciled human beings with God once and for all, so that in
future they no longer need the many little sacrifices (in the temple),
especially as this temple has been destroyed. Abraham gives this
statement the necessary legitimation within Judaism by already
showing by his conduct towards Melchizedek that an unbroken
priestly descent is not important for achieving reconciliation with
God. What is decisive is faith in Jesus Christ, who reconciled
human beings with God in a last, personal sacrifice, so that there
was no need of further sacrifice or further priestly service in the
temple.

III. Abraham is a model of true faith. Hebrews is not just a didactic letter; it also contains threats and reminders, as I already indicated at the beginning. And in this process of reminding, Abraham appears often. The climax is chapter 11, in which Abraham functions as part of a 'cloud of witnesses' (12.1) from Jewish history. What is to be remembered? True faith! What is this faith? Hebrews replies: 'Faith is the assurance of things hoped for, the convictions of things not seen' (11.1).

With this guideline, the author now reads Jewish history as a history of faith. Abel, Enoch and Noah, the men of old before Abraham, already had this faith. So did the great witnesses after Abraham: from Isaac through Moses to Daniel and the prophets. But even more, Abraham and Sarah did:

By faith Abraham obeyed when he was called to go out to a place which he was to receive as an inheritance; and he went out, not knowing where he was to go. By faith he sojourned in the land of promise, as in a foreign land, living in tents with Isaac and Jacob, heirs with him of the same promise. For he looked forward to the city which has foundations, whose builder and maker is God. By faith Sarah herself received power to conceive, even when she was past the age, since she considered him faithful who had promised. Therefore from one man, and him as good as dead, were born descendants as many as the stars of heaven and as the innumerable grains of sand by the seashore . . .

By faith Abraham, when he was tested, offered up Isaac, and he who had received the promises was ready to offer up his only son, of whom it was said, 'Through Isaac shall your descendants be named.' He considered that God was able to raise men even from the dead; hence, figuratively speaking, he did receive him back (11.8–12, 17–19).

Certainly for the author of the Letter to the Hebrews, Jesus Christ finally and definitively shows what faith means. For Jesus – the culmination of the long history of Israel's faith – is called the 'author and perfecter' of faith (12.2). But at the same time the author could have left out the whole 'cloud' of Jewish witnesses, had his view not been:[34]

– For Christians, true faith does not first come through Christ; there was already true faith in Israel throughout its history. Therefore:

– Anyone who as a Christian believes in God in Jesus Christ, at the same time believes like Abel and Noah, like Abraham and Sarah, like Jacob and Moses, like David and the prophets.

– For Christians too, true faith means holding firm to what one hopes for, being convinced of what one does not see, being able to depart from familiar ties, to surrender certainty, and live as a stranger in a land which is not one's own homeland; even to be able to give what one loves most in trust that God has the power to raise the dead to life.

Thus it is clear that when it came to Abraham, all the Christians in the period after Paul who have been mentioned here (Matthew and the author of the Letter to the Hebrews as Jewish Christians and Luke as a Gentile Christian), were concerned to do one thing: to relate the history of Jesus Christ not as an event of inheriting from or replacing an Israel which had been definitively rejected, but as a part, indeed as a new pinnacle, of God's history of covenant and blessing with and for his people. However bitter the conflict between the first Christian communities and the 'present Jerusalem', the Israel of this generation, may have been, God's surprisingly new action in Jesus Christ was still to be for the benefit of Israel, even if Israel had not (yet) recognized this offer. For even after the Christ event, the promises of God to Israel have not been annulled; the covenant has not been repealed. Certainly there is a division within Israel itself, but there is no definitive repudiation of all Israel.

In other words, according to these New Testament witnesses, Christians who believe in the action of God in Jesus Christ are not 'inventing' any new faith but again living out what the 'patriarchs of Israel' practised in their own way. No new covenant which has completely abolished the old covenant is beginning with Jesus Christ; rather, with Jesus Christ the primal covenant which God made with the 'fathers of Israel', and of which he is constantly mindful, is renewed once more.[35] God again shows his unspent power and freshness – specifically in the interests of the Gentiles who hitherto stood outside this covenant. The new covenant in Jesus Christ is the covenant with Israel renewed by God – for Israel and the nations it is the new covenant in the old.[36]

4. Christians claim Abraham for themselves: John

But there is a counterpoint. In one community of primitive Christianity we encounter a completely different conflict situation. It is not comparable with the dispute in which Christians associated with the Sayings Source were involved because of the different kind of table-fellowship with Abraham. Nor can it be compared with Paul's dispute over Abraham's faith outside the law and the blessing of Abraham for the Gentiles. Finally, it is not to be compared with the controversies over Abraham which are reported by Matthew (John the Baptist's polemic), Luke (the parable of the rich man and Lazarus) and the author of Hebrews (the withdrawal of legitimation from the priestly class). What is it about?

Anxiety and crisis: the situation of a marginal community

We cannot reconstruct the whole complex history of this community here.[37] But if we are to understand chapter 8 of the Gospel of John, which is so decisive for our question, at least some comments must be made. The Johannine community originally consisted predominantly of Jewish Christians who had heard a final no to Jesus as the Messiah of Israel from the synagogue and had been excluded – probably in the course of the redefinition of boundaries by the Pharisaic authorities who were left after the downfall of the Second Temple in 70. I gave a brief account of this in the chapter on Judaism. Presumably the reason for this was a charge of blasphemy, since presumably the Johannine community had countered the synagogue's 'no' with an extremely 'high' christology: Jesus Christ as God's exclusive mediator of salvation, the Son sent by the Father who is the only one really to know God. From the Jewish side, this must have felt like blasphemy (John 10.30–39).

The whole fatal problem of the relationship between Jews and Christians in this Gospel, which had immeasurable effects on theology and church history, can thus only be described in appropriate historical terms if we understand the Johannine community as a minority being discriminated against in the context of a Jewish authority demarcating itself off in a rigid way. For exclusion from the synagogue was not merely a 'purely religious' measure. To be branded as heretics and excluded from the community of faith above all had social and economic consequences which changed the whole life of those involved: 'Rabbinic passages insist on cutting off ties with heretics, stopping all personal and business relations and excluding help in any direction' – thus the Protestant theologian Klaus Wengst, who has written the most thorough study of the situation of the Johannine community in the German-speaking world.[38] Moreover, in the Gospel itself potential exclusion from the synagogue is present as a constant threat (16.2; cf. 9.22; 12.42). This explains the atmosphere of anxiety that may have surrounded the Johannine community: the parents of the man born blind cannot concede that Jesus was the miraculous healer 'for fear of the Jews'. Leading men of Israel do not dare to confess their faith in Jesus openly 'so as not to be cast out of the synagogue' (12.42); Nicodemus finds it better to go to Jesus by night, and even Joseph of Arimathea remains only a 'secret disciple of Jesus' – 'for fear of the Jews' (19.38).

This is probably also an explanation, finally, of the extreme dualism which has become the sign of the existence of the Johannine Christians. For the Johannine community evidently feels threatened not only by 'the Jews' (here 'the Jews' appear for the first time in the New Testament not as individuals or as a group but as a collective stereotype), but even more: they also believed themselves to be rejected and hated by 'the world' generally. Therefore Jesus' appearance is judgment on the world (9.39; 12.31); the world is inhabited by 'sons of darkness' and hates those who are not 'of this world' (17.14). Jesus himself refuses to pray for 'the world' (17.9), has 'overcome the world' (16.33), and driven out the Satanic prince from this world (12.31;14.30). In short, John depicts Jesus' person and message as the great crisis for Israel and the world, which requires a decision between truth and lie, light and darkness, life and death, freedom and servitude.

No hostility to the Jews in principle

However, before we come to the climax of the polemic between the Johannine Christ and 'the Jews' in chapter 8, it is worth also noting the noting the overtones in the Gospel. For on close inspection there can be no question of the relationship between Christians and Jews having been painted in black and white, or even of any hostility to the Jews in principle. The Gospel leaves no doubt that in addition to

Gentiles there are time and again Jews who follow Jesus. These even include 'many of the leading men' of Israel (12.42): Nicodemus, a scribe from the Pharisees and member of the Sanhedrin (3.1–10); Nathanael, explicitly called by Jesus 'an Israelite indeed, in whom is no guile' (12.47), not to mention Joseph of Arimathea, who sees to the burial of Jesus (19.38–41). What is theologically more decisive, however, is that despite all the distance from God and the law 'of the Jews', the Johannine Christ explicitly confirms that the God whom he calls 'his Father' is also the God of the Jews and Israel is the origin of salvation. For in the conversation with the Samaritan woman this Christ explicitly declares:

> You (the Samaritans) worship what you do not know; we worship what we know, for salvation is from the Jews (4.22).

That makes the conflict with 'the Jews' in this Gospel all the more tragic. The dispute is not over the question whether the Jews in principle recognize the true God, but over whether they recognize in Jesus the one who newly discloses this God to them. So the issue between the Johannine Christ and the Jews is not one of an unknown God, but of the God known in Israel. The dispute is not over the person of the God of Israel, but over the place where he is present now. This dispute over the place of the presence of God is intensified into a sharp either-or about the knowledge of God: 'anyone who disputes the presence of God in Jesus is challenged as to whether he knows God'.[39]

The break: children of the devil instead of children of Abraham

All the conflicts are focussed as through a magnifying glass in chapter 8 of the Gospel. There is only one new element. Here the Johannine Christ discusses not only with the Jews, at this point specifically the Pharisees who attack Jesus' message a priori, but also with 'Jews who believed in Jesus' (8.31), which further heightens the confrontation. For both groups are confronted here with the same exclusive claim to revelation – and deterred. Specifically what seems to be happening is this. The Pharisees are told that there is no knowledge of God that does not go through Christ. Indeed, that knowledge of Christ is synonymous with knowledge of God: 'You know neither me nor my Father; if you knew me, you would know my Father also' (8.19) – a statement which is very much in line with the exclusive Son christology which occurs throughout the Gospel: 'No one has seen the Father except him (the Son) who is from God; he has seen the Father' (6.46; cf. 14.6–13).

Moreover there is the same christological exclusivism, the same confrontation with 'Jews who believed in him'. For they, too, entangle the Johannine Christ in a dispute. Remarkably, in it they refer to Abraham:

> 'If you continue in my word, you are truly my disciples, and you will know the truth, and the truth will make you free.' They answered him, 'We are descendants of Abraham, and have never been in bondage to any one. How is it that you say, "You will be made free"?' Jesus answered them, 'Truly, truly, I say to you, every one who commits sin is a slave to sin. The slave does not continue in the house for ever; the son continues for ever. So if the son makes you free, you will be free indeed. I know that you are descendants of Abraham; yet you seek to kill me, because my word finds no place in you' (8.31–37).

What group of people are these 'Jews who believed in him'? Commentators have made the well-founded conjecture that here John has in mind Jewish Christians of his time who because of Jewish counter-propaganda may have been in danger of lapsing from their belief in Christ. Indeed we must probably assume 'that the lapse has in fact taken place and the evangelist has the aim of deterring those who still remain from similarly taking such a step'.[40] This is presumably why the same conversation-partners in this chapter are quite naturally once again called 'the Jews' from v.48 on. From the perspective of the evangelist, these may therefore have been Jewish Christian apostates. They evidently had not seen why their previous state had been a state of 'slavery', since as Jews they had had Abraham as their father. But the Johannine Christ overtrumps this counter-argument once again by suggesting that these Jews (i.e. those who believed in him) had wanted to kill him.

Here at the latest it becomes clear that verbal clashes of this kind cannot be the reflection of real conditions, but must be back-projections: projections of the conflict of the Johannine community with the prevailing synagogue into the time of Jesus. For literally speaking, it would be quite absurd to suppose that the very Jews 'who believed in Jesus' wanted to kill him. No, 'Jesus' and 'the Jews' can only be code names for two hostile groups in the time of the community. The charge about wanting to kill him made here can therefore adequately be understood only as an anxious reflex action of a marginal community of Christians who feel slandered and threatened, and who react to the cursing and excommunication by the synagogue by vilifying the opposition. So we can say that the unprecedented claim to exclusive knowledge of God now made by this Christian community may have been a reaction to the experiences of their own exclusion. This is what this looks like in chapter 8:

1. The Johannine Christ reacts to the supposed intention to kill him by saying that while he does not dispute that the Jews are descended from Abraham (*sperma*, 8.37), he does dispute that they are children of Abraham (*tekna*, 8.39f.). For the first time in the history of early Christianity the scheme is turned round polemically. The Jews are no longer the true descendants of Abraham; rather, Christians are now the only children of Abraham left, although they cannot demonstrate that they are descended from Abraham. What was not yet decided in the negative for Paul is now clear once for all in John – to the disadvantage of the Jews:

> They answered him, 'Abraham is our father.' Jesus said to them, 'If you were Abraham's children, you would do what Abraham did, but now you seek to kill me, a man who has told you the truth which I heard from God; this is not what Abraham did' (8.39f.)

2. The Johannine Christ disputes not only that the Jews are children of Abraham but even that they are children of God. For in people who do not recognize the truth of Jesus, the 'devil' has taken God's place. Moreover with what S.Schulz has called this 'uniquely sharp saying' and J.Becker 'the most anti-Judaistic statement in the New Testament', the polemic against the Jews has reached its climax:

> If God were were your Father, you would love me, for I proceeded and came forth from God; I came not of my own accord, but he sent me. Why do you not understand what I say? It is because you cannot bear to hear my word. You are of your father the devil, and your will is to do your father's desires. He was a murderer from the beginning (8.42–44).

This saying is indeed uniquely sharp, because what it means is: 'It is not the repudiation of Jesus which has put the Jews on the side of the devil, but rather the fact that the Jews were always on the side of the devil, so they had to reject and kill Jesus.'[41] So in John's view the Jews were never God's children. And this now becomes abundantly clear in their hostile reaction to Jesus.

3. The Johannine Christ counters the Jewish charge of claiming to be 'greater than our father Abraham' (8.53) by appealing to Abraham as his forerunner. For this Christ, Abraham is no longer 'the father of us all before God', as Paul understood him. Rather, Abraham is 'the forerunner of us all' before Christ, a figure who no longer has any significance within Judaism, but merely points the way: 'Your father Abraham rejoiced that he was to see my day; he saw it and was glad' (8.56).

The beginning of a disheritance of the Jews

But that is not all: in order to demonstrate his absolute superiority to Abraham and thus to any legitimation by Abraham within Judaism, the Johannine Christ refers to his pre-existence with God. The circle of theological argument is thus closed, and the claim of 'Christian truth' is presented consistently and without a gap: this is a condensed system of argument. If in the early Christian discussion it was possible as it were to 'explode' established traditions by referring to the chronological priority of Abraham – Abraham was before the Torah (Paul), before the temple (Hebrews) – this chronological priority of Abraham which is critical of the system is once again surpassed by the Johannine Christ: although Jesus of Nazareth 'as man' was first born in time, as Son of God he existed before time and thus also before Abraham. And to be 'before Abraham' means to be before all claims to Jewish election, before all promises of salvation by God. Thus the Johannine pre-existence christology is the keystone in an argument about the exclusive truth needed for the Christian truth finally to be able to triumph over Jewish truth. That is the only way in which we can understand the next sentence:

> The Jews then said to him, 'You are not fifty years old, and have you seen Abraham?' Jesus said to them, 'Truly, truly, I say to you, before Abraham was, I am.' So they took up stones to throw at him (8.57–59).

After all this, the breach between Jews and Christians seems irreparable. Stones instead of dialogue; speechlessness instead of communication. Indeed, the whole of chapter 8 can be described as an ongoing process of loss of communication and understanding, which ends where such processes usually end: in speechless aggression. And the reason is that Christians here have denied Jews what for centuries has made up Jewishness, namely being children of Abraham and thus standing in a history of covenant and salvation. Christians have made themselves the only legitimate 'children of Abraham' and thus have deprived Abraham of any significance within Judaism. He is now no more than a 'forerunner' of Christ.

The Catholic New Testament Rudolf Schnackenburg has therefore rightly pointed to the difference between the picture of Abraham in Paul and that in Hebrews: 'The Johannine picture of the Jewish patriarch is no longer interested in the features which are important for the apostle Paul (Abraham as the prototype and father of believers), and is also different from that in Hebrews. Its orientation is christological and it is a riposte to the claim of the Jews. For John, Abraham is essentially a witness to Christ, a voice urging faith in Christ and an accuser of non-believers. The Jewish-Christian argument shows through.'[42] Furthermore, it is recognized that the dialogue between Jews and Christians has broken down. Nowhere is this break, this complete lack of understanding, expressed more symbolically than in the brief dialogue: 'The Jews said to him, "Who are you?" Jesus said to them, "Even what I have told you from the beginning"' (8.25).

So we cannot avoid the conclusion that in John we are confronted with the first exclusive Christianization of Abraham. Granted, in principle the Johannine Christ recognizes that salvation comes 'from the Jews' (4.22). But at the same time, in this Gospel the hallmarks of Judaism – covenant, Torah and temple – 'are only perceived appropriately if they are not taken as intrinsic values but as testimonies to the revelation of salvation by Jesus Christ which lies outside them. They are stripped of reality in favour of the reality of Christ which alone brings salvation.'[43] And to strip Israel of these realities means to disinherit Israel. Moreover such a theology is unique in the New Testament. Worse still, outside the Gospel of John it was to have a fatal effect when the Christian church unexpectedly developed into a factor of social and religious power in the world of late antiquity.

5. The Christianization of Abraham in the early church

Once again, history and historic effect need to be kept separate. The Gospel of John is a document from the passionate controversy between Jewish Christians and the orthodox synagogue and other Jewish-Christian groups. Its polemic can be explained not least from its situation of persecution: an exclusivism 'from below' in reaction to the experience of one's own exclusion. This must be noted if we are to judge correctly the anti-Jewish Christian exclusiveness associated with Abraham, which emerges for the first time. Here a marginal group of powerless Christians, struggling for their identity, was fighting a twofold battle for recognition: against the apostolic church on the one hand (the Johannine community was not part of the mainstream church at this time), and against Jewish orthodoxy on the other (from which it had to accept excommunication).

Abraham – the exclusive witness to Christ: the Letter of Barnabas

The situation becomes quite different from the second century on in a Christianity which now consists only of Gentile Christians, whereas Jews have to live in remnants scattered all over the world. We should be clear that the earliest post-canonical Christian writings, composed at the beginning of the second century, already take for granted the conviction that Israel must be thought to be superseded in salvation history, replaced by the Christian church and rejected by God. The destruction of the temple? What was this if not God's punishment for the rejection of the Messiah Jesus? The expulsion from the promised land? What was this if not the repealing of the covenant by God himself? The Hebrew Bible? What does this contain if not constant promises of the Messiah Jesus Christ and his church? There is no doubt that the process of the Christianization of the heritage of Israel and thus also of the 'fathers' of Israel is now continuing step by step. Here we can only demonstrate this by a few less central works. Here, too, we shall concentrate on the role of Abraham.[44]

Already around 130 CE, one of the earliest post-canonical Christian documents, presumably written in Western Asia Minor by a Gentile Christian, the Letter of Barnabas, leaves no doubt that the 'traditions' of Israel (scripture, the covenant, the fathers, the prophets) fundamentally never had anything to do with the elect people, but exclusively belong to Christians and the church. Moreover commentators have emphasized as a 'peculiarity of the Letter of Barnabas' that what the prophets had said and intended has 'in no way and at no time' been fulfilled in the history of Israel. In Barnabas, the holy scripture of the Jews has been radically 'detached from the history of the people of Israel' and has degenerated into the 'mere letter', whose timeless meaning is not known by 'them', the Jews, but by 'us', the Christians.[45]

In other words, going beyond the well-known apologetics and polemic to be found elsewhere among the authors of the early church, in the letter of Barnabas we have the 'assumption that Israel never was the people of God, since because the Jews were not worthy as a result of their sins (the making of the Golden Calf), Moses had broken the tables of the law (Ex.32.19) and the covenant had not come into being at all, but rather was first given to the Christians'.[46] Thus Israel has already been eliminated as the bearer of the history of God with his people, attested by scripture before this history ever began.

It is obvious that this also inevitably had consequences for the picture of Abraham. Moreover, the author of Barnabas did not hesitate to detach Abraham completely from Judaism and utilize him exclusively for Christian purposes. Even Abraham's circumcision had nothing to do with the Jewish observance of the law but exclusively pointed forward to the true, spiritual circumcision which Christians enjoyed. For Barnabas – here structurally following the line of the Gospel of John – Abraham exclusively functions as a witness to Christ. He is father of the Gentile Christians alone and no longer father of the Jewish people. Here is the key passage (note, too, the excessive use of typological-allegorical scriptural exegesis):

Dear children of love, here is the full explanation of it all. Circumcision was given to us in the first place by Abraham; but he, when he circumcised himself, did so in a spiritual prevision of Jesus. He got his instruction from three letters of the alphabet; for the Scripture tells us that out of his own household Abraham circumcised eighteen and three hundred. How does his spiritual intuition come into this? Well, notice how it specifies the eighteen first; and then, separately from this, the three hundred. Now in writing eighteen, the ten is expressed by the letter I and the eight by E; and there, you see, you have IE(sus). And then, since grace was to come by a cross, of which T is the shape, it adds 'and three hundred'. Thus it indicates 'Jesus' with two of the letters and 'the Cross' with the third (9.7–8).

The letter of Barnabas is no random and peripheral document of the early church. It was widely received and had a considerable influence within the church: 'It was used, directly or indirectly, by Justin Martyr, Irenaeus, Clement of Alexandria, Tertullian, Origen and some other authors. What found a following was not least the one-sided way of evaluating biblical passages already developed further here, which derives appropriate positions from developments within the Bible, and ignores statements to the contrary.'[47]

Judaism as a dead religion: the letters of Ignatius

The letters of Ignatius give us detailed information about the faith, ethics, life and organization of Christianity in Asia Minor and Syria around the beginning of the second century.[48] Ignatius was bishop of the important Syrian city of Antioch, presumably between 70 and 107/8. In the course of a persecution of Christians he was arrested, and taken under escort to Rome. The seven letters which have come down to us from Ignatius were written by him on his journey as a prisoner, addressed to friendly Christian communities. He died as a martyr in Rome, presumably around 110.

In Ignatius we already find a christology and ecclesiology which is quite different from the New Testament. At numerous points in this letter Christ is quite naturally called 'God' in a way which betrays a complete lack of sensitivity and indifference to the Jewish Christian heritage. At the same time there is marked emphasis on a monarchical episcopate, supported by a theology of the episcopate in which the bishop is the representative of God and Jesus Christ before and over against the community. Among other things the bishop has the task of safeguarding the purity of doctrine. The bishop alone is the stronghold of orthodoxy, and only the community with the bishop guarantees Christian orthodoxy. So it is not suprising that we find a good deal of polemic in the letters of Ignatius against heretics of all kinds.

For example, Ignatius must have come up against the problem of Judaizing mission or Jewish propaganda in the community of Philadelphia in Asia Minor:

All the same, if anyone should make use of them to propound Judaism to you, do not listen to him. Better hear talk of Christianity from a man who is circumcised than of Judaism from one who is not – though in my judgment both of them alike, if they fail to preach Jesus Christ, are no more than tombstones and graves of the dead, which limit their inscriptions to the names of mere mortal men.[49]

It is clear that Christianity and Judaism are thus two completely distinct entities for Ignatius. Furthermore, Judaism is a dead religion compared with Christianity. It is no longer significant for a Gentile Chrsitian like Ignatius that Jesus Christ was once a Jew, 'under the law' (Gal.4.4). Alongside Christianity, Judaism as a living religion in fact no longer has any significance, except as a danger against which Christians must guard. Moreover, in Ignatius we do not have an Israel theology in the spirit of Paul but a combination of quotations from the Letter to the Hebrews and John with an anti-Jewish focus. The key passage, in which Abraham also appears, is:

The priests of old, I admit, were estimable men; but our own high priest (= Christ) is greater, for he has been entrusted with the Holy of Holies, and to him alone are the secret things of God committed. He is the doorway to the Father, and it is by him that Abraham and Isaac and Jacob and the prophets go in, no less than the apostles and the whole church.[50]

Can one speak out more clearly against Israel? It is not Abraham, Isaac, Jacob and the prophets who show the way to God, a line which is then taken up again and brought to life by Jesus Christ, but Christ (as pre-existent redeemer) is already the door through which all the fathers and prophets of Israel first came to God. There is no question that the systematic degrading, or more precisely the christological disinheriting, of Israel is in full swing.

'We Christians are children of Abraham': Justin's Dialogue

We find probably the most direct and harshest clash with a representative of Judaism outside the New Testament in the writings of a man who was born in the Samaritan city of Neapolis (Nablus) and was martyred in Rome in 165: Justin.[51] For in addition to two *Apologies* 'against the Gentiles', Justin left a fictitious dialogue with a Jew named Trypho. In fact Trypho functions less as a partner in a dialogue on equal terms than as a figure through which the superiority of Christianity can be demonstrated. Justin's *Dialogue* is probably the earliest anti-Jewish apologia we have; it was probably written in Ephesus between 155 and 160 and was addressed to educated Gentile Christians. In grandiose theological style and refined argument and rhetoric, this is to be a demonstration that Christianity is now the better and true Judaism.

Moreover, with its 124 chapters this *Dialogue* extends further and further and treats virtually all the themes which have meanwhile become highly controversial between Jews and Christians. Here the correct interpretation of scripture has become a central point of dispute. For Justin there is no doubt that if one interprets scripture 'rightly', Jesus appears as the promised Messiah of Judaism, and the law of Moses is detached from the old covenant and replaced by the new law of Christ in the new covenant. All this is further supported by a philosophical and theologial premise of Justin's: Jesus Christ is the pre-existent Logos from eternity. So great figures of history before Christ can already have had a share in this Logos, in particular Socrates, Heraclitus and Abraham. Through their knowledge of the truth they were fundamentally already Christians before Christ, and thus already anticipate later Christianity.

These, briefly, are the basic presuppositions which provide the context for Justin's picture of Abraham. Here, too, we shall concentrate on the key passage, which occurs in section 119 of Justin's *Dialogue*:

What larger measure of grace, then, did Christ bestow on Abraham? This, namely, that he called him with his voice by the like calling, telling him to quit the land wherein he dwelt. And he has called all of us by that voice, and we have left already the way of living in which we used to spend our days, passing our time in evil after the fashion of the other inhabitants of the earth; and along with Abraham we shall inherit the holy land, when we shall receive the inheritance for an endless eternity, being like children of Abraham through the like faith. For as he believed the voice of God, and it was imputed to him for righteousness, in like manner we, having believed God's voice spoken by the apostles of Christ, and promulgated to us by the prophets, have renounced even to death the things of the world. Accordingly, he promises to him a nation of similar faith, god-fearing, righteous and delighting the Father; but it is not you, in whom is no faith.[52]

'You Jews are not that people': more radically and fundamentally than others, Justin the Christian denies Israel precisely what has constituted its identity for centuries: being the elect people and living in an unabrogated covenant with God. For Justin, the elect people has fundamentally become a non-people before God: a people which never really existed before Christ was born. Why not? Because all the fathers and prophets of Israel exclusively point to Christ, are exclusive witnesses to the coming of Christ. History in between is fundamentally a non-history, a history of shadows, a prehistory, which is nothing in itself but constantly points away from itself to the future: to the church of Jesus Christ.

In other words, with the help of typological allegorical exegesis Justin, too, reduces the 'Old' Testament to a mere source of key words for the Christ-event, a quarry of 'proof texts' to support the truth of Christianity. And Judaism as a living religion? After Christ it is dead, useless and obsolete. Now it is like the 'sand on the sea shore', which 'produces nothing and bears no fruit'.[53]

Let us stop here for a moment and become clear: a good century after the death of the apostle Paul a normative representative of the theology of the church of his time already leaves no doubt that Judaism is a useless, extinct, barren, thoroughly dead religion. What is still left in Judaism has established itself as an enemy of Christ and Christians. For Jews have not only ceased to be children of Abraham (as a result of their behaviour towards Christ), but those who have survived continue to exist in a state of bitterness and godlessness, in a state in which the word of God is 'spurned'![54] Indeed, in a later chapter Justin will even make the Jews henchmen of the devil.[55] There is no doubt about it: in this philosopher, already in the second half of the second century we can find all the elements which would make ecclesiastical anti-Judaism fatally typical of the next centuries. Here was the preparation of a theological reservoir on which the antisemitism of the twentieth century could still shamelessly draw, given that in 1935 a Nazi ideologue could see Justin as the 'greatest antisemite of Christian antiquity'.[56]

Granted, this is a horrific misinterpretation of Justin (as we know, racial antisemitism only appears during the nineteenth century), but there is no doubt that Justin laid the foundations for the anti-Judaism of the church. So there is no disputing Heinz Schreckenberg's analysis: 'Justin is the first Christian author of any status to regard the Jews comprehensively as enemies of Christ and the Christians. They blaspheme the name of Jesus and want to kill and martyr his believers. They scorn and mock the Son of God.'[57] Indeed, Justin is the first Christian theologian and philosopher of status to deny the Jews any descent from Abraham in such an excessive way, through the slogan 'For the true spiritual Israel, and descendants of Judah, Jacob, Isaac and Abraham, are we . . .'[58] The journalist Elisabeth Endres has therefore rightly referred to the fatal consequences of this theology of disinheritance in the history of the church: 'They, the Christians, were the real spiritual sons of Abraham. In antiquity the consequence of that was that theologians, from the author of the Syrian Didascalia to Augustine, asked themselves whether the Jews could still call themselves Jews. For they had lost their religion. Their religion was the shadow of Christianity cast forward; their prophets and saints merely types of the original which only came into the world later in time, Jesus Christ.'[59]

6. The paradox: the non-Christian Abraham is made a member of the church

It is no coincidence that the name of Augustine appears in this context. For if there is a theologian who could sum up the great legacy of more than the theology of the Western Latin fathers and form a brilliant new synthesis it was Aurelius Augustine, who was born around 200 years after Justin's death in Hippo Regis, North Africa (354–430). Furthermore, with Augustine we have the patriarch of all Western Latin theology, whose work had effects on theology and the church throughout the Middle Ages which are almost impossible to overestimate. That is reason enough for concluding our short history of the Christian reception of Abraham with Augustine's theology of Abraham (that is all that we can go into here). In this work the Christian Abraham theology found a 'classic form' which was handed down almost unquestioned until the twentieth century (at least in Catholic theology).

The mystery of Abraham: Augustine and the Jews

Augustine passionately persecuted two groups of people, the heretics and the Jews. Here it is idle to argue whether in his polemic against the heretics Augustine had not sometimes been even more bitter. Whereas he continually presents the Jews as 'opponents of the church', he even presents the heretics as 'the worst enemies',[60] especially since all his Christian life, above all as a bishop, he had to do with specific heretics, but never – as far as we know – with specific Jews.

Be this as it may, there is no denying the fact that Augustine, too, stands in the tradition of a Christian anti-Judaism which had become a firm ingredient of Christian theology from the second century on. For Augustine, too, wrote a work (originally homilies) against the Jews, in which he castigates the Jews for their 'blindness', 'shame-lessness' and 'blinkered view'. Indeed, all the topics of anti-Jewish Christian polemic recur unbroken in Augustine: their guilt for the crucifixion; their hardening; their justified dispersion among the peoples; their bitterness towards the church.[61]

But why are the Jews so blinkered? Why are they so 'blind'? Because they do not see history with 'spiritual eyes' but with fleshly eyes. According to Augustine, anyone who looks at history with 'spiritual' eyes looks at it with the eyes of Christ. For Christ is the Logos who was before all time. He is the Son of God through whom the world was called to life. For Augustine, all history is to be thought of in the light of Christ and is directed towards Christ. All history has a mystery in it: Jesus Christ.

So it is not surprising that the Gospel of John occupies a key role in Augustine. And in the Gospel the focus is again – as far as our question is concerned – on the famous chapter 8, in which the evangelist John made his Christ say: 'I say to you, before Abraham was, I am.' It is understandable that Augustine can pick this up in order to give his theology of history a biblical foundation. Moreover in his exegesis of the Gospel of John Augustine does not hesitate to bring out Christ as the mystery of Abraham in a 'spiritual', i.e. allegorical, way:

And the Lord: 'Verily, verily, I say unto you, Before Abraham was made, I am.' Weigh the words, and get a knowledge of the mystery. 'Before Abraham was made.' Understand, that 'was made' refers to human formation; but 'am' to the divine essence. 'He was made', because Abraham was a creature. He did not say, 'Before Abraham was, I was; but, 'Before Abraham was made,' who was not made save by me, 'I am'. Nor did he say this, 'Before Abraham was made I was made'; for 'In the beginning God created the heaven and the earth'; and 'In the beginning was the Word.' 'Before Abraham was made, I am.' Recognize the Creator – distinguish the creature. He who spake was made the seed of Abraham; and that Abraham might be made, he himself was before Abraham.[62]

All these texts are important preliminary steps in understanding the great theological synthesis which Augustine presents at the end of his life, shaken by crises and full of combat, and in which he also gives the final contours to his picture of Abraham. This is of course his gigantic work *The City of God*.

Jews now serve Christians: the City of God

Apart from the crises over the 'heretics' Pelagius and Donatus, no event shook Augustine's life so much as the conquest of the capital, Rome, by the West Goths under Alaric in 410. To counter pagan polemic that Christianity as the new religion was to blame for the fall of the great city, in his old age Augustine once again turned to a great defence of Christianity – this time in the form of a grandiose philosophical view of history, unprecedented in Christianity. For thirteen years (from 413–426) Augustine worked on this account comprising twenty-two books, which bears the title *De Civitate Dei*, *The City* (or *State*) *of God*. It is governed by a basic dualism, the opposition and conflict between the *Civitas Dei* and the *Civitas terrena*, the city or state of this world. Here Augustine does not see the history of the world as an eternally recurrent cycle – which is known elsewhere in antiquity – but as a series of six periods of salvation history with an increasingly acute conflict between the two realms, which will only be separated in the last divine judgment.

For Augustine, the climax and centre of history is the appearing of Christ in the sixth period: the end time, which extends from Christ's birth to the Last Judgment. At the same time it is clear that all the previous five periods are no more than pointers, shadowy outlines, forecasts of the appearance of this God-man in whom God and man have entered into the only possible reconciliation. How else would Augustine himself have written: 'The centuries of past history would have rolled by like empty jars, if Christ had not been foretold by means of them.'[63]

Peter Brown, the distinguished American biographer of Augustine, has therefore rightly referred to the remarkable hermeneutics of history in the *City of God*: 'Augustine always believed, with all the Christians of the Early Church, that what was most significant in history was that thread of prophetic saying and happenings that culminated in the coming of Christ and the present situation of the church. As in a kaleidoscope, patterns charged with prophetic significance would suddenly crystallize, only to dissolve again and be replaced by a more vivid grouping: the ark of Noah, the Promises to Abraham, the Exodus, the Captivity of Babylon.'[64]

This was in fact the decisive thing: in history, for Augustine a battlefield between two powers, there are always as it were 'prophetic' times, breaks in which God's counsels shine out in a quite special way. The great sacrifices were such 'prophetic' turning points: the sacrifices of Abel, Melchizedek and also Abraham. So it is no coincidence that in the *City of God* Augustine is dealing at length with the history of the old covenant 'from Noah to David', and in it at length with the history of Abraham. For Augustine has no doubt that with Abraham's entry into history the process of the 'City of God' has moved forward. This now already has clearer contours, since all these events – understood spiritually – point to the future culmination of history in Christ. In concrete that means:

– The promise of God to Abraham: it is certainly to be understood – at a lower level – in a 'fleshly' way (after Abraham there was a people of the Jews), but 'far more gloriously'. In a spiritual sense, it means that Abraham is the 'father of all nations' who follow in the footsteps of his faith.[65] And it was a matter of course for Augustine that these peoples are the Christian peoples, since the promise that the nations would be blessed through Abraham was fulfilled in Christ.[66]

– Circumcision as a sign of the covenant. According to Augustine this must be understood even more in a spiritual way, in the light of grace. If that is done, it is clear that circumcision means none other than 'renewed nature after shedding the old being'. The eighth day of circumcision points to that: to Christ who rose after the end of the seven-day week.

– Abraham's sacrificing of Isaac. This tremendous scene in particular is completely under the sign of God's grace and God's promise. For since Isaac is saved by God's grace, he is such a child 'of promise'. He 'promises' the future which God has prepared for later. If today as a Christian one looks at this future, then Isaac's sacrifice by his father can only point to the mystery of Jesus Christ who really sacrificed himself on the cross. Here, too, it is clear that for Augustine the Abraham stories are not really stories about Abraham, but at the deepest level anticipations of the life and work of Jesus Christ. Everything in the Old Testament already proclaims 'newness, and the new covenant is shadowed forth in the Old'.[67]

But what about the people of the Jews? Do the covenant promises of God to Isaac, son of Abraham and father of Jacob/Israel, no longer have any role? Already in his homilies against the Jews Augustine had left no doubt on this question. After Christ's death and resurrection the church has finally replaced, totally superseded, the synagogue. It is clear that this process is seen as complete in the *City of God*. Here Augustine speaks quite plainly about the relationship of Jews and Christians in terms of the relationship of Jacob and Esau. Just as God prefers the younger brother to the older, so now he prefers Christianity, which is historically younger, to Judaism, which is older. Indeed through God's will the 'elder people of the Jews' must now serve the 'younger people of the Christians'.[68] The consequence is that Christians are now the 'Lord's people', who rule over the servant people of the Jews. Jews can continue to exist, certainly, but only because by their scriptures they continually give new proof of the truth of the Christian religion; they provide the dark contrast against which the Christian truth stands out all the more splendidly and convincingly. This is what we read in the *City of God*:

> Christ, I say, who is ours is blessed, that is, truly spoken of out of the mouths of the Jews, when, although erring, they yet sing the law and the prophets, and think they are blessing another for whom they erringly hope.[69]

From the inclusion of the Gentiles to the exclusion of the Jews

With Augustine, the theological foundations of a Christian anti-Judaism had been cemented once and for all. With his charge of bitterness and hardness, with his typological christological exegesis of the Hebrew Bible, Augustine had deprived the Jewish people once and for all of any theological legitimation. As the Israel after the flesh which had been left behind, Jews had lost everything which had once singled them out: their election through God, the covenant, the commandments, scripture and the Messianic promises. All this has now passed over to the 'spiritual Israel', the church. The *ecclesia* has finally triumphed over the synagogue; the Jewish heritage has finally been Christianized, indeed incorporated into the church.

Thus we find a paradoxical situation in Christian history which shows structural analogies to the development in Judaism. For just as in Judaism a split could be noted between universalists (the 'Yahwist', Philo and Josephus) and exclusivists (Jubilees, the Apocalypse of Abraham, the rabbis), so now a split can be noted in Christianity. One group of Christians (Paul, Matthew, Luke, the author of Hebrews) saw the reference to Abraham not as a sign of a new exclusiveness but as the continuity of God's history of covenant and blessing from Abraham to Jesus Christ – ultimately in favour of Israel. For them, Abraham remained in principle the father of Israel, though after the appearance of Jesus Christ, with true universality he also became the 'father of the nations', from whom all people could learn what it means to believe in the one true God. In the light of faith in Jesus Christ they recognized what significance the faith of Abraham already had: before God it does not depend on descent from a people or privileges in salvation history but solely on justifying faith. Therefore through Abraham, people from the Gentiles, if they so believed, had become descendants of Abraham and had thus been accepted into God's history of covenant and blessing with his elect people. For them, Abraham does not stand for the exclusion of Jews but for the inclusion of Gentile Christians in the history of the one true God, which began with the fathers and prophets of the people of Israel.

Another group of Christians (the author of the Gospel of John, the early Christian Apologists, Justin, Augustine) used Abraham exclusively to legitimate Christian faith as the true faith. Instead of the Gentiles gratefully recalling their inclusion in God's history with his elect people, now Gentile Christians exclude Jews from the true faith. Only the line from Christ to Abraham counts. Through a particular pre-existence christology and a typological christological exegesis of the 'Old Testament' the Jewish people is now refused its own approach to its original scriptures. The Jewish people is theologically disinherited. The church alone is the heir to the synagogue, and the more it becomes the monopoly of Gentile Christians, the more it has an anti-Jewish profile. Abraham is no longer the father of the Jewish people but the exclusive witness for Christ to truth. To be a child of Abraham is no longer a sign of the people of Israel but the preferred characteristic of those who have inherited from Israel, the Christians. It follows from this that if in the Jewish tradition there is a tendency to associate Abraham increasingly narrowly with the halakhah, in Christian tradition already from the second century there is a broad process of disinheriting the Jewish people, which is matched by a process of the Christianizing of Abraham, i.e. of incorporating him into the church.

We should be clear what this development within Christianity has led to: the non-Jew Abraham, who received promises from God of a great people and its descendants, is used by Christians to force this elect people to the margin, to obliterate it from salvation history. And centuries later this obliteration from salvation history was followed by a physical obliteration. Theological anti-Judaism and racial antisemitism combined in a fatal mix to which, moreover, the Jewish people as a whole was almost to fall victim.

III. Abraham and Islam

But no one, whether Jewish Christians like Paul or Matthew, or Gentile Christians like Ignatius or Augustine, could have dreamed that once more a great religious power would emerge in world history which would again attach supreme importance not only to justifying its own understanding of faith by Abraham but also to claiming Abraham for itself.[1]

1. Ishmael – an enigmatic son of Abraham

How could this be? Hadn't the Christian churches done everything possible to establish themselves as the true heirs of Abraham – at the expense of the Jews? Hadn't Christian theologians attached supreme importance to establishing once and for all that Christians were the true children of Abraham? After all, history had been 'seen through' with the help of christology, and seemed to have been decided once and for all in favour of the Christian claim to truth and salvation. Christ ruled as king in heaven. And on earth pope and emperor were his representatives.

What no one could have suspected

But barely two centuries after the death of Augustine (in 430), the world-historical situation looked completely different. A new prophet appeared on the Arabian peninsula and with charism and power proclaimed a new message which then as a religion made a triumphal progress over large parts of the earth with unparalleled speed. In only 100 years after the death of this prophet, whose name was Muhammad (632), under the first four caliphs (632–661) and the first great dynasty of the Umayyads (661–750), Islam not only spread throughout the Arabian peninsula, but also conquered Syria, Palestine, Egypt, Persia and large areas of Afghanistan as far as

India: indeed Islam not only succeeded in conquering the whole of North Africa from Alexandria to Tangier, but also subjected almost all of Spain by force of arms. Here the emirate of Cordoba was established, which was to last for centuries. Only the military defeat at Poitiers, deep into France (just a century after Muhammad's death, in 732), prevented a further advance of Islam into Central Europe, where since the Frankish ruler Clovis had gone over to Christianity (he was baptized in Reims in 497/498 by Bishop Remigius) the Christian church had just begun to establish itself as a state church.

No, a man like the apostle Paul would certainly never have dreamed that Ishmael, the son of the Egyptian Hagar, about whom he had still spoken so disparagingly in an allegory in the letter to the Galatians (4.22–25), would have descendants who, having become great and powerful, would actually entangle the church in a life-and-death struggle. And while Augustine had mentioned the promise of God through Ishmael in the *City of God* ('I will also make the son of the maidservant a great people', Gen.21.13), he then completely ignored this, because for christological reasons only the covenant of God with Isaac, who as the 'son of the promise' was a model of Christ, was important for him. And now it was the descendants of Ishmael who arose to challenge the Christian church in an unprecedented way. It is a tragic irony that Augustine's homeland of North Africa also succumbed to the triumphal progress of Islam (Carthage was conquered in 698) barely 270 years after the death of the long-lived Bishop of Hippo. Since then there has been no North African Christianity worth mentioning.

Cast out – yet blessed

Here there can really be no doubt that the Hebrew Bible made significant statements about Ishmael – not only biographical but above all also theological. In the interest of an Abrahamic ecumene these theological statements urgently need evaluation. For Ishmael is the forefather of the Arabian tribes and thus of Islam. To continue to ignore this aspect theologically would be an indication of a pernicious blindness to God. According to the testimony of Israel, the God who guides the history of Israel also guides the destinies of all peoples. And this God evidently has special plans for

Ishmael, which can only be ignored by those trapped in a salvation-historical arrogance.

Certainly, Genesis is theologically far more interested in the history of Abraham's son Isaac, the father of Jacob/Israel, than it is in Ishmael. According to the 'Priestly Writing', which shows special theological interest in the line from Isaac through Jacob/Israel, God concludes his 'eternal' covenant with Isaac and not with Ishmael (Gen.17.19–21; cf. 21.12). Yet the reports about the other son of Abraham are remarkably ambivalent, fluctuating between demarcation and expulsion from God's covenant with his people and a theological revaluation on the one hand to a further existence blessed by God on the other. It is here in particular that Ishmael's position differs from that of the six sons which Abraham had by his second wife Keturah. These are recompensed by Abraham with no more than a gift at the end of his life, sent 'eastwards' so that they live 'far from his son Isaac' (25.1–6). There are no special theological statements about them. By contrast, things are different with Ishmael – according to Israel's own testimony:

1. However great the theological difference may be between Ishmael, the son of the 'flesh' (i.e. of human potential), and Isaac, the son of the 'promise' (i.e. God's grace), it is a fact that not Isaac, but Ishmael, is Abraham's firstborn son. For Abraham has this son by his Egyptian slave girl Hagar at the age of eighty-six – expressly at the desire of his legitimate wife Sarah, who had become old and remained barren (16.1–4). Moreover the literal meaning of the name Ishmael is 'God hears' (16.11). This status of firstborn is understandably of deep symbolic significance, if not for Jews and Christians, later for Muslims.

2. Ishmael receives the sign of God's covenant, circumcision, even before Isaac. For at the age of ninety-nine – at this time Isaac has not yet been born – Abraham circumcises himself and the thirteen-year-old Ishmael with this sign of the covenant with God, strikingly on the same day (17.23–26). Theologically this is of considerable significance. For by preserving this history, Israel itself has accepted the statement that before Ishmael, later to be the ancestor of the Arabian tribes, was cast out, by God's will he bore the sign of God's covenant (17.10). Thus he was a priori accepted into God's covenant with Abraham, Sarah and Isaac. Conversely, this means that Israel cannot absolutize its own election. Other children of Abraham, too, have been singled out

by God.[2] Two further elements in the history of Ishmael emphasize this.

3. Not only Isaac's life but also Ishmael's stand under God's special protection. For strikingly, Ishmael's life is twice safeguarded by God – against the will of his parents. We can follow this theologically in the case of the first expulsion (16.7–9) when the jealous Sarah literally sends her slave-girl Hagar, who has become proud, into the wilderness. There Hagar is rescued by an angel of God and sent home. For here the story is told according to a simple scheme: God thwarts an evil human plan. Moreover, God has Hagar told through his angel, 'I will make your descendants so numerous that they cannot be counted' (16.10), a statement which is given further theological value by corresponding to the promise to Isaac almost down to its wording (15.5). Moreover, the theological point of this scene is that it is explicitly not human will (that of Ishmael's parents) but God's will that he should come into the world at all.

However, the second expulsion scene (21.9–21) is theologically enigmatic – because of God's own behaviour. For here it is God himself (and no longer an angel) who explicitly encourages Abraham to put behind him his initial 'disgust' at the expulsion of Hagar and Ishmael and yield to his wife Sarah. The reason for this is that Abraham's descendants would now be named 'after Isaac' (21.12). However, anyone who sees theological triumphalism at work here and already wants to accept this humbly (according to the motto, God chooses whom he wills and rejects whom he wills) will be surprised at the next statement from God. For the same God who has just encouraged the expulsion of Hagar and Ishmael tells Abraham that he will make Ishmael, too, the son of the handmaid, 'a great nation'. Why? Because he too, Ishmael, is Abraham's 'descendant'. So the confused reader of this scene faces a riddle: how can this God do both at the same time? How can God accede to Hagar's and Ishmael's expulsion and at the same time have great plans for the future for them both?

Abraham's behaviour at this point is no less ambivalent. We have a farewell scene between Abraham and Hagar which is remarkably ambiguous. On the one hand, Abraham is firmly resolved to throw out Hagar and Ishamel, and indeed is encouraged to do so by God. On the other hand, Abraham's 'disgust' at this plan which comes from Sarah is not concealed, since Abraham has evidently still retained some awareness that in the end Ishmael is after all 'his son'

(21.11). Perhaps this is why this farewell scene is told as it were in slow motion down to the last detail, which cannot fail to have an effect: Abraham gets up in the morning, takes bread and a skin with water, gives both to Hagar, puts it all on her shoulder, hands over the child to her, and lets her go. He does not say a word to her about God's saving intent (21.14).

Here, too, the reader is left with an ambiguous feeling. How can Abraham both carefully stage the farewell and at the same time send the woman and 'his son' into the wilderness without even hinting by so much as a word what he already knows: that she and her son will not perish? Moreover Hagar and Ishmael are saved a second time by God's angel. We are expressly told: 'And God was with the lad, and he grew up; he lived in the wilderness, and became an expert with the bow. He lived in the wilderness of Paran; and his mother took a wife for him from the land of Egypt' (21.20f.). Note the parallels here, too: the proving of Isaac before the sacrifice corresponds to the rescue of Ishmael before he dies in the wilderness. Thus through the tradition of this story Israel expressed the fact that God's grace is not exclusively limited to the line Isaac-Jacob-Israel; it also embraces the other son of Abraham, not only individually but collectively. For:

4. Not only Isaac but also Ishmael stands under God's blessing as son of Abraham. For Ishmael, too, is given the prospect of fertility and countless descendants – similarly on more than one occasion (16.10; 21.13,18). Granted, the 'Priestly Writing' in Gen.17 once again explicitly emphasizes God's 'covenant' with Isaac, which is not matched by any covenant with Ishmael (17.21), and this covenant relates above all to the promise of land. But at the same time even according to this source God confirms to Abraham: 'As for Ishmael, I have heard you; behold, I will bless him and name him fruitful and multiply him exceedingly; he shall be the father of twelve princes, and I will make him a great nation' (17.20). This statement by Israel itself is of considerable theological significance. It confirms that God's blessing through Abraham continues not only in Isaac/Israel but also in outcast Ishmael and his descendants. That there are descendants despite all the plans of Sarah and Abraham to do away with them is an expression of God's will. Moreover the area in which they settle is explicitly described in Genesis, and again it cannot be a coincidence that Ishmael, too – in analogy to the twelve sons and finally the tribes of Jacob – also has twelve sons and tribes attributed to him; this can only enhance his position compared with Jacob/

Israel (25.12–18). So that is reason enough also to reflect theologically on the remarkable 'fate' of Ishmael: Ishmael, the man of the wilderness, cast out by his father, excluded from the specific history of the covenant – and yet sharing in God's blessing, manifestly loved by God, though differently from Isaac, who remained in the land.

5. Not only Isaac but also Ishmael is present at Abraham's burial. That is striking, since we do not hear a word about Ishmael in the book of Genesis after the expulsion of Hagar (ch.21), in complete contrast to Isaac, about whom we have extensive narratives, not only about the threat that he will be sacrificed (ch.22), but also about his marriage (ch.24). But suddenly (ch.25) Ishmael reappears in a deeply symbolic scene: in company with his brother Isaac at the tomb of his father Abraham, whom he buries in the cave of Machpelah near Mamre:

> These are the days of the years of Abraham's life, a hundred and seventy-five years. Abraham breathed his last and died in a good old age, an old man and full of years, and was gathered to his people. Isaac and Ishmael his sons buried him in the cave of Machpelah east of Mamre (Gen.25.7–9).

So if we reflect on all these statements about Ishmael, we can no longer avoid the impression that this son of Abraham is already an enigmatic figure. He is difficult to place, hard to classify, and Israel's theologians are visibly perplexed. For Ishmael is not, like Isaac, tribal ancestor of a people of the covenant, yet he is circumcised and bears the sign of the covenant; he has been cast out by Abraham and yet saved by God; he is to be done away with by his parents and yet remains under God's special protection and blessing. This is strange, enigmatic enough: God evidently wills even against the will of Ishmael's parents that there should be this son of Abraham and his descendants. So Ishmael occupies a strange hybrid position: he is neither like Isaac, the son of Abraham, nor is he like one of Abraham's sons by Keturah. Something special seems to have happened in his case. Evidently God still has special plans for him. And if we look at subsequent centuries, it does in fact seem odd that Judaism and Christianity always found it difficult to accept the descendants of Ishmael, with the very distinctive profile of faith which they had gained. At first these children of Ishmael seemed to be like all the other 'unbelievers' and 'Gentiles', yet they are indissolubly linked through Abraham with the biblical history of faith. So it is remarkable to reflect that the manifest theologcal confusion which we already find in Genesis as to how we are to understand God's purpose with this special son of Abraham is still reflected today in the perpelexity that there is the Islam of the sons of Ishmael, and has to be, when everything about God and the world seemed to have been made clear by Torah and Gospel . . . We shall be evaluating this state of affairs in the second part of this book, in the interest of an Abrahamic ecumene.

Ancestor of the Arabs: Jewish traditions

Isaac remained in the land, whereas Ishmael became a son of the desert (21.20). This, too, perplexed the theologians of Israel, indeed made them as it were ungracious. For they describe Ishmael with noticeable distaste not only as an 'archer' in the wilderness of Paran (21.20f.), but above all as a disturber of the peace.

> He shall be a wild ass of a man,
> his hand against every man and every man's against him;
> and he shall dwell over against all his kinsmen
> (Gen.16.12; cf. 25.18).

Thus already in the Hebrew Bible, Ishmael and the Ishmaelites are synonyms for wilderness dwellers and Bedouin. Granted, the Bible does not know the term 'Arabs', but we must assume that the area of settlement indicated here is the north-western desert of Arabia. Moreover the historical reliability of the biblical accounts is reinforced by other sources, since the tribes of Ishmael mentioned in Genesis regularly appear as Arab tribes in Assyrian inscriptions from different times, thus e.g. Nebaioth and Kedar, and Adbeel, Massa and Tema. Moreover, Tema and Duma are names of oases in the north Arabian desert.[3]

So it is not surprising that later Jewish tradition made Ishmael directly the father of the Arabs. The book of Jubilees already reports: 'And Ishmael and his sons and the sons of Keturah and their sons went together and they dwelt from Paran to the entrance to Babylon in all of the land which faces the east opposite the desert. And these mixed with each other, and they are called Arabs or Ishmaelites.'[4] So does Flavius Josephus in his *Jewish Antiquities*.[5] For him there is no doubt that Ishmael is the tribal ancestor of an 'Arab nation' which has called its tribes after the twelve sons of Ishmael, 'in honour of their own prowess and of the fame of Abraham, their father'.[6] The rabbis later will also identify the Arabs with the Ishmaelites.[7]

All these genealogies already have a deep theological symbolic value in Genesis. Deliberately placed at the end of the Abraham narratives, according to Claus Westermann these lists of peoples are meant to indicate that 'the ties of affinity of these tribes with Abraham are more important than the political separations and hostilities of later times. They have deep roots. Abraham is the father of both the religion of Israel and of Islam.'[8] But what is the precise character of the tie between Abraham and Islam? We shall be seeing this in the following sections.

2. The battle for the one God: the time in Mecca

First of all it is striking that whereas Jewish and later also Christian sources (Theodoret, Sozomen) report that the nation of the Arabs is descended through Abraham and Ishmael, there is nothing about this in the Arab sources from the pre-Islamic period known to us.[9] Yet historians recently have tended to see a historical nucleus in at least two Abraham traditions from the Muslim period which previously had been assigned to the realm of Islamic legend: the special social status of Muhammad's tribe, the Quraish, as a result of its descent from Abraham-Ishmael, and a monotheistic reform movement which already existed before Muhammad under the programmatic name 'religion of Abraham'.

Arab traditions about Abraham before Muhammad

First of all we should remind ourselves that Muhammad was born in Mecca in 570 into the tribe of the Quraish, which was not only the leading tribe in Mecca but also economically the most powerful tribe anywhere on the Arabian peninsula. Furthermore this tribe also enjoyed great social respect. Why? Because among other things the Quraish claimed that they were the richest and noblest descendants of Ishmael and thus had a unique descent from Abraham. That was important, because as a result of this genealogical legitimation they could claim to control Mecca and the sanctuary there, the Ka'ba. For according to tradition this sanctuary was founded by Abraham and Ishmael. We shall be hearing more of this.

The earliest biographer of Muhammad, Ibn Ishaq, a good century after the prophet's death, programmatically (like the Gospel of Matthew) begins his account of Muhammad's life by tracing Muhammad's death through Qusaij, the ancestor of the Quraish five generations before Muhammad, Ishmael and Abraham back to Adam.[10] Critical scholarship has more faith in these accounts than before. Thus the Göttingen Arabist Tilman Nagel writes: 'The adoption of the figure of Abraham's son Ishmael by the Quraish was doubtless the ideological expression of a far-reaching political revolution on the Arabian peninsula, the aim of which was to bring together all Arabs under the rule of the Quraish. Without going here into the many details of this process, some of which still cannot be explained satisfactorily, it should be pointed out that already in the lifetime of the Prophet numerous tribes had been caught up in this development . . . It is beyond question that even Muhammad himself was convinced of the correctness of the genealogical links between the Quraish and the tribes united with it, and Ishmael.'[11]

Furthermore, although for centuries they had been 'surrounded' by Judaism and Christianity as religious traditions and options, the Arab tribes had maintained their ancestral religious practices. And these were polytheistic through and through. In effect, that means that various Arab tribes worshipped various Arab deities at various places without making any concessions to the monotheism of Judaism and Christianity. Here the old Arab sanctuary of the Ka'ba at Mecca had a special significance, for there various old Arabian gods had been gathered in the form of a pantheon. Evidently no one had any thought of an original monotheism associated with Abraham and Ishmael. On the contrary, at the time of Muhammad, people in Mecca worshipped not only a high god (called 'Allah' by some), but above all three goddesses: Manat the goddess of fate and death; Al-Lat, the goddess of shepherds and caravan leaders; and Al-'Uzza, whose name means something like 'the strong, the mighty'. So polytheism was widespread in the Arabia of the time, and the Ka'ba, too, was drawn into the cults of the various gods and goddesses.

Yet already in the time of Muhammad there must have been a group of Arabs who rejected polytheism and reflected on the worship of the one and only God of Abraham. At any rate Ibn Ishaq already gives a list of such men, who are called *hanifs*: old Arab 'godseekers' or 'devotees', who wanted to return to belief in the one and only God – with explicit reference to the 'religion of Abraham'. 'Their view was that their people had corrupted the religion of their father Abraham and that the stone around which they ran had no significance; it could neither hear or see nor harm nor help. "Find a religion for yourself," they said, "for by God you do not have one." And so they went their different ways in the lands, in search of the Hanifiya, the religion of Abraham.'[12]

These reports, too, are now generally accepted by the biographers of Muhammad as accurate. For example, Rudi Paret, the Islamic expert and translator of the Qur'an, formerly from Tübingen, himself has 'no doubt' that 'here and there in ancient Arabia even before Muhammad there must have been thoughtful, meditative people who no longer found any satisfaction in their native religious tradition and all the more readily took up and appropriated ideas which were so to speak currently on offer from Christians and Jews. That they confessed monotheism in particular can indirectly be inferred from Qur'anic terminology. Here the expression *hanif* denotes something like "Muslim monotheist".'[13] All this means that for his own prophetic message Muhammad could link up with traditions which were already associated with Abraham. Simply from the point of view of tribal history, an 'Abraham consciousness' seemed to have appeared along the way. But what did he make of it?

Muhammad's battle against the idols and their cult

No matter precisely when Muhammad's calling to be a prophet is dated, how it is understood and what content may originally have been associated with it, one thing is certain: at the age of more than forty Muhammad, who in the meantime had established himself well both socially and economically as the husband of the widow of a rich merchant, appeared in his ancestral city of Mecca as the bearer of a new revelation: as a prophet who wanted to shake his fellow citizens out of their religious indifference, sheer rootedness in this world and social injustice. The well-established and also extremely profitable religious practice of pilgrimage to the Ka'ba and the cult centred on it was rejected by Muhammad as idolatry, to the perplexity of his people, and castigated with religious passion.

No wonder that at first the Meccans responded to Muhammad as the people of Nazareth responded to the 'prophet' Jesus or the Greek philosophers of Athens to the preacher Paul: they thought him mad. Who had ever heard of such a message? Anyone who preached like this had to be mad. The Qur'an itself contains an allusion to this: 'Hence, [be patient] even though they who are bent on denying the truth would all but kill thee with their eyes whenever they hear this reminder, and [though] they say, '[As for Muhammad,] behold surely he is a madman!' (Surah 68.51). Indeed the more Muhammad attacked the cult of the pilgrimage sanctuary of the Ka'ba, the more the fury grew over this unasked-for 'warner' who evidently acted like a 'magician'.[14]

So parallels to the story of Jesus of Nazareth are obvious here. They can also be seen where Muhammad responds to the rejection of his message of religious reform by sharpening his preaching of judgment – which is turned against his own people, whom he simply finds 'hardened'. That revives memories of the conflict between the Jewish Christians and the Jewish establishment which I reported earlier. It is also important here that Muhammad drew the material for his preaching of judgment above all from biblical tradition, which he may have come to know through contact with Jewish and Christian circles in Mecca and its surroundings.[15] Moreover early Meccan surahs also refer to the fate of Sodom and Gomorrah (53.54; 69.9), to Noah and the flood (53.53; 51.46), and to Pharaoh and his army destroyed in the waves of the Red Sea (85.18; 73.16; 79.17; 89.9; 69.9; 51.38ff.). Conversely, Muhammad feels a particularly close link with those biblical figures in whom he discovered an analogy to his own fight against polytheism and idolatry, and in whom he recognized the same pattern of reactions as among his Meccans: mockery and resistance to the prophet and his proclamation of true belief in God (43.6–8). Thus Muhammad was certainly not the only 'godseeker' who wanted to purge the old Arabian cult practices and to return to monotheism. But no one other than him was evidently in a position 'to proclaim this notion in such stirring language' and to depict to his fellow-countrymen 'the terrors of the Last Day in terrifying colours'.[16]

A new, old faith

All this already makes it clear that the prophet Muhammad did not want to abandon the biblical story of revelation and replace it with a completely new revelation by a hitherto unknown God. He explicitly brings it into line with the previous history of revelation as this had been handed down by Judaism and Christianity. He understands this as a unity, going back to a primal revelation, an eternal scripture with God which has been revealed to the different peoples one after another, each in its own language. Before this the Arabs had no written revelation, so Muhammad felt himself to be called to be prophet of the Arabs. Why shouldn't God give the Arabs a share in a revelation, as he had already done previously in the case of Jews and Christians? That was Muhammad's basic notion, which is articulated in the conviction that God's eternal word is now once again newly proclaimed in Arabic – through an 'Arabic' Qur'an (43.2f.; 42.7). What Muhammad wants to offer is not a simple 'translation' of age-old traditions of Jews and Christians, but Allah's authentic and ultimate word, directly from heaven, first of all for the Arab tribes who are still completely ignorant of religion.

So we shall understand Muhammad's message rightly only if we describe it, paradoxically, as a new, old, faith. What is new is the charisma and linguistic luxuriance of Muhammad's 'revelations': 'short, even elliptically abbreviated statements, reminiscent of loud cries and introduced by mysterious oaths, held together by striking prose rhymes, gripping images in rapid succession – this is the style of the prophets as the Arabs knew them'.[17] What is new is the concentration on monotheism which can already be recognized in what is probably the earliest surah: 'Read in the name of thy Sustainer, who has created – created man out of a germ-cell! Read – for thy Sustainer is the Most Bountiful One' (96.1–3). Another new feature is the eschatology, i.e. the preaching of judgment against the blindness of the idolators and the greed of the rich. What is proclaimed is paradise for the righteous and hell for the wicked.

By contrast, Muhammad's concern is an old one: a form of radical monotheism of a kind that he had found above all in Judaism. So it is no wonder that already in a surah of the first Meccan period (610–615) there is a programmatic allusion to the 'fathers of Israel', including Abraham. Indeed, this surah even indicates that the prophet must have been thinking of a special written revelation not only for Moses (Torah) but also for Abraham: 'Verily, [all] this has indeed been [said] in the earlier leaves [revelations], the leaves of Abraham and Moses' (87.18f.; cf. 53.33–41).

Here it is clear that at the beginning of his activity as a prophet Muhammad did not want to found a new religion. He did not think of doing so, any more than the rabbi from Nazareth. On the contrary, Muhammad wanted to recall an age-old faith and proclaim anew what had already been set down on earlier 'leaves'. The Prophet was still convinced that the Jews, who in the Qur'an are called the 'children of Israel', had preserved this age-old faith; the Christians knew it too, so that along with the Jews they could be called the possessors of scripture or the 'people of the book'. Here Abraham (Arabic Ibrahim) plays a decisive role as the 'prophet' common to all the 'people of the book'. He is mentioned in twenty-five surahs (he comes second in mentions in the Qur'an after Moses). One surah, no. 14, even bears the name of Abraham. Let's look at this more closely.

Key witness against the idols: Abraham

It is striking that in the period of his prophetic struggle in Mecca the figure of Abraham is especially important for Muhammad as a figure with whom he can identify in his own battle against polytheism and idolatry. Moreover, the key texts of the Qur'an, above all from the second Mecca period (615–620), show an Abraham who on his own impetus overcame polytheism, recognized the true God as the creator of heaven and earth by the aid of his own reason (Surah 6.75–79), and then engaged battle with his polytheistic surroundings (star worship). Thus Surah 19 reports a dispute between Abraham and his father over the idols; in the Qur'an his father is not called Terah but Azar:

> 'O my father! Do not worship Satan – for, verily, Satan is a rebel against the Most Gracious! O my father! I dread lest a chastisement from the Most Gracious befall thee, and then thou wilt become [aware of having been] close unto Satan!' He answered: 'Dost thou dislike my gods, O Abraham? Indeed, if thou desist not, I shall most certainly cause thee to be stoned to death. Now begone from me for good!' (Surah 19.44–46).

We can easily recognize here features of the Jewish tradition which we have already analysed. For Joshua 24, the book of Jubilees and the Apocalypse of Abraham had already mentioned a fight by Abraham against his idolatrous family, as does the great Genesis Midrash (38.19). And it had already been important for Josephus and Philo that Abraham had been able to recognize the true creator with the help of his reason by contemplating the heavens and the stars. But in Muhammad all this has a further biographical accentuation and is utilized for his own prophetic self-understanding. For him in particular the Abraham stories are reflections of the difficult situation with which he was confronted as a prophet in Mecca. We may follow Heinrich Speyer, who has subjected the biblical narratives in the Qur'an to a thorough investigation, when he says: 'According to the Jewish saga Abraham seeks to convert his father by referring to the nothingness of the idols, whereas according to the Qur'an he attempts to convert his people. Muhammad probably rendered the narrative heard from Jews so as to show Abraham playing the role of the Arabian prophet for his people.'[18] Indeed, the prophet evidently recognized himself in Abraham's fate, since apparently Meccans of his time worshipped their idols as did Abraham's family in their time. As a result, Abraham is no more a fossilized monument to faith from primeval times for Muhammad, the apostle to the Arabs, than he is for Paul, the apostle to the Gentiles; rather, he is a living figure who legitimates the prophetic struggle for the true faith.

Here we reach a first fixed point for the picture of Abraham in this phase of the Qur'an. Very much in line with a Jewish picture of Abraham which became classic and was familiar to Muhammad, the Prophet, too, makes it clear through Abraham that it is important for human beings to free themselves from the false religious views which have come down to them and in the face of the resistance of their own families to decide for the one true God. Abraham stands for consistent and strict monotheism, which has recognized that God is 'the Sustainer of all the worlds, who has created me and is the One who guides me, and is the One who gives me to eat and drink, and when I fall ill, is the one who restores me to health, and who will cause me to die and then will bring me back to him and who, I hope, will forgive me my faults on Judgment Day' (Surah 26.77–82; cf. also Surah 29.16–27; 37.38–98). Thus, for Muhammad, God is the sole giver of all human needs (Surah 29.16); God alone has unlimited power (29.20); God alone is eternal and imperishable: beside him there is no God.

There is a second fixed point: if God's divinity is obscured by idols, these must be cast down – after the model of Abraham, who already according to Jewish traditions was an iconclast, one who destroyed images of God. This tradition also appears in the Qur'an:

'By God, I [Abraham] shall most certainly bring about the downfall of your idols as soon as you have turned your backs and gone away!'

And then he broke those [idols] to pieces, [all] save the biggest of them, so that they might [be able to] turn to it. [When they saw what had happened], they said: 'Who has done this to our gods? Verily, one of the worst wrongdoers is he!' Said some [of them]: 'We heard a youth speak of these [gods with scorn]: he is called Abraham.' [The others] said: 'Then bring him before the people's eyes, so that they might bear witness [against him] . . .' He said, 'Do you then worship, instead of God, something that cannot benefit you in any way, nor harm you? Fie upon you and upon all that you worship instead of God? Will you not, then, use your reason?' (Surah 21.57–67).

In the light of this and other passages we can now understand better the charismatic persuasion of Islam as the confession of the one true God. It can also be seen as the foundation stone of Islamic faith that any form of religious veneration or glorification (*latria*) of earthly values or persons (idols) is radically rejected as 'idolatrous' and thus contrary to God. All values or persons are reduced before God to their true status: the work of human beings, nothing but the work of transitory men. Nothing and no one may come beside or take the place of God: no human being, no ideal and no cause, no collective and no nation. In the Qur'an, Abraham is the archetypal figure of this renunciation of idolatry. With the power of his own reason Abraham had already understood the powerlessness of astral figures and idols shaped by human hands and had rejected them in favour of the one true God (cf. Surah 6.75–79). Abraham had already recognized by himself the vanity and uselessness of any idolatry and had bowed to the creative power of the one true God. Moreover Surah 6 makes Abraham say:

'Behold, unto Him who brought into being the heavens and the earth have I turned my face, having turned from all that is false; and I am not of those who ascribe divinity to aught beside him' (6.79).

Thus in the Qur'an, too, Abraham is the one who trusts God. For the presupposition for Abraham's way to God was the trust that God would show him his way. Tilman Nagel has recently once again described the consequences of this basic attitude of Abraham for all Muslims like this: 'The person who follows the example of Abraham and turns wholly to the one creator God directs his face towards him in the same way as the pilgrims directed their faces towards the God of the holy places, and is taking the decisive step towards gaining salvation. With this step he is subjecting his whole life to the meaning which follows from the creatureliness that he now affirms: as creatures, human beings owe their Creator all-embracing gratitude. In the Qur'an, to refuse to offer thanks is the essence of unbelief.'[19]

A third fixed point is that, according to the Prophet, too, Abraham is the model of the rescue and exodus of a monotheistic champion of the faith by God himself, along with the promise of descendants. For the same Surah 21 has also handed down a scene which was similarly circulating in Jewish circles: the miraculous rescue of Abraham, who has cast down the idols, from the fire, his migration and the announcement of his elect descendants:[20]

> They exclaimed: 'Burn him, and [thereby] succour your gods, if you are going to do [anything]!' [But We said] 'O fire! Be thou cool, and [a source of] inner peace for Abraham – and whereas they sought to do evil unto him, We caused them to suffer the greatest loss: for We saved him and Lot [his brother's son, by guiding them] to the land which We have blessed for all times to come. And We bestowed upon him Isaac and [Isaac's son] Jacob as an additional gift, and caused all of them to be righteous men' (21.58–72; cf. also 11.69–73).

It is theologically decisive that in the Qur'an a motif recurs which Jewish (Sirach 44; I Macc.2) and Christian (Hebrews 11) tradition had associated with Abraham: God's blessing rests on Abraham because in faith in God, despite many trials, he was found 'loyal' and 'obedient'

A fourth fixed point, which belongs in the same context, is that the prophet uses Abraham so that he can appear before his own people with even more emphasis as one who is warning them against the divine judgment. The story of Abraham and Lot from Genesis 18 and 19 is also used for this purpose by Muhammad, who here largely takes over his biblical model: the visit of the angel to Abraham, the announcement of punishment on Lot's people and Abraham's intercession for the just, and finally the saving of Lot, who avoids the judgment, though without his wife (cf. Surah 11.69–83). It is important in these passges that Abraham is presented not only as one who warns but also as the merciful one who pleads before God for sinners, as also in the case of Lot. The decisive passage runs:

Abraham was most clement, most tender-hearted, intent upon turning to God again and again. [But God's messengers replied:] 'O Abraham! Desist from this [pleading]! Behold thy Sustainer's judgment has already gone forth: and, verily, there shall fall upon them a chastisement which none can avert' (11.75f.; cf. 9.113f.).

All this already makes clear what we may call the fifth fixed point of the picture of Abraham in the Qur'an in this period: the rediscovery and revival of the 'religion of Abraham', Arabic *millat Ibrahim*. Surah 16 from the late Meccan period (620–622) expresses this with epigrammatic brevity and clarity:

Verily, Abraham was a man who combined within himself all virtues, devoutly obeying God's will, turning away from all that is false, and not being of those who ascribe divinity to aught beside God: [for he was always] grateful for the blessing granted by Him who had elected him and guided him onto a straight way. And so We vouchsafed him good in this world; and, verily, in the life to come [too] he shall find himself among the righteous. And lastly, We have inspired thee, [O Muhammad, with this message:] 'Follow the creed of Abraham, who turned away from all that is false, and was not of those who ascribe divinity to aught beside God [*hanif*]' (16.120–123).

So programmatically we have here the word which already denoted followers of the 'religion of Abraham' in the pre-Islamic period, *hanif*. This denotes the resolute, unambiguous monotheist. Here and in the future it was also associated with the sharp negative demarcation 'not a heathen', i.e. not someone who has 'associated' something or someone else with God, someone who has yielded to the temptation of idolatry.

But talk of the 'religion of Abraham' contains yet a further dimension, which is equally typical of the late Mecca period. With the self-designation 'religion of Abraham', the Prophet lays the foundation for a later religious identity which differs from Judaism and Christianity. Surah 6 from this period already points in this direction by emphasizing the 'religion of Abraham' as the 'right faith' and Muhammad as the first 'right' believer:

Say: 'Behold, my Sustainer has guided me onto a straight way through an ever-true faith – the way of Abraham, who turned away from all that is false, and was not of those who ascribe divinity to aught beside him.' Say: 'Behold, my prayer, and [all] my acts of worship, and my living and my dying are for God [alone], the Sustainer of all the worlds, in whose divinity none has a share: for thus have I been bidden – and I shall [always] be foremost among those who surrender themselves unto Him' (6.161–163).

But things had not got so far; the Prophet still believed that in the dispute with the idolatrous Meccans he had allies, namely Jews and Christians. For in this phase Muhammad leaves no doubt that the 'people of scripture' enjoy his full sympathies. He leaves no doubt that the God whose revelations he receives is also the God revered by Jews and Christians. Thus 'Islam' is not yet a designation for a new religion, but a designation for the basic human religious attitude that is required. 'Islam' is still what it originally meant quite literally: human submission to the will of the one and only God, being guided rightly in living and dying. Surah 6 from the late pre-Meccan period again compiles a list of biblical-Jewish figures, all of whom are among those who are 'righly guided': not only Isaac and Jacob the sons of Abraham but also Noah and David, Solomon, Job, Joseph, Moses and Aaron. To these are added Zechariah, John, Jesus and Elijah and Ishmael, Elisha, Jonah and Lot (6.84–86). Indeed, in this phase the Prophet explicitly calls on his followers 'not to argue with the followers of earlier revelation otherwise than in a most kindly manner' (29.46). He unmistakably proclaims:

And say: 'We believe in that which has been bestowed from on high upon us, as well as that which has been bestowed upon you; for our God and your God is one and the same, and it is unto him that We [all] surrender ourselves.' For it is thus that We have bestowed this divine writ from on high upon thee [O Muhammad]. And they to whom we have vouchsafed this divine writ believe in it (29.46f.).

After all this there can be no question that even at the end of the Meccan period the Prophet was convinced that both the revelation granted to him and that handed down to the Jews and Christians had to be believed in the same way. Moreover he thought that he had found the strongest support for his new, old message specifically in the Jewish tradition. This explains the fact that in the early Meccan phase, in analogy to the Jewish tradition, Abraham is above all the well-tried, loyal champion of monotheism whose prophetic warning at that time Muhammad impressively revives for his own prophetic fight in Mecca. Yet the Prophet by no means takes over all that is in the Jewish tradition. This makes all the more acute the question how the different revelations are related. Hasn't this to be clarified in some way? Yes. But at the end of the time in Mecca Muhammad's way was still open for further developments. After twelve years 'a situation developed in Muhammad's relationship with the Jews which was capable of development in two directions: the Jews and their history are key witnesses (for the Prophet's cause), but the guideline and criterion is the revelation of the Qur'an. It was still an open question whether Muhammad would attach himself to the Jews or the Jews would submit to the Qur'anic revelation.'[21] So what happened?

3. Structures of a new religion: the time in Medina

Muhammad had moved to Medina with great hopes in 622, when the situation for him and his followers in Mecca had become untenable. Just as according to Jewish tradition Abraham had had to move from Mesopotamia because of persecution by the heathen King Nimrod, from there to go on to Canaan and Egypt, so too did Muhammad. Thus Muslims could later see Abraham's migration as the model for the Hijra (cf. Surah 9.114; 21.71). 622, the year of the 'exodus' of Muhammad and seventy-five of his loyal followers to the oasis city of Yathrib, just over two hundred miles away, marks the greatest internal break in Islamic history, so that in the Muslim calendar it is counted as year 1. From then on Yathrib was called Medinat Annabi, city of the Prophet, Medina for short. Moreover it was here that a majority of the Arabs came to accept the Prophet's message in just a few years.[22]

The break with the Jews

Muhammad set such great hopes on a change in his situation in Medina because in contrast to Mecca this city had a significant number of Jewish inhabitants. Indeed, originally Medina had even been a purely Jewish settlement. And even then at any rate three Jewish tribes (the Qaynuqa, the Qurayza and the Nadr) still lived there, in total around 10,000 people. They lived together with non-Jewish Arab tribes (the Aus and the Haraj), not without tensions and rivalries, since the Jews, too, did not form any political unity, but as owners of oases outside the city or as goldsmiths within it had considerable economic power and political influence. And it was from the Jews in particular that Muhammad had long promised himself allies for their common monotheistic cause – against the people of Mecca, who were still unbelievers.

Muhammad had been called to Yathrib as an arbitrator in tribal rivalries. Tactically skilful and diplomatically wise, the Prophet was able to exploit this situation for his own advantage. In a relatively brief time he succeeded in exercising political influence in Medina, and with the help of a 'community order' (second half of the year 623) making peace between the divided tribes. And what about the Jews? Here they were still treated quite naturally as an integral part of the community of Mecca: they were able to preserve their existing independence above all in the religious sphere, and this was explicitly confirmed for them. Furthermore, in the first phase in Medina Muhammad endorsed for the believers who followed him those religious practices in which he had hitherto drawn most strongly on Jewish tradition: times of prayer, sabbath rest (for Muslims on Friday), prayer towards Jerusalem and fasting on the Day of Atonement.[23]

Granted, the 'community order' of Medina is more a decree than a treaty between two parties with equal rights. But there can be no question of any hostility to the Jews. On the contrary, the Jews were expected to show solidarity, in particular to take part in the war that was expected against 'unbelieving' Mecca. Moreover article 37 of the community order states: 'The Jews have a duty to pay their taxes and the Muslims theirs. They will give mutual help to each other against those who wage war on the people of this document. Between them there is good friendship, goodwill and loyalty without deception.'[24]

But the more time went on, the more deceptive Muhammad's hopes of organizing a monotheistic alliance against Mecca proved. The Jews of Medina manifestly had no intention of recognizing Muhammad in his prophetic role – either politically (in the fight against Mecca) or in religious terms (conversion to Islam). On the contrary, the Qur'an itself indicates that the Jews of Medina must have reacted to Muhammad's prophetic claim in the same way as the 'heathen' in Mecca – with mockery and repudiation. What need do we have of a new prophet? None has come to us! (cf. Surah 5.19).[25]

Muhammad himself reacted to this repudiation by now massively intensifying his accusations against the Jews: they had falsified the scriptures; they had distorted God's word; above all, they had ignored or 'kept secret' those references from scripture which pointed to Muhammad's appearance (Surah 5.15f.). And Muhammad took a further momentous step. Whereas previously he had commanded his followers to pray towards Jerusalem and follow Jewish tradition in their customs of prayer and fasting, now he made a decisive change. From now on the direction of prayer (Arabic *gibla*) for all Muslims was to be Mecca, and the time of fasting was fixed in the month of Ramadan (Surah 2.136–145). Indeed, since Muhammad's political fortunes had also improved (he had been able to inflict a surprising defeat on his opponents from Mecca at the decisive battle of Badr in the second year of the Hijra), he no longer needed to take any political account of the Jewish tribes in Medina. Step by step over the next years they were excluded (depending on the changing fortunes of the Prophet in war). Those Jews who remained were finally slaughtered. 600–900 men were killed, and women and children were for the most part sold in the slave market in Medina.

Hand in hand with this went Muhammad's settling of accounts with the inhabitants of his home city of Mecca, which he had had to leave in such shameful circumstances. In any case the change of direction of prayer towards Mecca impelled the Muslims even more to capture it, and indeed the more time went on, the less even the Meccans could ignore Muhammad's powerful position. In 628 for the first time the Meccans made a treaty with Muhammad which guaranteed safety for making the Lesser Pilgrimage ('Umra) there. Thus the Prophet had at least been recognized as a treaty partner with equal rights. And barely two years later Muhammad achieved his political goal: he entered Mecca without resistance and also became ruler of this city. Having tidied up the political front, he could now tidy up the religious front, and in the year of his death (632) he already had unlimited rule not only over Mecca and Medina, but over all Arabia. In this process there were now significant shifts of accent in the picture of Abraham as well.

The new role of Ishmael

We can describe the phase in Medina which begins with the establishment of a Muslim community as a process of the intensified

Arabizing of the Prophet's message, provided that we do not lose sight of the universality of the message of the Qur'an. In that case a first visible sign of this process is the fact that now in the Medina phase the Ishmael traditions acquire a quite different status.

It is in fact surprising that Ishmael is mentioned all the more often in the Mecca surahs, but usually only as an individual figure, not yet connected with Abraham (6.86; 19.54f.; 21.85; 38.45–48). Moreover the Prophet quite naturally regards Isaac and Jacob as sons of Abraham – in analogy to Jewish-Christian tradition (6.84; 19.49; 21.72). By contrast, Ishmael does not seem to have been important to the Prophet as a son of Abraham, since in Mecca he is merely mentioned as one of the many sent by God: 'And call to mind, through this divine writ, Ishmael. Behold, he was always true to his promise, and was an apostle [of God], a prophet, who used to enjoin upon his people prayer and charity, and found favour in his Sustainer's sight' (19.54f.). Thus Ishmael is initially (independently of Abraham) one of the prophets for his people, for whom at the same time he performs two duties: prayer and almsgiving. However, the people mentioned here may already be Arabs (since the passage is about descendants of Ishmael, not of Isaac). It follows from this that while the Prophet indicates no awareness that all Arabs as a nation are children of Abraham and Ishmael, he is aware that Ishmael the son of Abraham belongs to Arabia, indeed is an Arabian prophet.

That makes it all the more understandable that now in the Medina phase, in the course of intensified Arabizing this knowledge becomes even more significant. If Ishmael still did not have a special role in the Mecca surahs, now he emerges from his 'isolated and shadowy existence'[26] and becomes Abraham's favourite son. Now he is mentioned before Isaac. Surah 2 is of key significance for this picture of Ishmael and thus also of Abraham. It reads:

And this very thing did Abraham bequeath unto his children, and [so did] Jacob: 'O my children! Behold, God has granted you the purest faith; so do not allow death to overtake you ere you have surrendered yourselves unto him.' Nay, but you [yourselves, O children of Israel], bear witness that when death was approaching Jacob, he said unto his sons, 'Whom will you worship after I am gone?' They answered: 'We will worship thy God, the God of thy forefathers Abraham and Ishmael and Isaac, the One God:: and unto him will we surrender ourselves' (2.132f.).

Furthermore, in the same surah the Prophet makes Abraham express the wish that God may 'raise up an apostle from among themselves (i.e. the descendants of Abraham), who will read to them (verses), teach the scripture and wisdom and purify them from the impurity of the heathen' (2.129). 'Among themselves' means none other than the Arabs. Thus Muhammad claims the person of Abraham for announcing to the Arabs a prophet of their own who is of course identical with him. He, Muhammad, is a descendant of Abraham and Ishmael and a prophet sent personally by God at Abraham's request. Thus the Abraham-Ishmael tradition of his tribe, the Quraish, could be used in a completely different way.

The new role of the Ka'ba in Mecca

A second, even more striking sign of an 'Arabization' of the Prophet's message is the fact that the Prophet now makes the Ka'ba also the centre of Muslim piety. For once Muhammad had finally taken military and political hold of Mecca, he set out on a radical monotheistic purification of his ancestral city. All the heathen sanctuaries were destroyed, and only the Ka'ba was left – again after appropriate purification. However, this was only in order to utilize its attraction afresh for Muslim faith. That was all the easier, since the Prophet now resorts to those traditions which report a primal link between Abraham, Ishmael and the Ka'ba – possibly taking up tribal traditions, indeed possibly in deliberate parallelism to traditions that Abraham had already stood at the origin of the Jewish place of worship, at the origin of the Jerusalem temple ('house of Abraham'), which indeed had been built on Mount Moriah, associated with Abraham and Isaac.

Be this as it may, it is unmistakable that now for the first time statements appear in the Qur'an which bring out a connection between Abraham, Ishmael and the Ka'ba. This could not fail to have consequences. For with Abraham at the origin of the Ka'ba this pagan sanctuary could much more naturally be claimed for the new, old 'religion of Abraham'. The paganism at the Ka'ba was then the very period of 'ignorance' between the primal Abraham of that time and those believing in Abraham in the time of the Prophet which he set out to purge. But what do we learn about Abraham and the Ka'ba?

– The house of God in Mecca is called 'the first Temple ever set up for mankind, rich in blessing', 'for all people'. The place on which it stands is called 'the place whereon Abraham once stood' (Surah 3.96f.).

– Abraham and Ishmael are commanded by God to make the place of Abraham a place of prayer in the framework of a pilgrimage. At the same time God bids them purge this house for those 'who will walk around it, and those who will abide near it in meditation, and those who will bow down and prostrate themselves [in prayer]' (2.125).

– The house of prayer as a pilgrimage place is called 'a goal to which people might repair again and again, and a sanctuary', probably an allusion to the peace in the land to be observed for four holy months during the pilgrimage (Surah 2.125; cf. 5.97).

– Abraham and Ishmael are termed those who 'raised the foundations' of the Ka'ba. In connection with this both utter the prayer:

> O Our Sustainer! Accept Thou this from us: for, verily, Thou alone art all-hearing, all-knowing! O our Sustainer! Make us surrender ourselves unto Thee, and make out of our offspring a community that shall surrender itself unto Thee, and show us our ways of worship, and accept our repentance: for, verily, Thou alone art the Accepter of Repentance, the Dispenser of Grace! (Surah 2.127f.).

In terms of the history of religion, this link between Abraham, Ishmael and the Ka'ba is similarly a 'cult legend'.[27] But how is it to be evaluated? May we go so far as to depict this link as a purely political ploy on the part of Muhammad in the process of his controversy with the Jews in Medina?[28] Or should we even speak of 'two Abrahams in the Qur'an', one of Medina and one of Mecca, who are fundamentally incompatible?[29] Understandably Muslims themselves regard these theses, which are popular among non-Muslim scholars of religion, as a degradation of the Qur'an and a devaluation of its authority. And purely in terms of the exegesis of the Qur'an, as we saw, already in the Mecca surahs Abraham is praised as the model of pure faith in God: the connection between Abraham and the Ka'ba need not first have been 'invented' by the Prophet in Medina, as though Muhammad had hit on this 'brilliant idea' purely for political reasons.[30] In the case of the Prophet its roots probably lay in the history of his tribe. Indeed Surah 14 once again confirms that Muhammad must have known of traditions that the inhabitants of the valley of Mecca were descendants of Abraham. How else could we understand Surah 14.37, when Abraham can say here:

> O our Sustainer! Behold, I have settled some of my offspring in a valley in which there is no arable land, close to Thy Sanctified Temple (i.e. the Ka'ba), so that, O our Sustainer, they might devote themselves to prayer.

On the other hand, in the light of the Qur'an it is quite clear that only in Medina is there express mention of the biblical patriarch as the founder and reformer of the Mecca sanctuary, and at another point even as its 'inhabiter' (Surah 22.26f.). Only in Medina do Abraham and Ishamel stand at the beginning of the Muslim pilgrimage to Mecca (Arabic *haj*). And the pilgrimage in particular is an impressive demonstration of how little the Arabization of the prophetic message is identical with a provincialization. The pilgrimage in particular emphasizes the universal dimension of the prophetic message, since according to the Qur'anic self-understanding the Ka'ba was set up by God 'for a blessing and guidance to people throughout the world', and the pilgrimage place is a 'goal to which people might repair again and again'. No distinction is made here.[31] On the contrary, to the present day the pilgrimage in particular leads Muslims to gather 'at the places in which the prophets Abraham and Ishmael lived and served God, from whom Muhammad descended in order to preach Islam to all the world'. Pilgrimage in particular conveys the 'great and decisive experiences of the brotherhood of Islam, a brotherhood which does not accept limitations of either race or language nor any differences of nationality; which in the face of God does away with the opposition between rich and poor'.[32]

4. Abraham – the model Muslim

We have seen that Muhammad makes his deepest religious concern clear specifically through Abraham and Ishmael: rejection of any form of idolatry, obedience to the will of the one true God. For Muhammad, 'faith' is not justification of the godless, as it is for Paul, but – as it is for Jewish tradition and particular Christian witnesses (Hebrews) – withstanding trial by God, proven trust in God, faithfulness in following God's will.

The sacrifice: understanding what 'Islam' is

What scene from the Abraham tradition could be more appropriate for illustrating this kind of faith than the scene on 'Mount' Moriah! No wonder, then, that the Qur'anic Abraham theology reaches its climax in the reception of this narrative from Genesis 22. Here, too, a demonstration is made by the model of Abraham of what true faith is and of how those who withstand such a testing by God can understand themselves as those who are blessed by God.

> And [Abraham] said: 'Verily, I shall [leave this land and] go wherever my Sustainer will guide me!' [And he prayed:] 'O my Sustainer! Bestow on me the gift of [a son who shall be] one of the righteous!' – Whereupon We gave him the glad tidings of a boy-child gentle [like himself]. And [one day,] when [the child] had become old enough to share in his [father's] endeavours, the latter said: 'O my dear son! I have seen in a dream that I should sacrifice thee: consider, then, what would be thy view!' He answered: 'O my father! Do as thou art bidden: thou wilt find me, if God so wills, among those who are patient in adversity!' But as soon as the two had surrendered themselves to [what they thought to be] the will of God, and [Abraham] had laid him down on his face, We called out to him: 'O Abraham, thou hast already fulfilled [the purpose of] that dream-vision!' Thus verily do we reward the doers of good: for, behold, all this was indeed a trial, clear in itself. And We ransomed him with a tremendous sacrifice, and left him thus to be remembered among later generations: 'Peace be upon Abraham!' Thus do We reward the doers of good (Surah 37.99–109).

There are two traditions of interpretation of this passage of the Qu'ran in Muslim exegesis – made possible by the fact that the name of the young man is not initially mentioned. Loyal to the biblical tradition, one group of commentators sees here the sacrifice of Isaac, since he is mentioned explicitly at least in the next verse (37.112). Another group deliberately wants to see Ishmael as the son whom Abraham wants to sacrifice. That is understandable, since this version is very much in line with the priority of Ishmael in later Islam. Thus Ishmael had already shown himself to be an exemplary Muslim, someone who submits unconditionally to the will of God, is found pious in testing and is therefore blessed by God.[33]

Moreover Abraham's sacrifice is also the model of the ritual sacrifice which forms the climax of any great pilgrimage to Mecca (cf. Surah 37.107; 2.124), the original, moreover, of the sacrificial feast which is celebrated throughout the Muslim world on the tenth day of the month of pilgrimage. When the pilgrims perform the prescribed rites, i.e. slaughtering sacrificial animals like camels, oxen, sheep or goats (cf. Surah 22.28,30) in the village of Mina about five miles from Medina, then in the truest sense of the word 'Islam', not just individually but also collectively, they are imitating what they understand to have been Abraham's readiness to sacrifice. Furthermore, in performing the sacrifice and reliving Abraham's pilgrimage the Muslim is actualizing both physically and spiritually what it means today to believe like Abraham: to abjure any idolatry and to respond to the one true God.[34]

The primal model of the true believer

This process of laying claim to Abraham becomes even more concentrated in Medina. For now Abraham is not just presented as the one who laid the foundations for and purified the Ka'ba, but also as the one who already fulfilled all the obligations of a pious Muslim. For now four of the basic pillars of Islam as a religion (with the exception of the fast in the month of Ramadan) are attributed to Abraham: not only the pilgrimage and the obedience of faith to the one and only creator God, but also ritual prayer and offerings for the poor. All this is an expression of the 'religion of Abraham':

> O you who have attained to faith! Bow down and prostrate yourselves, and worship your Sustainer [alone], and do good, so that you might attain to a happy state! And strive hard in God's cause with all the striving that is due to Him: it is He who has elected you [to carry His message], and has laid no hardship on you in [anything that pertains to] religion, [and made you follow] the creed of your forefather Abraham. It is he who has named you – in bygone times as well as in this [divine writ] – 'those who have surrendered themselves to God', so that the Apostle might bear witness to the truth before you, and that you might bear witness to it before all mankind. Thus, be constant in prayer, and render the purifying dues, and hold fast unto God. He is your

Lord Supreme: and how excellent is this Lord Supreme and how excellent this giver of Succour! (Surah 22.77ff.)

At the same time we have to see that, for the Qur'an, to be an 'exemplary Muslim' is not a limitation but a possibility for anyone in space and time. Abraham stands specifically for this temporal depth of Islam, and beyond Abraham even the first man, Adam, who in the Qur'an is already regarded as the bearer of revelation and the first prophet (Surah 20.122). This is merely to emphasize that according to the Qur'an, from the begining of creation people have lived by the true faith, and have recognized their true relationship to God. The Qur'an knows nothing of a primal history of human disaster (Adam, Cain) which then has to be changed by a 'salvation history' (Noah, Abraham). From the beginning there is 'Islam', true faith. Certainly this true faith is obscured in the course of history, but it has now been restored by Islam in its original purity and clarity – in the interest of all human beings. So Abraham as the primal image of Islam demonstrates the universality of the truth restored in its purity by the Prophet:

> He [God] said: 'Behold, I shall make thee a leader of men.'
> Abraham asked: 'And [wilt Thou make leaders] of my offspring as well?' [God] answered: 'My covenant does not embrace the evildoers' (Surah 2.124).

This passage is particularly illuminating. For Abraham's invitation to God also to relate his promise (of many descendants) to his physical descendants (i.e. the people of Israel) shows the thrust of the whole statement: in the Qur'an Abraham is not the possession of a single community of believers, but the model in faith for all human beings. Muhammad does not know an understanding of salvation restricted to salvation history and genealogy any more than the New Testament does. That physical descent from Abraham is the basis for any position or even precedence in salvation is completely alien to the Qur'an, since there was already 'right faith' before Abraham.

Thus the orientalist Heribert Busse is right in saying: 'Two things are spoken of in Surah 2.124: the promise and the covenant. In the Bible the covenant relates to the land (cf. Gen.15.18–21). In the Qur'an this has become the expectation of salvation through faith. Here Abraham is seen with the eyes of the Christian tradition. Jesus argues with the Jews who take their stand on their descent and derive their certainty of salvation from it (Matt.3.9). But descent from Abraham is no use for salvation if faith is lacking. Paul says that 'Abraham is the father of believers' (Rom.4.16). The covenant made with Abraham relates to believers, not to physical descendants. In the Qur'an things are put right immediately: Abraham as a matter of course does not relate the covenant to his physical descendants, since he is to be a model "for all humankind". As he is concerned about his physical heirs, he wants them to be included in the covenant, and his wish is granted. But sinners remain excluded. Those whose leader is Abraham are the righteous and believers; physical descendants can also be among them. They form a group of believers and have no higher claim than other believers. Faith justifies, not physical descent from Abraham.'[35]

Against the claims to possession by Jews and Christians

The decisive turning point in Medina as opposed to the Mecca period may thus lie here: Abraham is more than a well-tried, loyal monotheistic champion of the faith; he is the archetypal embodiment of Islam as an independent faith (*hanif, muslim*) which is brought to light again in the present in a new way, free from all distortions and falsifications, by the Muslims. For it must have become increasingly clear to the Prophet in the course of his controversies, above all with the Jews of Medina, that the religious message which he presented is not completely compatible with Judaism and Christianity. If in the Mecca period Muhammad had still believed that he was merely presenting a purer form of Judaism, at all events a form of faith which was compatible with Judaism, now he came to demarcate his religious message increasingly strongly from Judaism (and Christianity) without fully disputing the truth-claims of either. Even in Medina, Muhammad insisted that Jews and Christians have received the Torah and the Gospel from God, which in themselves contain 'right guidance and light' (Surah 5.44, 46), i.e. the Word of God. So Jews and Christians have an obligation to keep the laws of their holy books, as the Muslims have a right to keep theirs:

> Say [to the Jews and the Christians]: 'Do you argue with us about God? But He is our Sustainer as well as your Sustainer – and unto us shall be accounted our deeds, and unto you, your deeds; and it is unto Him alone that we devote ourselves' (2.139).

But there is also no disputing the fact that the Prophet recognized increasingly clearly that Jews and Christians had no credibility beause they were constantly disputing with each other (cf. Surah 23.53). The Prophet had to note with abhorrence how Jews and Christians had each become set in their exclusivism, and that Christians, too, had succumbed to dogmatic disputes among themselves. So they are threatened with judgment:

> Furthermore, the Jews assert, 'The Christians have no valid ground for their beliefs,' while the Christians assert, 'The Jews have no valid ground for their beliefs' – and both quote the divine writ. Even thus, like unto what they say, have [always] spoken those who were devoid of knowledge; but it is God who will judge between them on Resurrection Day with regard to all on which they were wont to differ (2.113).

The consequences which Muhammad drew from these experiences were far-reaching. Judaism and Christianity could no longer be a model for truth. A different religion had to take over this role, a religion which had really already been there from the beginning of humankind, but had then been falsified and obscured by disputes among Jews and Christians.

> Behold, the only [true] religion in the sight of God is [man's] self-surrender unto Him; and those who were vouchsafed revelation aforetime took, out of mutual jealousy, to divergent views [on this point] only after knowledge [thereof] had come to them (3.19).

In other words, in Medina the prophetic cause now increasingly became a new religion in the framework of a new legal order. And Abraham is now claimed increasingly firmly as a key witness for this religion against Judaism and Christianity. The effect of this is that Muhammad now directly counters the Abrahamic exclusivism of Jews and Christians. And his strongest lever here is the recognition that the 'religion of Abraham' was there before Judaism and Christianity and is again taking new form in Islam after Judaism and Christianity. This undermines the claim of Jews and Christians that each alone is the way to salvation:

> And they say, 'Be Jews' – or, 'Christians' – 'and you shall be on the right path'. Say: 'Nay, but [ours is] the creed of Abraham, who

turned away from all that is false, and was not of those who
ascribe divinity to ought but God' (2.135).

We shall see what consequences this has.

5. The paradox: the non-Muslim Abraham is made a Muslim

Does this now mean that Muhammad similarly claimed the patriarch Abraham exclusively for himself and his cause, as Jewish and
Christian theologians had done in the course of the centuries? We
need to differentiate here. In principle, Abraham was never
monopolized as excessively by Muhammad as happened in Judaism
and Christianity. Nowhere in the Qur'an is there any statement that
the Muslims are now exclusively the true children of Abraham.
Nowhere are Jews and Christians in principle denied their claim to
be children of Abraham, as happened to Jews at the hand of
Christians.

Abraham – Muhammad: the line of the true religion

Yet the picture of Muhammad's understanding of Abraham would
not be complete unless we also show the monopolizing, exclusivist
tendencies in the way in which Muhammad deals with Abraham. For
although the Prophet does not claim that Muslims are exclusively
children of Abraham, he leaves no doubt about the following:

1. While Muhammad has no special status in salvation history, he
does *de facto* have a special position as the 'son of Abraham' who is
in fact better than all the previous prophets of history. Already in
Surah 2 Abraham had been made to express the wish to God that
from his descendants, the Arab people, their own prophet might
arise. Moreover in the Qur'an the numerous prophets and apostles
of God before Muhammad are traced back to Isaac. But the last and
definitive prophet, Muhammad, is traced back to Abraham's first
son, Ishmael, the co-founder of the Ka'ba. This indicates that
'Muhammad means as much in the history of revelation as all the
other prophets from the family of Abraham put together'.[36]

2. The Muslims are closest to Abraham. The Prophet acutely saw
through the Jews' and Christians' exclusive claim to Abraham. And
with great skill he attempted to undermine precisely this claim to
possess Abraham, especially as Jews and Christians were still

disputing over it. Muhammad, rejected equally by Jews and Christians, defends himself by unerringly emphasizing the weak point of Judaism and Christianity: there is Torah and Gospel only after Abraham, so that any exclusivity about Abraham must collapse. Once again Surah 3 makes the decisive point here:

> O followers of earlier revelation! Why do you argue about Abraham, seeing that the Torah and the Gospel were not revealed till [long] after him? Will you not, then, use your reason? Lo! You are the ones who would argue about that which is known to you: but why do you argue about something which is unknown to you? Yet God knows [it], whereas you do not know: Abraham was neither a 'Jew' nor a 'Christian' but was one who turned away from all that is false, having surrendered himself unto God (3.65–67).

But with the utmost self-confidence, the Prophet now counters the traditional Abraham exclusiveness of Jews and Christians with the objective priority of Abraham for the Muslims. For Surah 3 continues:

> Behold, the people who have the best claim to Abraham are surely those who follow him – as does the Prophet and all who believe [in him] – and God is near unto the believers (3.68).

Thus Muhammad does not dispute that Jews and Christians are children of Abraham, but he does challenge their exclusive grip on Abraham. At the same time he claims the utmost proximity to Abraham for his religion, and this means, conversely, that while Islam does not regard itself as being exclusively true (Judaism and Christianity also have a share in the truth), it does hold itself to be the better religion, whose appearance in history was necessary because Jews and Christians had obscured their original 'knowledge' of God in disputes. Here Abraham is neither the first nor the only biblical prophet, but he is the exemplary figure who moreover can be given the honoric title 'friend of God' (*al-halil*) in the Qur'an, a title which he is also given by Christians and Jews (James 2.23; Isa.42.8):

> And who could be of better faith than he who surrenders his whole being unto God and is a doer of good withal, and follows the creed of Abraham, who turned away from all that is false – seeing that God exalted Abraham with his love? For, unto God belongs all

that is in the heavens and all that is on earth; and indeed, God encompasses everything.

Islam as the earliest and most authentic religion

Here we reach the decisive point in the self-understanding of Islam as a religion, and this has to do with the question of truth and history. For from the perspective of the history of revelation, Islam is in the same situation towards Judaism and Christianity as Christianity had been towards Judaism. As a faith-community emerging later in history it needs to legitimate itself towards what has gone before. This is all the more necessary, since the Prophet Muhammad did not want to leave the biblical history of revelation but explicitly wanted to give himself a place in the history of revelation so far. That makes it all the more necessary for him to justify his own faith in the face of Judaism and Christianity – especially towards the numerous Christian and Jewish opponents with whom he had to struggle.

Muhammad solves the problem by referring to Abraham. For if Abraham was the model of the true believer (before Moses and Jesus) and also the model Muslim, then Islam as the religion of the Muslims can legitimate itself as both the youngest and the oldest religion. For with Abraham it is clear that there was an 'Islam' before Islam. And Islam's universal claim to truth as a religion is rooted precisely in this notion: Islam, submission to God, is 'the primal form of human worship of God, the primal form with which the founding act of Abraham and Ishmael in Mecca became historical reality and has remained effective since then, though it has often been concealed'.[37]

Therefore Islam understands itself not as a religion founded on a particular historical event (Jesus Christ), or on an ethnic group (the people of Israel), but as a universal and original truth which always has been and always will be. Thus one of the most prominent Muslim philosophers and historians of our time, Seyyed Hossein Nasr, who continues: Islam 'understands itself as a return to this truth which stands over and beyond all historical fortuitousness. Morever the Qur'an refers to Abraham, who lived long before the historical manifestation of Islam, as both a Muslim and as a Hanif; in other words, Islam is part of that original monotheism which has survived among some few people despite the apostasy of the majority of men and women in the later Arab society which preceded the rise of Islam, to a crass form of idolatry and polytheism which Muslims identify with the age of innocence.'[38]

And we have to add that here Islam differs from Judaism and Christianity. For both Jews and Christians maintain that God wanted a special history of revelation for a particular people, enters into a covenant relationship with this people, and communicates his blessing for the other nations through this people. Here Muhammad's Abraham theology also differs from that of the apostle Paul. For Muhammad did not want to argue for the inclusion of the Gentiles (say his Arabs) in God's history of covenant and blessing with his elect people through faith in Abraham and thus confirm the continuity of Israel's history of covenant and blessing from a Muslim perspective. Rather, he understands Abraham a priori as the model of true faith, which anyone can practise, quite independently of belonging to a people or having a place in salvation history. So the Qur'an is not interested in a 'salvation-historical' continuity, but in original authenticity, without thus rejecting Israel's and the Christians' claim to faith. According to the Qur'an, 'Islamic Abrahamism has been bequeathed by its founder to his children without distinction, but with a preference for Jacob. However, such a formulation is far from making it the privilege of the descendants of Ishmael, i.e. the Arabs, and in no way excludes the Jews.'[39]

Moreover, nowhere is the prophetic consciousness of Muhammad which he gained in Medina expressed more vividly than in a saying about him which has become famous, decribing him as the 'seal of the prophets' (Surah 33.40). It is important to see that here too the Prophet is attempting to overturn an exclusive claim previously made by Christians. For if we follow the study by the Berlin historian of religion Carsten Colpe, talk of the 'seal' of prophecy is not at all of Islamic but already of Christian origin.[40] The earliest Latin church father Tertullian (c.160 to c.220 CE) had already described Jesus Christ as 'seal of all the prophets' in his *Adversus Judaeos*. This is what he wrote:

That all prophets ever announced of him that he was to come, and had to suffer. Therefore, since the prophecy was fulfilled through his advent, for that reason he said that 'vision and prophecy were sealed'; inasmuch as he is the seal of all prophets, fulfilling all things which in days bygone they had announced of him. For after the advent of Christ and his passion there is no longer 'vision or prophet' to announce Him as to come.[41]

Thus it is quite conceivable that Muhammad picked up this formula in circles which believed that they had secured Christianity's truth-claim once and for all. Faithful to his practice elsewhere of taking up biblical traditions and going beyond them, here, too, he adopted this formula and saw it as a summary of the prophetic self-understanding which he had newly gained in Medina. He preaches not only the new-old but also the 'last word' about all earlier reflections. This raises a claim to finality over against Judaism and Christianity which now gives his own religion a sharp profile. For the one who has the 'last word' has the fullness of truth and can thus make everything previous a forerunner. But at the same time Islam also claims – here in an analogous way to the pre-existence christology in Christianity ('Before Abraham was, I am', John 8.58) – the first word, in which Muhammad proclaims none other than the original religion of Abraham, who was a Muslim before Muhammad, as were all the other fathers and prophets of Israel.

Thus Islam as a prophetic-historical religon also has a cyclical structure of time which is simply meant to symbolize the perfection of its truth-claim (the circle as a symbol of perfection). Just as in the Gospel of John Jesus Christ was at the same time before and after Abraham, so too is the cause of Islam: it was present before Muhammad (embodied in particular in Abraham) and with Abraham again comes into history, in the course of which it had been falsified and distorted. In other words, through this doctrine of an Islam before Islam, Muslim theology has as it were created its truth-claim – with an analogous structure to that in Judaism and Christianity – and protected it from rival attacks based on salvation history. It is theologically decisive that much as Islam explains its historical breakthrough in terms of the conflicts between Jews and Christians on the one hand and the disputes within Christianity on the other, its origin is not to be grasped purely historically. The origin of Islam is God himself, as Jews claim God as origin for the Torah and Christians for the Christ event.

Processes of idealization: Muslim traditions

After all this it can hardly be surprising that in an analogous way to

Judaism and Christianity the process of universalizing and idealizing the Prophet as the son of Abraham continues in later Islamic tradition – to the point of theories about the inerrancy and sinlessness of Abraham.[42] We can only hint at all this briefly and show that developments have taken place in three directions – here historians like Muhammed Al-Tabari (died 923) and Qur'an commentators like Mahumud Al-Zamakhsari (died 1144) were the greatest authorities.[43]

1. The development of the relationship between Abraham and Ishmael. Both the Bible and the Qur'an are very sparse in their information about the relationship between Abraham and his son Ishmael. Whereas the Bible even reports an expulsion of Ishmael, the Qur'an knows only the relationship between Abraham and Ishmael in connection with the foundation of the Ka'ba in Mecca, at best traditions which connect Ishmael with the valley of Mecca. However, nowhere is there any report of communication between father and son, of a more personal relationship.

We can understand how later Muslim tradition was not content with this – given the significance that Abraham and Ishmael had now attained for Islam as a religion. Moreover the relationship between Abraham and Ishmael is developed in the post-Qur'anic tradition. Thus for example the flight and rescue scene (Hagar with Ishmael) reported in Genesis 19 is moved from the wilderness of the Negeb to the valley of Mecca. It is said to have been there that Hagar sought water for her son. In desperation she ran seven times to and fro between two rocks (al-Marva and as-Safa) looking for help. Finally she received from an angel the comforting message which saved her life and that of her son. For a spring sprang up at her feet, called the spring Semsen. And at this spring Abraham finally founded a sanctuary at God's bidding, the Ka'ba, when he once visited Hagar and his son Ishmael. Thus the link between Abraham and the Ka'ba is explained more smoothly than in the Qur'an. And for centuries this running of Hagar between the rocks al-Marva and as-Safa has been part of the Muslim pilgrimage ritual round the Ka'ba in Mecca.

2. All Arabs are children of Abraham. However, all these Arabian traditions about Abraham and Ishmael leave one question unresolved: where do the Arabs as a people originally come from? From the line of Abraham-Ishmael? This was well known at least from Jewish sources, and the Qur'an itself also contains references, though as we saw these are sparse (Surah 14.37). So here, too,

Muslim theologians in the subsequent period tried to close the still-remaining gaps in the explanation. They began to identify well-known founder figures of Arab tribes with figures which were known from the biblical genealogies and thus to provide a link between the 'patriarchs' and the Arabian peninsula. Here Montgomery Watt has summed up the evidence: 'According to the biblical tradition (Gen.25.12–18), certain northern Arabian tribes were descended from Ishmael, and the fact that while the Qur'an mentions descent from Abraham it does not place particular emphasis on it, perhaps indicates that the Arabs already had a vague notion of the biblical tradition. In the 150 years after Muhammad's death Muslim scholars worked out whole genealogies of the Arab tribes and linked them with the genealogies of the Bible. Adnan, the alleged progenitor of the so-called North Arabian tribes, was said to be a descendant of Abraham through Ishmael, whereas Qahatan, the progenitor of the so-called southern tribes, was identified with Yoqtan or Yaqtan, according to Genesis 10 a descendant of Shem of the fourth generation.'[44]

3. Muhammad had a physical resemblance to the figure of Abraham. The night ride and ascension of the Prophet shortly before the move to Medina, which became famous, are already handed down in Ibn Ishaq. The basic features of these stories can be quickly sketched out. While Muhammad was sleeping at the Ka'ba in Mecca the angel Gabriel awoke him by night, made him get on the miraculous horse Buraq and ride him to Jerusalem. There the prophet met 'God's friend Abraham' and Moses and Jesus among other prophets and prayed with them. Later a ladder was sent down from heaven and the Prophet could go through the various heavens. Already in the 'second heaven' he met those who had believed in the one and only God in former times: Jesus and John the Baptist. In the 'sixth heaven' he even met Moses, who is described as a 'man of dark colour, great build and a crooked nose'. Then he also had an encounter with Abraham, and made the surprising discovery that he evidently resembled Abraham not only spiritually but also physically:

And he (the angel Gabriel) brought me into the seventh heaven; there I saw a man of mature age sitting on a chair at the gate of paradise through which seventy thousand angels entered each day, who will only return on the Day of Resurrection. I never saw a man who more resembled me. And Gabriel said: this is your ancestor Abraham.[45]

With this we can conclude our survey of the picture of Abraham in the Qur'an and conclude that Islam developed from an originally prophetic message to a separate religion – just like Christianity. Moreover the development of Abraham theology in Islam displays a constant process of perfecting its own truth-claim, which finally does not fall short in any way of those of Judaism and Christianity. What was originally to have been a rediscovery and restoration of the 'religion of Abraham' involving Jews and Christians to the same degree developed into a new religion with a universal orientation which in fact feels itself superior to Judaism and Christianity, and in which Jews and Christians are now demoted to the role of those who are 'tolerated' and whose 'protection' is commanded (Arabic *dhimmi*). As people of the book they are no 'unbelievers', and enjoy legal protection in Muslim society. But at the same time, compared with Muslims they are of 'another faith', are compelled to pay taxes, and are in no way on the same legal footing as Muslims.[46]

6. Abraham – the possession of any religion

Thus we come upon a remarkable fact in the history of religion, that in Islam, too, the pattern of development over Abraham has the same structure. The tendency already recognizable in Judaism and Christianity for each religion to claim Abraham as its possession is continued in the Qur'an. So here too we face a paradoxical constellation. Let us remind ourselves of the structure once again.

Abraham and the halakhah: Judaism

In Judaism, over and above the canonical text of scripture (Genesis), after the exile above all in the non-canonical literature (Jubilees, Apocalypse of Abraham) and in the rabbinic tradition (Talmud, Midrashim) there is an increasingly strong tendency to make Abraham exclusively Jewish. In concrete this means that Abraham comes to be an exclusive follower of the halakhah, the exemplary Jew of the Torah. Paradoxically enough Abraham the non-Jew, living without the Torah, becomes an exclusively Jewish figure, a kind of primal rabbi and arch-priest and thus the archetype of 'halakhic man'. Indeed, with the conviction that there was already Torah and halakhah before Moses (here Abraham is the key witness), orthodox rabbinic theology as it were dehistoricized the Jewish truth-claim, perfected it and thus immunized it against any criticism from outside.

Abraham and the church: Christianity

In Christianity – beginning in the New Testament (John) but essentially after the canon – Abraham became more and more Christian. In other words, Abraham was claimed exclusively for the church as an exemplary Christian before Christ. Paradoxically enough, the non-Jew and non-Christian Abraham becomes an exclusively Christian figure with whose help the Jews are now deprived of their status as being the people of the covenant and of God. Indeed, with the conviction that there was Christian faith before Christ (here Abraham is the key witness), moreover that Jesus Christ even existed before Abraham, orthodox Christian theology similarly dehistoricized the Christian claim to truth, perfected it and thus immunized it against any criticism from outside.

Abraham becomes a Muslim: Islam

Finally, in Islam, after the initial emphasis on the 'religion of Abraham' common to Jews, Christians and Muslims, in the second phase of Muhammad's prophecy Abraham was portrayed with increasing emphasis as a model Muslim – segregated from Jews and Christians. Paradoxically, here too Abraham the non-Jew, then the Jewish and Christian hero of faith, becomes an exclusively Muslim figure with whose help Muslims now dispute that Jews and Christians have the true faith. Indeed, convinced that there was already 'Islam' before Muhammad (here Abraham is the key witness), Islamic theology dehistoricized the Muslim truth-claim, perfected it, and thus immunized it against any criticism from outside. And for centuries the three monotheistic religions have persisted in this situation of non-relationship, exclusivity, claims to absoluteness. All appeal to Abraham, and all claim Abraham as their own possession.

What then? Against this horizon does it still make sense to seek an Abraham dialogue between Jews, Christians and Muslims? Isn't it utterly naive in the face of this evidence still to want to talk seriously of an 'Abrahamic ecumene'? Furthermore, at least for Christians, isn't it theologically inadmissible to talk of 'Abrahamic religions' or even of an 'Abrahamic ecumene'? Doesn't this completely level out the special status of the religions? After all, with Jews, Christians affirm a special 'salvation-historical' status for the people of Israel. And for Christians, too, despite their repudiation of Jesus as Messiah, the people of Israel remains 'loved by God for the fathers' sake'. And for Jews and Christians, Abraham in particular stands for this special history of revelation through which Judaism and Christianity are linked together in a special way.

Islam differs. As the Catholic theologian and Islamic specialist Hans Zirker rightly points out, it has no salvation-historical perspective. 'For it Abraham stands in the vast mass of prophets of all peoples, and thus in the Muslim estimation he occupies a far more comprehensive typological position than in Christian theology, where he represents only the three special religions of revelation (in so far as here Islam is taken into account alongside Judaism).'[47]

So isn't Zirker right in warning against all too easy 'theological misinterpretations' in talking of the three 'Abrahamic religions', as though 'Muslims, too, could recognize a special line of origin and affinity from salvation history here'?[48] He soberly concludes: 'Thus Abraham is not only a link figure between between biblical and Muslim faith but also, with an eye to the future of humankind, one who separates.'[49] Indeed, doesn't Abraham in particular show that the three religions have moved infinitely far from one another and have no intention of coming together again? I shall attempt to give an answer to all these difficult questions in the second and third parts of this book.

B. Perspectives for an Abrahamic Ecumene

I. Presuppositions for an Ecumenical Awareness

Can this paradox of the commandeering of Abraham be resolved? Anyone who attempts this and wants to talk without any 'theological misinterpretation' of an Abrahamic 'ecumene', anyone who despite everything wants to present a critical and creative ecumenical theology of peace, must begin by clarifying in principle the meaning of ecumene and ecumenical consciousness. This consciousness can be defined only by describing the changed horizon of today's world. The very word 'ecumene' demands this, since etymologically it means 'the whole inhabited earth'. Therefore ecumenical awareness is a matter of thinking in a global network with other cultures and religions, in mutual responsibility within a world community. Those who think ecumenically thus think in universal connections, in terms of human history, human responsibility. Those who think ecumenically attach importance not only to their region, nation or religion, but to the fate of all religions, to the future of humankind as a whole.

1. The new horizons of the world

But in order to be able to assess the change, first of all we need to reflect briefly on the disastrous history of mutual aggression and rejection, since shared remembering often creates an awareness of the urgency of ecumenical understanding today. Without a will for the ecumene there is no ecumene; without mourning a failed ecumene there will be no will for a future ecumene.

The necessary recollection of a disastrous history

For centuries after the death of the Prophet Muhammad, the three religions, Judaism, Christianity and Islam – apart from isolated fruitful encounters – have existed in self-isolation, partly in aggressive confrontation with one another. Their shared history embraces the whole spectrum, from cultural fertilization and religious understanding to war and catastrophe. Judaism, as numerically the smallest of the religions, was mostly the victim here. Whereas in lands under Muslim rule (above all in Spain up to 1492, and then in the Ottoman empire) on the whole Jews could live under legal protection as 'people of the book' (think of the splendid Jewish-Muslim symbiosis in Spanish Cordoba in the tenth and eleventh centuries), Jews in Christian central Europe in the high and late Middle Ages were constantly swamped with waves of cruel oppression and persecution. Here pogroms, forced baptisms and burnings of the Talmud were only the tip of a policy of legal discrimination against a people which in the eyes of numerous Christian theologians even in the Middle Ages (following Augustine) had 'really' forfeited its right to exist.

The relationship between Christianity and Islam was different yet again. Here in the course of the centuries two political and military power blocks struggled for influence and rule. And Christian theologians in particular did all they could to disqualify Islam in spiritual terms also: either as a mere Christian heresy (John of Damascus, c.675–753) or as an object of rejection with a Christian foundation: thus Peter the Venerable (1094–1156), Abbot of Cluny, who in 1143 commissioned the first Latin translation of the Torah and with further polemic and apologetic works influenced the later missionary strategies of the church. The warlike clashes between the Christian and Islamic powers thus took on a fanatical aspect.

Whereas Christian rulers sought confrontations with Muslims in Palestine in the course of seven Crusades (First Crusade 1096–1099 – Seventh Crusade 1270), conversely Muslim leaders time and again sought the opportunity to bring the rest of Europe under their control through Spain. And after the Arab-Islamic thrust was stopped in the West at the fatal battle of Poitiers in 732, the campaigns of conquest now continued in the East, led by the Turkish rulers of the Ottoman empire. For a long time large areas of the former Christian Byzantine empire in the Balkans lay conquered, and then in 1453, after a long siege, Constantinople, that city which had a symbolic significance for the whole of Christendom, finally fell in 1453.

Since then there has been widespread fear of an aggresive Islam in Europe. It was intensified when barely a century after the conquest of Constantinople the Muslim Turks were even at the gates of the imperial city of Vienna: in 1529, during the lifetime of Martin Luther, who condemned Islam as polemically as he later condemned Judaism. The Turks were beaten, but they conquered Budapest in 1541, and Belgrade before that. And barely 150 years later they were besieging Vienna for a second time (in 1683), suffering final defeat only after decades of campaigns. Since these confrontations in Europe there has been not only 'an incredible contempt for Islamic faith' (L.Gardet) and a 'rabid fury against the Qur'an which has blinded people' (G.C.Anawati),[1] but also a political anxiety about Islam which has time and again been utilized by particular Christian groups to serve their own political interests. Christian fundamentalists are fond of conjuring up a battle between the dark sons of Ishmael and the elect sons of Israel, which is supposed to be a matter of historical destiny, a universal 'battle over inheritance' under the crazy alternative of 'world conflagration or world peace'.[2]

At all events, these military and political confrontations had devastating effects on the image of Islam in the West.[3] Countless people in Europe in particular believed and still believe that Islam is a religion of violence, which preaches nothing but 'fire and sword' and follows a prophet who was obsessed with power and greedy for conquests, who constantly provoked or legitimated holy wars. Here insufficient note has been taken of isolated voices supporting an ecumenical theology of peace like that of the great cardinal Nicolas of Cusa (1401–1464), voices which already at a time of cruel atrocities (the conquest of Constantinople) had argued for a peace in faith (*De pace fidei*) and developed the vision of the peoples of the earth being capable of reconciliation through religion without having to be unfaithful to their own confessions.[4] But these voices went unheard. Here, given the self-isolation of mediaeval rabbinic Judaism, the disinheritance theology of countless Christian theologians and the militancy of the Muslim thrust for conquest, there was no thought of an 'Abrahamic' ecumene, a reconciling reflection on the common father of faith which would bring peace.

But after centuries of military, political and religious expansion the dynamic of the Ottoman empire gradually became exhausted. And at the latest from the 'Christian' reconquest of Belgrade by the Habsburgs in 1717 on, even the 'High Gate' in Istanbul had an urgent interest in securing the possessions of its giant empire and consolidating it within. But at the same time, in the course of European modernity during the eighteenth and nineteenth centuries, Christian European powers (above all France, Great Britain and Germany) succeeded in taking leading positions in almost all the decisive fields: above all in the spheres of science, technology, economics and industry. The exploitation of colonies, particularly in Africa and Asia, was decisive here. Indeed the influence of Christian powers now assumed a universal, global dimension once Great Britain above all had succeeded step by step during the nineteenth century in building up an 'empire' which finally reached from South Africa through India and Sri Lanka to Australia and Canada. And the countries of South America had also long been under Christian domination.

The end of Eurocentric modernity

No wonder that the Christian churches at the end of the nineteenth century hoped that they would become the beneficiaries of the process of modernity. Nor was this hope an unrealistic one. For had not Christianity in particular 'won' a unique position in the world at this time, in the course of the policy of colonialism, imperialism and expansionism which began from Europe? Indeed, a combination of Western culture and Christian religion seemed to have taken hold of the old civilizations. Politically and economically India was under English control and seemed to be spiritually exhausted. The Ottoman empire had become politically powerless, and Islam seemed incapable of reform. China was economically and spiritually defeated, the plaything of European powers. Japn was isolated, Africa largely colonized. In short, with the globalization of technology, economics and industry Christianity seemed to have the best prospects of establishing itself all over the world, as the only religion with power and dynamism.[5]

However, after two World Wars the world looked different, and even the role of Judaism and Islam began to change. Specifically, after centuries of persecution and discrimination, at the end of the nineteenth century, under the leadership of the Austrian journalist Theodor Herzl, Jews had begun in an unprecedented way actually to return to the 'promised land', the land promised to Abraham in primeval times. This 'Zionist' plan was implemented. And as the crown of numerous immigration movements to Palestine, in 1948, under the charismatic politician David Ben Gurion, an independent state was founded in Israel. Thus almost nineteen centuries after the destruction of the Second Temple (in 70 CE by the Romans) Judaism again had a political centre. And with this centre Judaism also became stronger as a religion, especially as significant thinkers like Martin Buber, Franz Rosenzweig, Abraham Heschel and Joseph Soloveichik were able to translate the old message of Yahweh and his people for a modern age.

And what about Islam? At the latest after the oil crisis at the beginning of the 1970s, the world public had become aware of the economic power of the Arab states stamped by Islam. And at the latest with the end of the Shah's regime in Iran in 1979 and his replacement with the most significant leader of Shi'ite Islam, Ayatollah Khomeini, anyone could see that Islam as a religion was still be in a position to write political history on a world scale. Moreover the increase in political and economic power in Muslim countries also meant a reinforcement of Islam as a religion (especially in Africa). Today Islam numbers around a billion adherents, from Indonesia (157 million) through Pakistan (118 million) and Turkey (57 million) to Algeria and Morocco with 25 million each.

During the course of the nineteenth and twentieth centuries Islam, too, has produced significant reformers who have been capable of translating the message of the Qur'an into a new time and thus proving the capacity of Islam for spiritual change: in the India of the nineteenth century already Sayyed Ahmed Khan and, following him, the spiritual father of Pakistan, the poet-philosopher Muhammad Iqbal. Mention should also be made above all of Jamaladdin al-Afghani, the charismatic father of a modern Islam orientated on reform in the Middle East.[6] And the increased importance of Islam as a religion can also be seen from the fact that at the end of our century, particularly in the Muslim lands most open to the West like Turkey, Egypt and Algeria, fundamentalist trends are attracting more and more people in the course of a broad wave of re-Islamicization.

What follows from this development? The expectations of Christianity that during the twentieth century it would become the dominant universal world religion in the course of Eurocentric modernity have failed all along the line. Not only has the world not been Christianized; on the contrary, at the end of the twentieth century, generally speaking, the other religions of humankind are stronger than they were at its beginning. The world-view of Eurocentric Christian modernity has been replaced. As Hans Küng has remarked, we have entered a postmodern age.[7]

For relations between the religions in the paradigm of postmodernity (a makeshift heuristic term primarily meant to describe the difference in experience from modernity), this means:
– Attempts to do away with a religion by aggressive mission strategies have failed; so too have all attempts at the arrogant and triumphalist rule of one religion over all other religions;
– Subtle attempts to take up other religions into one world religion or models for syncretistic fusions with the aim of the one universal religon made up of parts of other religions have also failed.

And instead? There has been a growing awareness that the religions must come together in a peaceful co-existence and pro-existence, in mutual respect, in a readiness for dialogue and co-operation. Ecumenical awareness can therefore be defined like this: comprehensive knowledge of one another, respect for one another, responsibility for one another and co-operation with one another. The basic theological presupposition for this is that in the religions men and women regard one another as members of the one family of humanity, each of which has a special way to God and a special task from God. This is true in a special way of the monotheistic religions, Judaism, Christianity and Islam, all three of which refer to the faith of Abraham and the God of Abraham. So even a Jew or a Muslim may at least accept as an ideal what the Second Vatican Council (which is binding on Catholic Christians) has said about the relationship of the religions to one another:

In this age of ours, when men are drawing more closely together and the bonds of friendship between different peoples are being strengthened, the Church examines with greater care the relation which she has to non-Christian religions. Ever aware of her duty to foster unity and charity among individuals, and even among nations, she reflects at the outset on what men have in common and what tends to promote fellowship among them.

All men form but one community. This is so because all stem from the one stock which God created to people the entire earth; and also because all share a common destiny, namely God. His providence, evident goodness, and saving designs extend to all men against the day when the elect are gathered together in the holy city which is illumined by the glory of God, and in whose splendour all peoples will walk (*Nostra Aetate*, no.1).

The decisive key words for defining ecumenical awareness are present here:
– the perception of an ever closer and interwoven world of nations;
– the need to further unity and love among the nations and thus make them into a community;
– the awareness that this community has a religious basis: God himself as the ground and goal of the whole human race.

2. Self-criticism of the religions as a way to peace

However, the fact that the community of nations is endangered by a lack of world peace is an everyday experience. And every day there is the terrifying, shameful insight that religious forces also lie behind the lack of peace in the world.

The declaration of the World's Parliament of Religions

Is there a way of conversion here? There is such a way only through the capacity to exercise self-criticism, i.e. to reflect self-critically on the share of one's own religion in the blame. More than formerly, there seems to be some readiness for this today. Here the 'Declaration on a Global Ethic' passed by the Parliament of the World's Religions in Chicago on 4 September 1993 laid down some criteria.[8] For this declaration, signed by representatives of all the great religions (including Christians, Jews and Muslims) aims at bringing out a basic consensus at least in the ethical sphere, regardless of all unbridgeable doctrinal differences: a consensus on binding values, irrevocable standards and personal attitudes. The starting point of the Chicago Declaration is that in all the great religions – despite the differences in content – there are the same or similar basic ethical demands and irrevocable instructions which should be brought out more strongly than before. There is, for example, the basic demand 'Every human being must be treated humanely', which is made concrete in the famous 'Golden Rule'. Put positively, this runs: 'What you wish done to yourself, do to others.' This 'Golden Rule' can be found in Confucius and in Rabbi Hillel and Jesus of Nazareth, in Islam and in Jainism, and in Buddhism and Hinduism. On this

basis all religious traditions could contribute four irrevocable directives from their own sources of faith:
– Commitment to a culture of non-violence and respect for life;
– Commitment to a culture of solidarity and a just economic order;
– Commitment to a culture of tolerance and a life of truthfulness;
– Commitment to a culture of equal rights and partnership between men and women.

Against religious fanaticism

We cannot go into detail here. But for our purpose it is important to note that the Declaration also contains above all criticism of all religions. For in all religions there is a significant proportion of fanatics, who instead of ecumenical understanding practise militant demarcation, instead of collaboration and understanding practise an arrogance about religious truth and aggressive confrontation. Here the Declaration gives an explicit warning:

> Time and again we see leaders and members of religions incite aggression, fanaticism, hate, and xenophobia – even inspire and legitimate violent and bloody conflicts. Religion often is misused for purely power-political goals, including war. We are filled with disgust.[9]

So particularly for the representatives of the religions, this means an obligation to a culture of tolerance and a life in truthfulness. Moreover the 'representatives of the religions' are unambiguously told:

> When they stir up prejudice, hatred, and enmity towards those of different belief, or even incite or legitimate religious wars, they deserve the condemnation of humankind and the loss of their adherents.[10]

So ecumenical awareness presupposes the will to truthfulness, the readiness to counter caricatures of others in one's own tradition, to fight ignorance of the other and strengthen those forces which are convinced that:

> Every human being without distinction of age, sex, race, skin colour, physical or mental ability, language, religion, political view, or national or social origin possesses an inalienable and

untouchable dignity . . . Every people, every race, every religion must show tolerance and respect – indeed high appreciation – for every other. Minorities need protection and support, whether they be racial, ethnic or religious.[11]

However, the best way of demolishing intolerance and a lack of respects for others is to resist any temptation to exclusivism. For as long as any religion lays exclusive claim to the whole truth and to all the means of salvation at the expense of all other religions and thus devalues them, the gate is wide open to a latent or open arrogance about the truth and salvation. This is then used to justify feelings of superiority, militant attempts at conversion or the contemptuous exclusion of others. What is needed is a theology which makes it possible for people in the religions to maintain their own claim to truth without excluding or even vilifying other truth-claims. Work is being done today in all the great religious traditions on such a theology of the religions. In this book I can do no more than refer to it. Here we are concentrating on the relationship between Judaism, Christianity and Islam. Only a few basic theological elements of such a theology of religions can be and need be mentioned in what follows, as they are the indispensable presupposition of any meaningful talk of an 'Abrahamic ecumene'. And in no tradition have such basic elements ever been totally suppressed. We can go on to relate a counter-history.

3. Judaism: salvation for others in the sign of Noah

Alongside Abraham there has always been a second great biblical figure in Judaism who makes it possible for orthodox Jews, too, to enter into relations with other religions. For in contrast to Christianity and like Islam, even Orthodox Judaism has never developed the notion that outside Israel there is no salvation. In this way Judaism has a priori avoided any missionary aggressiveness towards other religions. Here Noah plays an even more marked role than Abraham. We might recall that even before Abraham, God made a first covenant with Noah, the progenitor of 'all the nations of the earth' (Gen.9.19): God committed himself to preserving all creation. At the same time God imposed specific commands and prohibitions on Noah and his sons (Gen.9.4–6).

Why the commandments to Noah are important

In rabbinic discussions these commandments, the so-called Noachide commandments, are understood as God's command for the whole of humankind, since the whole of the human race is descended from Noah and his sons.[12] There are seven rules, six of which are prohibitions (idolatry, murder, fornication, blasphemy, theft and brutality against animals) and one a commandment (the duty to establish courts). We can read the decisive rabbinic debate on this in the tractate Sanhedrin of the Babylonian Talmud:

> Our Rabbis taught: seven precepts were the sons of Noah commanded: social laws; to refrain from blasphemy; idolatry; adultery; bloodshed; robbery; and eating flesh cut from a living animal. R.Hanania b.Gamaliel said: also not to partake of the blood drawn from a living animal. R.Hidka added emasculation. R.Simeon added sorcery. R.Jose said: The heathens were prohibited everything that is mentioned in the section on sorcery (bSanhedrin 56a/56b).

Thus according to the rabbinic view it is clear that the whole of humankind is obligated to avoid polytheism and blasphemy, murder and theft, fornication and brutality to animals and to set up courts to settle disputes. The decisive theological point here is that if the peoples of the world observe these commandments, then according to rabbinic doctrine, as the righteous from the non-Jewish people they can receive a 'share in the world to come'. So in the orthodox Jewish view no one need become a Jew to attain salvation. Israel alone has a duty to observe all 613 commandments and prohibitions of the Torah. For the 'Gentiles', these seven are enough. Here too we are indebted to the great mediaeval Jewish scholar Moses Maimonides for connecting the question about the portion of the righteous among the non-Jewish people in the world to come with the Noachide commandments.[13]

Thus the foundation has been laid for the capacity of Judaism to engage in inter-religious dialogue. Christians and Muslims, indeed all peoples, can also be called 'sons of Noah' if they observe the commandments of Noah. Thus the existence of the Noachide commandments serves towards universal understanding and inter-religious tolerance. And the notion of a common ethic supported by all religions that is expressed in the Declaration of the Parliament of the World's Religions in Chicago cited here, which was also subscribed to by Jewish theologians, has both its biblical foundation and its foundation within Judaism at this point. For Jewish theologians, today the covenant theology connected with Noah, along with the covenant theology connected with Abraham, represents a welcome legitimation of Jewish universalism and inter-religious understanding in a world which is characterized by a plurality of religions.[14]

What being a Jew means today

However, one of the most impressive testimonies to this dimension of Jewish existence is to be found not in a Jewish theologian but in the *New Union Prayer Book* of American Reform Judaism, published by the Central Conference of American Rabbis. This contains an impressive chapter on 'Israel's mission in the world'. Meditative texts set out what the election of Israel can mean today – in the light of a changed world situation:[15]

> The sense of being chosen impressed itself deeply on the soul of our people. And yet they did not consider themselves superior to other nations, for they knew that all humans are God's children. It was not their lineage but the possession of Torah that made them a choice people. For centuries they stood alone in upholding divine truth and the way of Torah in a world steeped in ignorance, superstition, and cruelty. Yet they always believed that others, too, might be chosen, if only they would choose the way of God.
>
> Only one privilege did they claim, that of serving God and His truth. And with that privilege came an exacting responsibility: 'You, of all the families of the earth, have known Me best; therefore I will hold you all the more accountable for your iniquities.'
>
> Israel gave birth in time to other religions that have brought many to God, but our responsibility continues, for our mission remains unfulfilled. It will continue until the earth is full of the knowledge of the Lord as the sea-bed is covered by water.

This is followed by a reflection on what it means to be a Jew today, including a reflection on the special task of being a Jew in the world:

I am a Jew because the faith of Israel demands of me no abdication of the mind.

I am a Jew because in every place where suffering weeps, the Jew weeps.

I am a Jew because at every time when despair cries out, the Jew hopes.

I am a Jew because the word of Israel is the oldest and the newest.

I am a Jew because the promise of Israel is the universal promise.

I am a Jew because, for Israel, the world is not completed; we are completing it.

I am a Jew because, for Israel, humanity is not created; we are creating it.

I am a Jew because Israel places humanity and its unity above the nations and above Israel itself.

I am a Jew because, above humanity, image of the divine Unity, Israel places the unity which is divine.

And what does the development look like in Christianity? How has the capacity for inter-religious relations developed here?

4. Christianity: the possibility of salvation for non-Christians

From the time of Augustine, who even propagated the forced conversion of unbelievers ('*Coge intrare*')[16] and the Council of Florence (1442), inspired by Augustine, Catholic Christianity has been committed to the harsh dogmatic statement: 'No one, neither Gentile nor Jew, neither unbeliever nor one separated from the church, can partake of eternal salvation, but will rather suffer eternal fire, unless he joins the Catholic Church before his death.' Nor did the Reformation bring any progress in matters of religious freedom: the *Extra ecclesiam nulla salus* became an *Extra Christum nulla salus*. Here the main concern of the Reformation was the freedom of specific Christians or churches, and not a general freedom of religion, which moreover is only a typical product of modernity. It goes without saying that against this background no positive religious evaluation of Judaism and Islam could arise. For centuries both religions were regarded as the products of error, unbelief and self-deception. For a long time Islam in particular was denounced as a 'diabolical religion' which clad itself 'according to the usual manner of Satan in a few truths, so as to deceive people all the better'.[17]

Co-operation instead of polemic: the Protestant churches

The late consequences of such a dogmatism within Christianity can be traced right down to our time. In 1984 the Conference of Confessing Communities in the Protestant Churches of Germany and the Working Party for Protestant Missions published a statement entitled 'Christian Confession and Biblical Command in the Face of Islam'. Right at the beginning of this paper the concept of an ' "Abrahamic ecumene" of the three monotheistic world religions' allegedly in the making is greeted sceptically. A liberalism within the churches is attacked which is said to have led to an 'excessive emphasis on the humanist and social' and to a crippling of 'biblical theological doctrine'. Christians are said to be 'either benevolently credulous and indifferent or even helpless and anxious in the face of Islam'. In this 'emergency' a clear word must be spoken. And this follows the old pattern:

Demonization: 'We recognize in Islam an anti-Christian seduction of the end time (I John 2.18,22) which challenges both the old covenant people of the Jews and the church of Jesus Christ.'

Deception: 'It is dangerous because it deceptively imitates the biblical revelation. So we call upon all Christians to study Islam watchfully, to confront its followers clearly with the gospel and to meet its errors in a readiness to offer spiritual defence (Ephesians 6.10–17).'

Distortion: 'We attack the view that Christians and Muslims believe in "the same God". Certainly the Creator has made himself known to all people in his works (Rom.1.19f.). But we cannot overlook the fact that Islamic faith reflects important features of God's self-revelation. Muslims claim to worship the one, true, God. But a careful examination in the light of the whole of the biblical witness proves that the Islamic notion of God as the one Creator, Judge and All-Merciful – despite the similarity of the terms – is a human caricature of the true God.'[18]

But other voices have been raised in Protestantism, calling for a new relationship both between Christians and Jews and between Christians and Muslims. Their approach is represented by the Berlin New Testament scholar Peter von der Osten-Sacken, whose description of the relationship between Israel and the church I cited in the chapter on 'Abraham and Christianity': 'Israel's origin is founded on the word of promise to Abraham. The present time of the people of God is characterized by the unbroken validity of his election (Rom.9.1–5; 11.29). Its future is defined by the unshakable certainty that 'all Israel will be saved' (Rom.11.26). All this is true, although and even if the majority of the Jewish people rejects the gospel as a means of eschatological salvation. This is the view expressed in Rom.9–11 and thus the perspective of a testimony which is part of the now canonical gospel of the early period. The right of Israel, the people of God, to exist and its abiding gifts emerge so clearly from this testimony that current theological talk of the "end of Israel" and suchlike is pure heresy by the standard of Paul's gospel, however many Lutheran, Protestnt, Catholic, Orthodox or other Christian advocates of this view there may be.'[19]

The pioneering 1979 study by the Council of the Evangelical Church in Germany which appeared under the title 'Christians and Jews' was composed in the same spirit. So too have been countless statements since then by synods and bodies in German and international Protestantism.[20] Common to them all has been a concern to stop describing the relationship between Israel and the church in categories like inheriting, replacing or surpassing. On the contrary, the counterpoint to all these statements is a farewell to a fatal theology of disinheritance. However, lamentably they only became possible after the dreadful experience of the National Socialist policy of terror and the annihilation of Jews which opened the eyes of Christians to the anti-Jewish shadow side that their christology and ecclesiology often displays.

Instead of this, within Protestantism we have a historically unparalleled re-reception of the apostle Paul's Israel theology which already in his day – as we saw – called on Gentile Chrisitans not to show any superiority towards Jews and constantly to remind themselves: 'It is not you who bear the roots, but the roots bear you.' So it became possible to reflect theologically on the way in which Israel and the church are independent of each other, yet are referred to one another before God.[21]

The same can be said of the relationship between the church and Islam. In contrast to Protestant churches which demonize Islam as the 'anti-Christian power of seduction in the end time' and write off the faith of Muslims as a 'deceptive imitation of the biblical revelation' and a 'caricature of the true God', a work-book published in 1990 by the United Evangelical Lutheran Church of Germany contained a 'Christian evaluation' of Islam. For all the 'obligation to witness' it is also necessary to 'listen to one another'. Granted, this statement does not take a specific stand on the question of salvation for Muslims and thus reflects a theological confusion which has prevailed for years even at the highest level of the Protestant church, in the World Council of Churches.[22] All that the WCC has been able to offer is a vague, ambiguous formula: 'Therefore for Christians, salvation is bound up with the experience of the love of God which took form in Jesus Christ. Outside this love they can recognize no salvation. However, faith has always recognized that human beings cannot define the limits of the love of God.'[23] But at the same time the Evangelical Lutheran Church leaves no doubt that Jews and Christians stand in 'the same tradition of faith' and have much in common.

> An evaluation from the Christian side first of all has to begin from the mutual proximity of the two religions. That cannot be taken for granted, given the centuries of controversy in which there was emphasis only on dividing factors. But the Islamic confession of the one God is inconceivable without the biblical commandment 'I am the Lord your God, you shall have no other gods but me' (Exod.20.2f.). This proximity is an expression of the fact that Christianity and Islam – together with Judaism – stand in the same tradition of faith. So Christians and Muslims have much in common in central questions of faith and life: gratitude for creation and responsibility for preserving it, confident belief in God, expectation of judgment on human actions, criticism of the idolatrizing of this-worldly aims and goods, commitment to righteousness and peace, solidarity with the weaker.[24]

This reflection on the same tradition of faith is followed by a call for more appropriate behaviour, which consists in listening to one another and respecting one another. Hospitality, neighbourliness, friendliness and readiness for peace can be specific testimonies of faith on both sides:

> Listening to one another and respecting one another makes possible an open encounter between Christians and Muslims which includes the testimony of faith . . . Christians and Muslims can give a concrete and vivid testimony to their faith if they live together as good neighbours. From of old, in both the Islamic ethic

and in many Christian testimonies, hospitality and neighbourliness have had a high status. They should also govern the form of encounter and relationship between Christian and Muslim communities in the same place, so that Muslims and Christians can live together in a friendly and peaceful way.[25]

High respect for Jews and Muslims: the Catholic Church

An even greater change can be recognized in the sphere of the Catholic Church. For the Second Vatican Council represents an epoch-making breakthrough both in the theological relationship of the church to non-Christian religions and in the question of the salvation of non-Christians.[26] Nothing comparable has come about in the other Christian churches at a world level, and this has also been noted from the Muslim side: 'Nothing has yet come from an authoritative Protestant body such as the World Council of Churches, the National Council of Churches around the world, from the Greek and Russian Orthodoxy, or any Sanhedrin or Rabbinic court.'[27] What did Vatican II actually say?

In its key dogmatic document, the Constitution on the Faith (*Lumen Gentium*), the council no longer defines the relationship between the church and non-Christians confrontationally, but relationally, using a model of concentric circles. For all the problematic aspects of this model, this is decisive theological progress. Specifically, it means that the Christian promise of salvation first of all applies to those who want to live as disciples of Christ in the community of the church. And if Christ forms the centre of the circle, the first rings are logically the Christian churches. Around them are the other religions, depending on the degree of their proximity to Christ at the centre: first Judaism, then Islam, and then the non-Abrahamic religions. This is what Chapter 16 of the constitution says on the relationship between Jews and Muslims:

Finally, those who have not yet received the Gospel are related to the People of God in various ways. There is, first, that people to which the covenants and promises were made, and from which Christ was born according to the flesh (cf. Rom.9.4–5): in view of the divine choice, they are a people most dear for the sake of their fathers, for the gifts of God are without repentance (cf. Rom.11.28–29). But the plan of salvation also includes those who acknowledge the Creator, in the first place amongst whom are the Muslims: these profess to hold the faith of Abraham and together with us they adore the one, merciful God, mankind's judge on the last day.

From this basic theological definition (God's will for salvation) there then follows a statement about the possibility of salvation for people who can have no knowledge of the gospel of Jesus Christ and his church for no fault of their own. In the same section the Gospel continues:

> Nor is God remote from those who in shadows and images seek the unknown God, since he gives to all men life and breath and all things (cf. Acts 17.25–28), and since the saviour wills all men to be saved (cf I Tim.2.4). Those who, through no fault of their own, do not know the Gospel of Christ or his church, but who nevertheless seek God with a sincere heart, and, moved by grace, try in their actions to do his will as they know it through the dictates of their conscience – those too may achieve eternal salvation.

It follows from this that according to Vatican II even Jews and Muslims will no longer fall into 'the eternal fire which is prepared for the devil and his angels'; they can attain eternal salvation – even in their own way. Thus in fact Judaism and Islam are recognized as what Karl Rahner has called 'legitimate ways of salvation', by which God leads people in his own way to the consummation destined for them. And in particular it is of epoch-making significance for Muslims that the council put an end to the anti-Muslim polemic of centuries, to the effect that Allah, as God is called in the Qur'an, is not identical with the God of the biblical revelation but is his demonic caricature. The Council explicitly says that Muslims worship the one God with 'us' Christians.

Here we have the basic data for a Christian theology of religions which we can develop in the interest of the Abrahamic ecumene. But what about Islam? Can there be any talk of a capacity for inter-religious dialogue here?

5. Islam: no compulsion in faith

It should be said to all those, especially Christians, who keep on with their clichés about the intolerance of Islam: certainly Islamic theology has interpreted itself in absolutist and exclusivist terms in its history. But in contrast to Christianity, it was never possible in Islam for a universally widespread and binding doctrine to become established, according to which Jews and Christians would be definitively excluded from salvation if they had not first been converted to Islam. Islam no more has a doctrine that there is no salvation outside it than does Judaism. Indeed in a comparison of the three monotheistic religions Christianity has always been by far the most intolerant!

Universalism instead of exclusivism

So it should not surprise Christians that classic Muslim theologians since the time of Mohammad Al-Tabari (died 923) or Abu Muhammad b.Ali b.Hazm (died 1064) have constantly asserted the absoluteness of Islam as the only true and perfect version of the original Abrahamic monotheism. Such theologians were doing no more than what Christian theologians did for centuries with the Jews, whose religion was declared to have been 'superseded' by Christianity. One passage from the Qur'an in particular has constantly been cited as justification for such an exclusivist claim to salvation: 'For if one goes in search of a religion other than self-surrender to God, it will never be accepted from him, and in the life to come he shall be among the lost' (3.85; cf. also 9.33). This passage was interpreted with the help of the theory of abrogation and supersession (transferred from legal ordinances to religion) to the effect that a former revelation was 'abrogated' (Arabic *naskh*) by a later one. Thus the revelation given to Jews and Christians could be presented as having been 'overtaken', 'superseded' by Islam. So these religions had forfeited their claim to salvation: there is salvation only through conversion to Islam.

However, unprejudiced study indicates that the Qur'an itself is silent on the question of superseding former Abrahamic revelations. There is neither direct nor indirect evidence in which the Qur'an understands itself as 'abolishing' earlier writings of revelation. Granted, it is claimed that the primal revelation has been falsified and distorted by Jews and Christians, but this does not mean that the validity of these revelations is completely disputed. In the words of the Muslim theologian Abdulaziz Sachedina, who lives in the United States of America: 'It is accurate to maintain that the Qur'an does not see itself as the abrogator of the Judaeo-Christian revelation. Yet some Muslim exegetes of the classical age, who were engaged at one level in providing an exclusive and independent identity for the Muslim Umma and at the other in defending Islam's claim to being the unadulterated version of the previous revelations, developed hermeneutical devices to extrapolate such a theological position. Thus in verse 3.85 they took the word *islam* as the proper name of the historical religion brought by Muhammad rather than as a generic term indicating the act of "submission" to the will of God.'[28] Moreover the basic tenor of the revelations in the Quran is that salvation is promised to all who 'believe in God and the Last Day and do righteous deeds' (Surah 2.62). And according to the same surah that is true not only for Muslims but especially also for those who belong to Judaism, indeed for 'all' people.

So it is not fortuitous that, as in Jewish and Christian theology, so too in modern Muslim theology, the development towards a comprehensive theology of religions is in full flood. And this is happening for a genuinely theological reason. For it would correspond to the universality of divine revelation to humankind if while Jews and Christians were allowed salvation in their way, millions of others were not. Muslim theologians, male and female, who are open to dialogue, like Mahmud Ayoub, Ismail al Faruqi, Khalid Duran, Mohammed Talbi, Mohammed Arkoun, Fathi Osman, Riffat Hassan and Abdoldjavad Falaturi are in the forefront here.[29] According to Seyyd Hossein Nasr, above all reflection on the Qur'anic doctrine of the universality of revelation and on Islamic mysticism (Sufism) and the Islamic metaphysicians leads to such a theology and to insight into the 'transcendent unity of religions'.[30]

Dialogue in faith: zeal over the good

From this we can understand why present-day representatives of Islam argue for friendly dialogue not out of feigned feelings of tolerance but out of a real conviction of faith. Thus Smail Balic, a Bosnian Muslim living in Vienna who has done great service for dialogue between Christianity and Islam in Europe, remarks: 'Despite the different standpoints adopted by Islam on the one hand and Judaism and Christianity on the other over certain central questions of faith, according to the theology of Islam a peaceful coexistence of the religions of revelation is quite possible. In a sense it is even a religious commandment. Islam is in favour of dialogue and open to common concerns. Collaboration is possible. Indeed, today it is a demand which cannot be ignored.'[31]

In other words, while in Islam, too, there is an exclusivist formula, 'One God, one religion', at the same time the Qur'an recognizes the older ways of salvation which preceded Islam. Granted, the Qur'an expresses massive criticism of certain representatives of Judaism and Christianity, but neither religion is simply vilified as error or 'unbelief'. Granted, for the Qur'an not all religions are of equal value, and Jews and Christians are invited to convert to Islam as the only true religion. But at the same time the Qur'an speaks out from beginning to end for a co-existence of Torah, Gospel and Qur'an. Granted, there is a tension between Surah 2.62 and Surah 13.85. But according to what is said by one of the most distinguished Muslim scholars, the Pakistani Fazlur Rahman, this can be resolved as follows: according to the Qur'an it is indeed better to accept the message of Muhammad which is incumbent on humankind, but where this does not happen, life after one's own prophetic message is thought sufficient, even if this does not fulfil the whole divine commandment.[32]

In other words: in contrast to traditional Judaism, which rejects Jesus and Muhammad as prophets, and in contrast also to traditional Christianity, which believes that Moses is superseded in Christ and rejects Muhammad with his claim to be a prophet, Muhammad always taught that Moses and Jesus should be revered as messengers of God. So Judaism and Christianity are indispensable elements of the Islamic way of salvation. Furthermore, according to the Qur'an, Jews and Christians are obliged primarily to follow their own scriptures (Surah 2.62); only those who do not observe anything are wicked (Surah 5.43–48) and threatened with judgment. Over everything stands the principle 'In religion there is no compulsion' (Surah 2.25) – and here Muhammad clearly differs from Augustine. Rather: 'Call thou [all mankind] unto thy Sustainer's path with wisdom and goodly exhortation, and argue with them in the most kindly manner: for, behold, thy Sustainer knows best as to who strays from His path, and best knows He as to who are the right-guided' (Surah 16.125).

The statements in Surah 5 beyond doubt have a key significance for Muslim tolerance,[33] which of course equally often has been and still is betrayed in the concrete practice of particular cultures and societies, just as righteousness is by Jews or love by Christians. And once one has read this, one immediately remembers the parable of the ring in the great drama of reconciliation by the German poet Gotthold Ephraim Lessing, *Nathan the Wise*. Here, within the framework of a play, the three great Abrahamic religions are depicted as parts of a single family. Moreover, the point of this play is that at the end of the action the different persons recognize one another as members of a single great family. All are related, and because they understand this, in the end they are also prepared for reconciliation. Here Lessing may have brilliantly recognized the spirit of Muslim tolerance and given it appropriate expression.[34] Moreover Surah 5 states:

> Unto every one of you have We appointed a [different] law and way of life. And if God has so willed, he could surely have made you all one single community: but [He willed it otherwise] in order to test you by means of what He has vouchsafed unto you. Vie, then, with one another in doing good works! Unto God you all must return; and then he will make you truly understand all that on which you were wont to differ (Surah 5.48; cf. 2.111f.; 4.95).

Thus according to the Qur'an, the difference between the three Abrahamic religions is not an expression of human sin and imperfection which must be restored by the efforts of a religion. The plurality of the three Abrahamic religions corresponds rather to God's will. Each religion has been shown its own way by God. Granted, the individual religions are subject to a divine 'test'; they also have to prove themselves by contributing their faith towards the others. But no one is required by God to go over into the camp of another (certainly not by force). Rather, all are invited to compete with one another over the 'good things'.[35] And finally: only in the eschaton will God abolish the differences between the religions. Therefore a relaxed attitude is appropriate towards the Abrahamic brother and sister religions, a relaxed Muslim attitude which draws on the conviction that 'Our and your God is one' (Surah 29.46).

I have been able to demonstrate that in all three religious traditions there is a theology 'beyond exclusivism'. Here beyond question Christianity has had to undergo the greatest development. So it is particularly significant that an important official dialogue document of the Catholic Church produced in 1981 makes it clear that inter-religious encounter must not be an attempt at mission in a subtle guise. Taking up Surah 5.48 it states: 'Only a deep and open dialogue between Muslims, Jews and Christians can lead these, in faithfulness to the faith of Abraham, to recognize the reasons for their differences and to discover the way to their religious points of contact . . . Therefore dialogue can in no way have the aim of wanting or attempting to convert the other to the religion of the partner at any price, or of leading him to doubt the faith by which that partner lives. Quite the opposite. In the framework of a holy "spiritual struggle" in which the believers "compete for the good things" (Qur'an 5.48), they will mutually help one another to surpass themselves, to correspond better to what their Lord has required and so come nearer to him and increase the weight of good in the world.'[36]

Such a farewell to exclusivism also provides the theological presupposition for an ecumenical theology of peace in the spirit of Abraham. For talk of an Abrahamic ecumene cannot be completely meaningless if there are theological foundations on which Jews, Christians and Muslims can come together. Indeed such an encounter can become concrete in quite a different way in the light of Abraham. But before we develop perspectives for such an ecumene, let us make clear what Abrahamic ecumene should not and cannot be.

II. What Abrahamic Ecumene Cannot Be

Right at the beginning of this second part, I remarked that on the basis of its original Greek meaning, 'ecumene' denotes the whole inhabited world. Anyone who thinks ecumenically thinks in global, universal terms, in terms of human history, human responsibility. To those who think ecumenically, it is not just their region, nation or religion that is important but the fate of all religions, the future of humankind as a whole.

1. The difference from the Christian ecumene

Talk of ecumenism has its historical context in the Protestantism of the end of the nineteenth century. The first Parliament of the World's Religions in Chicago in 1893, and then the World Missionary Conference in Edinburgh in 1910, later the first World Conference on Life and Work (Stockholm 1921) and finally the first World Conference of Faith and Order (Lausanne 1927) are steps on the way towards an institutionalization of the ecumenical movement within Protestantism which in 1948 – under the impact of the genocidal Second World War – came to a climax in the foundation of the World Council of Churches with headquarters in Geneva.[1] Those who initiated this movement (above all John R.Mott, Robert Gardiner and Archbishop Nathan Söderblom) had begun with the aim of bringing together the Christian churches in the spheres of mission, practical action and confession and church order. The aim was, as it was later to be expressed, unity in difference. The one centre was Jesus Christ, who according to the Gospel of John had himself already summoned Christians to unity: 'Holy Father, keep those whom you have given me in your name, that they may be one as we are one' (John 17.11).

Granted, for a long time the Catholic Church rejected the ecumenical movement. For centuries, being Catholic and being ecumenical were mutually exclusive, since the Catholic Church understood itself in an exclusivist way as the sole source of salvation. In 1928, in his encyclical *Mortalium animos*, Pope Pius XI still spoke out resolutely against any participation by Catholics in the ecumenical movment. Those committed to ecumenism were branded 'pan-Christians', who were encouraging a false understanding of the church. But here, too, the Second Vatican Council produced a decisive change. In the pioneering 'Decree on Ecumenism' (*Unitatis redintegratio*) it was even said to be one of the 'main tasks' of the Council to help to restore the unity of all Christians. Now the ecumenical movement was no longer discredited, but was understood as a product 'of the grace of the Holy Spirit'. The split among Christians was regarded as contrary to the will of Christ, as a 'stumbling-block for the world and damaging to the sacred cause of the proclamation of the Gospel'. Since this decree one can now also define the Christian ecumene like this: the Christian ecumene aims at a common confession, practice and church order among the different Christian churches which together confess Jesus Christ as their Lord and Redeemer.

Now can one transfer this Christian understanding of unity to the relationship between Judaism, Christianity and Islam, and speak of an ecumene of Abrahamic religions? No. For the differences in belief existing in the self-understandings of Islam, Christianity and Judaism and which have become differentiated and deepened in a theological process of reflection over the centuries cannot be compared with the differences between the different Christian churches. For Judaism, Christianity and Islam are three different religions, not simply three different confessions of Abraham. And whereas one can speak of a common Christian tradition, one cannot speak in the same way of a common Jewish-Christian-Muslim tradition. This would in fact be a 'myth'[2] – to adopt the term used by the American Jewish scholar Jacob Neusner – and no concessions should be made here for well-meaning ecumenical reasons.[3]

Furthermore, as we saw, the three religions are not the same in their internal relationship with one another either. Judaism and Christianity are bound together in a special way through the Hebrew Bible in terms of 'salvation history'. That is not true in the same way for Islam. So theologically speaking, according to the Christian self-understanding, through its common covenant history Christianity does not have the same relationship with Islam as it does with Judaism. In short, talk of an 'Abrahamic ecumene' may not overplay or level down the structural theological differences either in the relationship between the three religions or in their relationships with others. In important theological and anthropological questions Jews, Christians and Muslims are so far removed from one another that there can be no question of a unity in confession, praxis and community structure, and on this earth presumably there never will be.

2. No enthusiastic 'back to Abraham'

But wouldn't the existence of the great and sometimes burdensome differences be sufficient reason for finally leaving behind the disastrous demarcations and exclusions and returning to the simple faith of Abraham? Wouldn't an Abrahamic ecumene be conceivable and desirable as a return to the original faith of Abraham, whom all three religions worship as their father in the faith? Why not firmly dispense with all institutions – dogmas and rites, the halakhah, canon law and the Sharia – which have come between the sons and daughters of Abraham, and regain the great simplicity of life before God as Abraham lived it? Why not found a 'community of Abraham' and take this as a challenge finally to unity and reconcile Jews, Christians and Muslims under the sign of Abraham?

There is one good reason why not: no one can leap out of the history of his or her faith community. Those who do this are working with a fatal and false hermeneutic of decadence where history is concerned. As though there had only been 'apostasy' in the faith between Abraham and today, only alienation, caricature or obscurity! As though there had not been a legitimate, i.e. divinely willed, development of faith, brought about by the Spirit, in all three religions between Abraham and today, expressed in law, in worship and in doctrine! As though despite all the perversion in religions unleashed by history, the essentials had not been known and practised! As though God's spirit – despite all human demonry – had not established itself in all places and times, in all people and nations! As though Abraham's faith had not been taken up by Moses, Jesus and Muhammad, the prophets and messengers of God, and made definitively specific for each particular community! It is not only meaningless in practice but also theologically illegitimate to seek to detach and abstract the 'historical' Abraham from the faith communities in order to play him off against these communities. Abraham was and is simply a part and function of a faith community. Therefore we must be clear that in speaking of an ecumene between Jews, Christians and Muslims under the aegis of Abraham we are not seeking to replace Moses, Jesus and Muhammad by Abraham nor to detach Abraham from synagogue, church and Umma. What does that mean in practical terms?

3. Abraham does not replace Moses 'our Master'

It means recognizing that the foundations which Abraham laid were developed by 'Moses' once and for all for Jews in the Torah: in instructions for life, specifically in commandments and prohibitions. If Abraham shows how human beings can come to believe in the one and only God and how this faith can be preserved throughout a long life, so the Torah from Sinai brings instructions by which one can order and structure one's life before God. If Abraham shows, especially at 'Moriah', the meaning of tested belief in the enigmatic God who is incalculable in his grace and surprising in his humanity, the Torah shows how one should live before this God in the community of the one people – every year (the great festivals), every week (working days and sabbath), every hour (prayer times, regulations for cleanness and food). The Torah from Sinai, both written and oral, is a process of learning which is in principle open, in which the Jew hopes to come to know in increasing depth God's revealed will, God's purpose with creation, history and people. In a word: without the structure of Sinai the Jewish people will not realize the faith of Abraham in the everyday world.

The Judaist Reinhold Mayer may be said to have made the decisive point here for Judaism: 'The decisive period begins with Abraham, who perceived the call of God in a special way. By going from his security into insecurity, from his times into freedom, he has become the model of all believers and also their father. The Abraham element has always remained important for Israel, since without faith the commandment would be fossilized. And Moses led his people Israel from its slavery in Egypt into the wilderness of Sinai in freedom, and as a result became their master and teacher. Because faith has no existence without the commandment, above all there is emphasis on the contemporaneity of all that is later with Moses, the man of the commandment.'[4] So the Abrahamitic and the Mosaic, faith and commandment, Moriah and Sinai, belong very closely together in Judaism. Abraham cannot simply be played off against Moses. Furthermore, with the Torah the Jewish people claims to have been given God's definitive revelation. However, many Jews think that they can conclude from this that this Torah can be lived out without sparing a thought for Christianity and Islam. In complete self-confidence they assert that Christianity and Islam need Judaism for their self-understanding, but Judaism does not need either Christianity or Islam.

4. Abraham does not replace Jesus 'the Christ'

Christians understand themselves – or at the latest since Paul's theology of Abraham and Israel have understood themselves – as children of Abraham in the spirit. But it would be wrong to play off being a child of Abraham against being a child of Christ. The slogan 'Abraham's faith is enough' cannot be a slogan for Christians, any more than it can be for Jews. Granted, according to Paul Abraham's faith is a justifying faith. But the same apostle has left no doubt that only faith in Jesus as the risen Lord makes Christians children of Abraham. As former Gentiles they have no claim to this honorific title. According to their own self-understanding, only through faith in the crucified Lord who has been raised by God are they incorporated into God's history of blessing and covenant with his elect people: 'But if you belong to Christ, you are descendants of Abraham, heirs of the promise' (Rom.3.29).

Moreover, here is the decisive point of dissension between Orthodox Jews and Christians over Abraham to the present day. Gentiles have no right to call themselves children of Abraham unless previously they have formally confessed Judaism, have been formally converted. So Christians are wrong in claiming this honorific title. Masses of Gentiles illegitimately regard themselves as 'children of Abraham' through faith in Christ without submitting to the 'works of the law'. In the eyes of orthodox Jews that must seem presumptuous.

But at this point Christians must argue patiently, in the spirit of the freedom and love of God. Therefore from earliest times the decisive Christian question to Jewish orthodoxy has been: isn't God free to create other children of Abraham for himself, even outside his elect people? Is the omnipotent and all-gracious God subject to the halakhic system? According to the original wording of the Torah didn't God will to bless 'all peoples' through Abraham? 'Is God then a God of Jews only, and not also of Gentiles?' (Rom.3.29). Indeed, since earliest times the Christian counter-thesis to orthodox Jewish exclusivism based on Abraham has been: 'God can raise up children of Abraham from these stones' (Matt.3.9), or even more specifically: 'Many will come from the east and the west and sit down at table with Abraham, Isaac and Jacob in the kingdom of God' (Matt.8.11).

Yet for Christians it is important to be a child of Abraham in the Spirit, and much cruelty would have been spared the original children of Abraham had Christians always remembered this, remembered the very first sentence of their 'New Testament': 'Genealogy of Jesus Christ, the son of David, the son of Abraham.' But what is decisive for Christians is that Jesus Christ, and no one else, is their Lord. Abraham's history of faith may be the anticipation of the gospel of a God who also justifies the godless. The Gospel itself is embodied in the person and cause of Jesus Christ. Here Christians are shown what it means to live and to die before God. Here the concrete meaning of faith, love and hope become clear for the everyday world. Here above all Christians have the foundation of their freedom from all works of the law, so that they are justified once and for all without obligation to the halakhah.

Certainly – already according to the very first sentence in the New Testament – Jesus Christ is and remains a 'son of Abraham', and all those who believe and live in his spirit can proudly call themselves sons or daughters of Abraham. Abraham is and remains 'the father of us all – in the presence of God'. However, for Christians 'the way, the truth and the life' remains Jesus, the crucified and risen Lord who is present in the Spirit, whose disciples they attempt to be in the everyday world. For Christians, Jesus Christ is and remains 'the author and perfecter of faith' (Heb.12.2). Many Christians think that they can conclude from this that through the revelation in Jesus Christ the revelation of God in the Torah is 'surpassed', so that it has meaning only in respect of Christ. Then Judaism is 'allowed' only as a prehistory to Christianity, and Islam is said to be theologically irrelevant.

5. Abraham does not replace Muhammad 'the Prophet'

The Prophet Muhammad also claims for Muslims that they are
children of Abraham in faith. Here he is no different from Paul when
the latter asserts the independence of the Jewish Christians from the
traditionalists of the Jewish establishment. Certainly Muhammad
even claims to be a physical child of Abraham through Ishmael. But
the renewed faith of Abraham which the Prophet seeks to revive is
independent of this. All can attain it, from whatever people they may
come. Therefore Islam rightly understands itself, like Christianity, as
a universal religion of humankind. Furthermore, no one called with
such radical directness for a return to Abraham as the Prophet did.
Even Paul only claimed to see the anticipation of the gospel in
Abraham. Muhammad asserts more: Islam as a religion is the
religion of Abraham. Indeed, Abraham as a *hanif* is 'Islam' in person:
trusting surrender to the will of God.

And yet Islam, too, leaves no doubt that the Qur'an of the Prophet
cannot simply be replaced with Abraham. Though the Qur'an may
not contain anything other than the religion of Abraham, this book is
nevertheless necessary to make this religion of Abraham concrete for
a new faith community. Though the Prophet himself may only be one
who warns against all deviations from this original religion, warns
against all idolatry, his instructions for concrete life are indispensable. What is important for a Muslim in living and dying is shown
not only by Abraham but by the whole further history of revelation
which embraces Moses and Jesus equally and which reaches its
climax in the Prophet Muhammad and the Qur'an which he brings.
Here the Muslim is given the light of the truth which cannot deceive,
the norms for correct action, a comprehensive order for life.
Abraham may be the beginning of all prophecy; Muhammad is its
'seal'.

However, many Muslims think that they may conclude from this
that Islam has taken up and surpassed Judaism and Christianity.
What Christians did to Jews for centuries, Muslims do to Jews and
Christians: they claim that they are the 'prehistory' of Islam. So the
polemic pattern of exclusion reaches its climax: Jews declare
Christianity and Islam to be irrelevant to their faith; Christians
declare Judaism to be superseded and Islam to be heretical; Muslims
declare the faith of Jews and Christians to be surpassed in Islam.
What then? If ecumene in the sign of Abraham is not simply a matter

of passing over histories of faith in a naive enthusiastic 'back to Abraham'; if Abraham cannot be played off against Moses, Jesus and Muhammad; if particular claims to validity cannot simply be ignored with reference to Abraham, what can be the positive significance of the 'Abrahamic ecumene'?

III. What Abrahamic Ecumene Can Mean

As a theological presupposition of ecumenical awareness I have been able to demonstrate that Jews, Christians and Muslims have learned to understand themselves as faith communities each of which has been given its own way by God. The mediators of the will of God differ, as do the concrete forms of the way to God. But reflection on the normative messages and primal documents shows that an exclusivism of truth and salvation can no longer be justified – regardless of ongoing claims to validity.

1. Abraham – an abidingly critical figure

As far as Abraham is concerned, it is theologically decisive that although he does not replace Moses, Jesus and Muhammad, conversely the Torah, the Gospel and the Qur'an do not do away with his significance. On the contrary, precisely according to the self-understanding of these holy scriptures Abraham remains the primal image of faith. Consequently he is also a critical figure for all the faith communities which have grown up. Why?

An abiding primal image of faith

In all traditions Abraham shows what is most important for human beings before God: not legal religious achievements, but dedication to the will of God, a well-tried trust in God. Only in this way do human beings stand before God justified, are they in the truest sense of the word '*hanif*', '*muslim*'. Conversely, however, that means that Torah, Gospel and Qur'an are concretions of the faith of Abraham, attempts to revive it. They did not set out to replace the faith of Abraham by a religious system but to bring it to light for everyday human life. They seek to show in their own way that, like Abraham, Jews, Christians and Muslims have to do with a God who calls into being that which is not and expects from human beings only *emuna*, *pistis*, *islam*: dedicated trust. In short, any talk of Abrahamic ecumene cannot be a suspension which forgets the origins but is rather a concretion of the faith of Abraham which is relevant to the present – in the light of Torah, Gospel and Qur'an. Abraham remains a point of reference by which the later traditions of synagogue, church and Umma can and must be measured critically.

So Abrahamic ecumene can only mean a revival of the faith of Abraham, made concrete in Torah, Gospel and Qur'an and reflected under the conditions of new times – a revival in the spirit. Now to bring Abraham's faith alive also means to take seriously the alien character of Abraham which I reported at the beginning of this book, on the basis of Genesis. The legacy of Abraham is no deposit, no system, no dead material, but a dynamic history of faith which needs constantly new critical re-reading. Abraham's legacy needs time and again to be freed from the petrifications of tradition. Abraham is not a memorial to faith, a religious giant from distant millennia. Abraham is not a man who possesses faith, but the movement of faith; he is not the security of faith, but the quest for faith; not the arrogance of faith, but the humility of faith.

Abraham the stranger – a criticism of all traditions

So if Jews, Christians and Muslims take Abraham seriously as the primal model of their faith, he can still surprise them. For in all the traditions of synagogue, church or Umma, what Abraham's faith means according to the original accounts is by no means exhausted. All traditions have a particular image of Abraham, but this is dependent on their specific theological or institutional interests. In many traditions, as we saw, nothing is left of the original 'strangeness' of Abraham. He has been commandeered, functionalized, politicized. He has been elevated and idealized, and as a result the Abraham of Genesis has been considerably changed.

But those who want to speak ecumenically of Abraham today will only avoid simple self-confirmation if they are prepared to adopt a critical standard from the original texts, see through the constrictions and discover Abraham in all his dimensions. Without recognizing the normativity of the original Abraham traditions in the book of

Genesis (the original 'historical' Abraham remains once and for all in the shadows of history) there can be no critical re-reading of the Abraham traditions that have grown up. The New Testament and the Qur'an are not opposed to this, since they recognize the authority of the Hebrew Bible as a source of revelation. So those who reject this critical hermeneutic shut themselves off from liberating openness to Abraham himself. They reject the criterion which opposes the misuse of Abraham for religious or political ends. And how much Abraham has already been abused for religious, pedagogical or even military interests![1] In that case, what is expressed is not the Abraham of the original document, but the Abraham whom people have made the projection of their wishes, interests and lusts for power. But to use the normative Abraham texts in Genesis as a criterion means no less than to engage in a radical, healthy critique of all exploitations and narrow-minded applications of Abraham by synagogue, church and Umma, and above all a radical critique of all idolatry of Abraham.

A reminder of responsibility for one another

For faithfulness to Abraham is more than a slogan only if people in all three traditions are still ready to listen to the Abraham of scripture as he has been handed down in all his dimensions, neither in the Talmud nor in the New Testament nor in the Qur'an, but in the book of Genesis. With Claus Westermann we will be able to say: 'To the degree that traditio-historical and archaeological research have demolished the superstructure of an idealizing figure of Abraham, the simple patriarchal figure of Abraham could gain significance for all three religions. The differences lie in the secondary interpretation, the superstructure. What is really common to all is the patriarch Abraham as he appears in the earliest strata of the traditions of Genesis.'[2]

Now if this is clear, and if – as I have already emphasized – ecumenical thinking means thinking in global dimensions, thinking in a way which takes account of one another and is responsible for one another, then the meaning of Abrahamic ecumene can be defined positively like this: Jews who direct their concrete life by Moses, their Teacher; Christians who direct their concrete life by Jesus, their Christ; Muslims who direct their concrete life by the message of Muhammad, their Prophet, set down in the Qur'an, recognize their special tie with one another, respect one another and are responsible for one another, because they take seriously their common historical origin: Abraham, Hagar and Sarah, the tribal ancestors of their faith. Those who think ecumenically in the spirit of the primal father and the primal mother cease to think only of the good of the synagogue, the church or the Umma. They are not indifferent to the fate of the other brothers and sisters. They practise authentic brotherhood and sisterhood in the best sense of the word.

Certainly the family metaphor should not be made all too idealistic, since a 'healthy' family has individuality, rivalry, distance and in some circumstances also disputes and partings.[3] Indeed Jews, Christians and Muslims have made rich use of this freedom in the past. But one indispensable notion is bound up with the metaphor of the 'family': for all the respect for each member's independence there is an awareness of belonging together, of responsibility, indeed of care for one another and solidarity with one another.

2. Recognizing Abraham's presence in others

But what are the theological foundations for such an Abrahamic ecumene? Despite all the structural differences in internal relationship between them, are there genuinely theological reasons, indeed is there a real need, for talking of a special link between Jews, Christians and Muslims? We must now bring together what was said about Noah, Abraham, Isaac, Ishmael and Jesus in the first part of this book and evaluate it in the interest of a theology of the Abrahamic ecumene. As a second step we shall listen to voices from contemporary Judaism, Christianity and Islam which speak out directly or indirectly for an ecumene between Jews, Christians and Muslims. The aim is not to demonstrate statistically the occurrence of the term 'Abrahamic ecumene', which for many people is too new or too open to misunderstanding, but to document the voices of those who are committed to the cause.

Biblical foundations: Noah – Abraham – Ishmael – Jesus

The book of Genesis shows that Israel always also had to justify its position as God's elect people with respect to other peoples by the figures of Noah and Abraham. Noah is regarded as the ancestor of a new humanity to replace that annihilated by the flood. All the nations of earth descend from his three sons (9.19). With Noah God made a covenant in favour of all creation, and all members of all peoples are under the blessing of this covenant if they observe the 'Noachide' commandments. We also saw, secondly, that in Genesis Abraham is not only the bearer of the covenant for Israel but also the mediator of blessing of other peoples. Moreover, in Judaism – right up to rabbinic theology – there was a lively awareness that through Abraham even a non-Jew can enter into God's special covenant relationship with his people if he submits to this God as a proselyte.

So the binding testimony of scripture for Jews and Christians can once again be summed up in the following theses:

1. Among all those outside the biblical history of revelation there are 'just' people who observe the Noachide commandments. Without having to be Jews, they have a 'share in the world to come'. For Christians, too, God's universal will for salvation which is expressed in the covenant with Noah is decisive. It is endorsed in the New Testament with a saying from the first letter to Timothy: 'God desires all men to be saved and to come to the knowledge of the truth' (2.4).

2. The election of a people as God's people may not be absolutized. Abraham in particular attests that other people are affirmed and blessed by God beyond Israel.

3. The elect people of God may not claim God's grace exclusively for their own line of descent (Abraham/Sarah – Isaac/Jacob). Other people outside this line also stand under God's saving grace.

4. The people of God and the peoples stand in a relationship of mutual dependence. Just as the existence of Israel is a presupposition for the blessing of the peoples by God, so the existence of the peoples is a presupposition that Israel will not reduce God's salvation exclusively to itself. If the peoples experience salvation through their attitude to Israel, so conversely the nations liberate Israel from a disastrous encapsulation in a salvation-historical solipsism.

5. Christians believe that they have received the universal dimension of the promise and blessing of Abraham in their testimony to Jesus Christ. Faith in Jesus Christ has made it possible for numerous peoples to be confronted with the liberating reality of the true God. It has taught them that at its deepest, faith represents unconditional trust in the Word of God. And faith in Jesus Christ in particular has made those who are not descended from the special line of the covenant which runs through Abraham, Isaac and Jacob children of Abraham. In this way they have helped the universal

blessing of God originally promised to Abraham to achieve true universality.

The Ishmael texts of Genesis need to be evaluated theologically with as much care as the Ishmael texts of Genesis. I already indicated at the beginning of the chapter on Islam that Ishmael is the progenitor of the Arab tribes and thus also of Islam, which explicitly refers to him. To continue to keep this dimension out of theology today would be to be blind to history and to God. Only those who as Jews or Christians are trapped in a salvation-historical overestimation of themselves can fail to see that God, who according to the testimony of scripture is also the Lord of history and guides the fates of the nations, evidently has his plans for Ishmael and his descendants. This is not to dispute that Israel, and for Christians the church as the people of God, also stands in a special covenant relationship to God. So anyone who takes scripture seriously in all its dimensions cannot avoid noting that over and above the will to salvation guaranteed by Noah, Abraham and Christ the Arab peoples are promised a special blessing by God in so far as these peoples understand themselves spiritually or physically to be descendants of Abraham-Ishmael; and why should this blessing have ceased when members of these peoples began to practise 'Islam', submission to the will of the one true God of Abraham?

By contrast, if we analyse the texts in the light of our historical experience, it will become clear that with Ishmael and his descendants the Abraham-Isaac-Christ tradition of the synagogue and the church are evidently to be prevented from becoming rigid in an exclusivist claim to the truth and a satisfaction with salvation. Once again it reaches a new level of universality. For both Jews and Christians, the Ishmael texts of Genesis are the key to a theological understanding of Islam. In principle this is not a new idea, since particularly in the Christian theology of the Middle Ages the rise of Islam was always connected with the fate of Hagar and Ishmael — though for the purpose of polemical denunciation. The Muslims were mocked as Hagarenes and Ishmaelites, and their militancy was explained by the statements about Ishmael ('like a wild ass'). In the light of our historical experiences, however, it is now time to interpret the Ishmael texts constructively in the interest of an Abrahamic ecumene, since Jews and Christians simply cannot go on failing to note that Islam has existed for almost 1400 years. This fact can no longer be said to be theologically irrelevant.

Without losing sight of the special covenant relationship between God and his people Israel, and thus for Christians with the church, we may therefore make the following theological statements about the significance of Islam on the basis of the Ishmael texts in Genesis:

1. Through the line Abraham-Ishmael, the people of the faith mediated by Abraham's son Muhammad stand under God's special protection. The mere fact that Ishmael and his descendants exist at all is not due to human will but exclusively to God's will. That Ishmael survived is not in accord with human purpose but with God's plan.

2. The tribal ancestor of Islam, Ishmael, bears the sign of God's covenant that Jews also bear. In this way he demonstrates impressively that other children of Abraham also have a share in God's covenant history with his elect people – including his descendants. For:

3. Ishmael's descendants, too, stand under God's special blessing. Thus any exclusivism of blessing for Israel is done away with – not only through the existence of children of Abraham among the disciples of Jesus Christ but also through that of children of Abraham among the disciples of the Prophet.

4. Ishmael is the son cast out by Abraham in accordance with God's will who nevertheless seems, like Abraham, to have been specially loved by God. For in a memorable way the fate of the father is reflected in this son in particular: just as Abraham went into exile from his homeland at God's bidding, so Ishmael went into exile in the wilderness at the bidding of God and his father. Just as Abraham was promised fertility and descendants by God, so too was Ishmael, the banished son of Abraham.

5. From a present-day perspective we can say that Ishmael's fate enigmatically anticipates the ambiguous relationship of Jews and Christians to their brother religion, Islam. In despising and rejecting the descendants of their brother Ishmael, they once again drive 'Ishmael' into the wilderness.

All this means that even today the Ishmael traditions of Genesis are still a theological challenge for Jews and Christians, since both have so far usually reacted to this son of Abraham and to the faith of his descendants with theological perplexity or rejection. However, to an unbiassed approach, scripture leaves no doubt that with the figure of Ishmael any dualistic thought in terms of a history of salvation and a history of damnation is already ruled out. For Ishmael fits into neither of these categories. Present-day Old Testament exegesis takes account of this. For one of the most important Old Testament scholars of this century, the Protestant Gerhard von Rad, noted in his commentary on Genesis the 'strange salvation-historical theme' in this account of Ishmael in Genesis 21: 'the departure from Abraham's house, the origin of a by-way of salvation history'. Granted. Ishmael 'will not inherit the blessings of salvation promised to the legitimate son of Abraham', but strikingly, he is not 'deprived of Yahweh's protection and blessing'.[4] And Claus Westermann has rightly recalled that by preserving this narrative as part of its Holy Scriptures the people of Israel has told itself two things: 'The expulsion of Ishmael limits the people which calls Abraham its father to the single line, the descendants of Isaac. The particular history of this people demands that it be separated from the "son of the maidservant" as God himself had ordered. But God's blessing goes also with Ishmael: he is to be "a great people". Contrary to the friend-foe mentality, a relationship of Israel with other peoples is retained from the early period. Abraham as father, despite the emphasis on the one legitimate line through Isaac, has a significance which bridges the gap to other peoples.'[5]

This perhaps helps us to understand better why the spirit of Abraham which leads to the ecumene among Jews, Christians and Muslims could never be driven out, despite all the attempts. There have always been men and women of Jewish, Christian and Muslim origin who have used the recollection of Abraham, Hagar and Sarah for mutual respect and concern. So we can gratefully note that after centuries of a fatal Abraham exclusivism, ecumenically we face a new situation: Jews, Christians and Muslims are ready to recognize fully the members of each others' faith-communities as children of Abraham and to draw the necessary consequences.

Abrahamic ecumene: Jewish perspectives

In Jewish tradition, there has been constant recollection of God's blessing for the peoples through Abraham with its originally universal orientation. Jewish thinkers of the past with a universalist orientation like Philo of Alexandria and Flavius Josephus already described Abraham as a cosmopolitan and the embodiment of a knowledge of God which is possible for all human beings. These theologians could already show that through Abraham Judaism remains concentrated on itself and at the same time can remain universally open for people from the nations.

Certainly the tendencies of orthodox rabbinic Judaism to segregate itself cannot be trivialized. I have been able to show how in rabbinic Judaism Abraham has become an archetype of 'halakhic man', a primal rabbi and arch-priest. All that was left in rabbinic Judaism of the blessing for the peoples was the blessing for Israel and the proselytes. Only in so far as someone from the nations converts to the one true God of Israel, only in so far as someone wants to go over to Judaism, can he be incorporated into the blessing of Abraham. But even this should not just be seen in a negative way. For here even the rabbis, at least in principle, affirmed that being a child of Abraham is not just limited to physical descent. There are 'proselytes' and 'godfearers' who through Abraham and Sarah can make contact with the people of God. So this universal dimension of rabbinic theology should be recalled once again. Thus the midrash of Abraham and Sarah as the father and mother of the nations of the earth says: 'All Gentiles throughout the world who accept conversion and all Gentiles throughout the world who fear God spring from the children who drank the milk of Sarah. Therefore it is said of Sarah that she is a "joyful mother of children".' We might also recall the 'Sayings of the Fathers', where the one who is called a 'disciple of Abraham' has 'a good eye, a humble spirit and a modest soul'. Or Moses Maimonides, who says of Abraham that he 'took many children under the wing of the divine glory'. Finally we could recall the rabbinic theory of late circumcision: Abraham as the archetype of someone who does not 'possess' faith, but struggles for it in the course of a long life, who is not a believing Jew from the start but only becomes a Jew through circumcision at a great age. Indeed precisely through his late circumcision – also according to the rabbis – Abraham made it possible for all non-Jews to go over to Judaism in the future.

Today in particular, at a time when there is an awareness of a world-wide religious pluralism, this theology opens up ecumenical opportunities within Judaism, since even orthodox Judaism is capable of inter-religious relations through Abraham. Thus the orthodox Rabbi David Hartman, who lives in Jerusalem and is committed to inter-religious dialogue, emphasizes in his fundamental book on more recent Jewish covenant theology, *Living Covenant*: 'Abraham's covenant signifies rejection of the idea that covenantal faith commitments are defined by racial and biological conditions. The predominance of norms over biology and race is evident in the halakhic ruling that a convert who enters the covenant, of whatever sociocultural or racial background, may refer to Abraham as his or her father. The convert, like any Jew born of Jewish parents, may in prayer address God as "our God and God of our fathers, the God of Abraham, the God of Isaac". In singling out Abraham, God made covenantal religion accessible to all. Abraham is the father of any person who seeks to emulate his way of life and to practise its values, norms and beliefs.'[6]

In other words, according to present-day orthodox understanding, Christians and Muslims can also be regarded as 'children of Abraham' without Israel having to give up its original and unique role as children of Abraham – in particular the promise to Abraham and the Abraham covenant with a view to the land. As the meditation in the New Union Prayer Book says: 'In the course of time Israel bore other religions which brought many people to God, but our responsibility continues, since our task remains unfulfilled.' The Jewish theologian David Flusser has made the decisive point here: 'In the Jewish religion the existence of Christianity (and Islam) can be understood as the fulfilment of God's promises to Abraham to make him the father of many peoples . . . The Jews, moreover, can view Christians (and Muslims) as "God fearers", Gentile descendants of Noah who have rejected paganism and will be saved if they behave in an ethical way.'[7]

So it is a welcome ecumenical sign that not only representatives of Reform Judaism (alongside Flusser also Lapide and Friedlander)[8] but present-day representatives of Jewish orthodoxy also take the faith of Christians and Muslims theologically more seriously than before. The foundation for this is the more recent covenant theology represented not only by David Hartman and Eugene Borowitz but also by one of the most respected Orthodox American rabbis, Irving Greenberg. Moreover, in his most recent book, *The Jewish Way*, Greenberg pleads for an 'open covenant' which embraces the special obligations of Israel 'without denying the validity of other commitments and religions'. This model is of particular significance for the growing communication in the one world.

So Greenberg affirms not only the possibility granted by orthodox Judaism that each individual may voluntarily enter the family of Abraham, but even more: 'since the covenant is open, it is open to further revelations in history'. New redemptive events have confirmed the covenant and brought the world 'closer to the messianic age': 'Through the unfolding covenant, many Gentiles are brought into the messianic process and become partners in the covenant of God and humanity. This affirmation in no way undercuts the validity and integrity of the Sinaitic treaty with Israel. After the holocaust and in light of the pluralism of the postmodern world, Christianity and Islam will have to reject their own claims to supersede Judaism. And Jews will, more clearly than before, recognize these religions as outgrowths of the original covenant. Such development, far from disproving Judaism, only shows that the original covenant continues to bear fruit and bring life.'[9]

So Christians and Muslims – also according to the present understanding of orthodox Judaism, are living witnesses to a living covenant of God with Abraham. The contribution of another orthodox Jewish theologian from the United States, Michael Wyschogrod, may also be understood in these terms when he writes of Islam and Christianity: 'The demand of the hour is a drawing together of all those whose lives are led under the judgment of the God of Abraham. For the children of Abraham to learn to recognize the presence of the patriarch in the adherents of the other Abrahamic faiths is the demand of the teacher of Beer-Sheva. We ought not to reject this demand.'[10]

So if there is talk of an Abrahamic ecumene, the children of Abraham will have to learn to recognize the presence of the patriarch in the adherents of the other Abrahamic faith communities. Only in this way can the paradox of the commandeering of Abraham in all the traditions be overcome. Fortunately work is being done by numerous groups in dialogues and trialogues, in the state of Israel as well – signs of hope for a better future.[11]

Abrahamic ecumene: Christian perspectives

In fact for centuries Christianity in particular found it especially difficult to recognize the presence of Abraham in the other children of Abraham. As we saw, Judaism had been disinherited; Christians had regarded themselves as the only children of Abraham. So they were even less ready to share this role with the Muslims. Granted, they had appealed over against the Jews to God's freedom to make children of Abraham from any stones he chose, but they wanted to deprive God of this freedom if these 'stones' were no longer Gentile Christians but Gentile Muslims. For centuries, it was far beyond the horizon of Christian understanding that even after the death and resurrection of Christ the stem of Abraham could still put out living branches, that God could use his freedom to create new and other children of Abraham. In particular the faith of the Muslims was disparaged as a heretical human caricature of the true God, and Islam demonized as an 'anti-Christian power of seduction'.

But even where Christians (like the Catholic Church at the Second Vatican Council) made a 180-degree turn on the question of salvation for non-Christians and advanced to a relational, dialogical model for the relationship between the church and the world religions, theological perplexities, in particular in the relationship between the church and Islam, are unmistakable. They have deep biblical-historical roots. By means of a structural analysis of the declaration *Nostra Aetate* I want to show how the Second Vatican Council attempted to frame a new definition of the 'relationship of the church to the non-Christian religions' beyond *Lumen Gentium* no.16.

Already in *Lumen Gentium* 16 the Council had spoken of a relationship between non-Christians and the church, here 'in the first place' referring to that elect 'people' (the name 'Israel' was not mentioned). So there is a special relationship between 'Israel' and the church, which is here sweepingly identified with the 'people of God', of a kind that does not exist with any other religion. In that case, why did the Council not consistently put the closer relationship to Israel as part of the Constitution on the Church or the Decree on Ecumenism? In this way it would have been able to give impressive theological emphasis to its special relationship with Israel, which in fact is not simply comparable to that with the other world religions. There were plans in this direction, but for political and dogmatic reasons no such step was taken at the Council.[12]

Thus what the Catholic Church says about the Jews now appears in a decree on all the non-Christian religions, which again prompts the suspicion that relations between the church and Israel are not something special but on a par with relations with Hinduism, Buddhism and the nature religions. However, in terms of content the passages in this Declaration relating to Israel must be described as an epoch-making shift of the Catholic Church over the Jewish question. There is nothing even approximately comparable in the previous history of this church. For with the supreme authority of a council, it is explicitly declared that the church no longer wants to clarify its self-understanding without Israel or contrary to Israel, but only with thought about Israel (again the name does not appear, but only general formulae like 'stock of Abraham' or 'Jewish people'). Certainly the theological schemes of interpretation used to define the relationship between Israel and the church here are unmistakably traditional. Israel is still seen exclusively in its function for the church, to some degree utilized as part of 'salvation history'. The decisive categories are 'prefigured' and 'included'. Thus Israel is still regarded as a spiritual 'heir' of the church and commandeered for the process of the church's reflection on itself. There is not a word about living Judaism in this declaration.

Yet *Nostra Aetate* 4 leaves no doubt that there is a lasting spiritual bond between the church and Israel. Indeed with the apostle Paul's Israel theology it is maintained that despite their rejection of the gospel, the Jews are still 'loved for the sake of the fathers'; but 'their gifts of grace and their calling are irrevocable'. The decisive passage reads:

> Sounding the depths of the mystery which is the Church, this sacred Council remembers the spirtual ties which link the people of the New Covenant to the stock of Abraham. The Church of Christ acknowledges that in God's plan of salvation the beginning of her faith and election is to be found in the patriarchs, Moses and the prophets. She professes that all Christ's faithful, who as men of faith are sons of Abraham, are included in the same patriarch's call, and that the salvation of the Church is mystically prefigured in the exodus of God's chosen people from the land of bondage. On this account the Church cannot forget that she received the revelation of the Old Testament by way of that people with whom God in his inexpressible mercy established the ancient covenant. Nor can she forget that she draws nourishment from that good olive tree on to which the wild olive branches of the Gentiles have been grafted.

The foundations for a Christian theology of the Abrahamic ecumene are thus laid by the church's magisterium with the Jews. According to what the Council says, no Christian faith and no Christian church may forget that it began with the fathers and was integrated into the history of promise and covenant which begins with Abraham. But what about the relationship of the church with the Muslims?

It is remarkable that the same theological perplexity which was already recognizable in the fate of Ishmael in Genesis returns when the church seeks to define its relationship to the spiritual descendants of Ishmael, the Muslims. For on the one hand Islam (here for theological reasons the religion is not named and there is talk only of the faith of the 'Muslims') is discussed in the declaration before Judaism, which in the structure of this declaration is meant to indicate that it is the closest religion to the church. On the other hand a separate section is devoted to Islam, which does not seem as summary as what is said on the Asian religions of Hinduism and Buddhism. On the one hand Islam is put on the same level as any other world religion and thus subsumed under the general formula of recognition, that in this religion, too, often a ray of that truth which illuminates all people can be recognized. Thus the Muslims, like all the other 'Gentiles', are discussed outside the biblical history of revelation and left completely out of account for the church's reflection on itself.

On the other hand, the passage relating to Islam cannot deny that biblical traditions play a constitutive role in Islam, including key biblical figures like Abraham, Jesus and Mary. So Islam cannot simply be presented as a religion in which occasionally 'a ray' of truth shines forth. Rather, with *Lumen Gentium* 16 it is to be described as a faith community whose members 'confess the faith of Abraham and worship the one God with us' – theologically, we have heard, an epoch-making reassessment. The decisive passage (*Nostra Aetate* 3) reads:

> The Church has also a high regard for the Muslims. They worship God, who is one, living and subsistent, merciful and almighty, the Creator of heaven and earth, who has also spoken to men. They strive to submit themselves without reserve to the hidden decrees of God, just as Abraham submitted himself to God's plan, to whose faith Muslims clearly link their own. Although not acknowledging him as God, they venerate Jesus as a prophet, his virgin Mother they also honour, and at times even devoutly invoke. Further, they await the day of judgment and the reward of God following the resurrection of the dead. For this reason they highly esteem an upright life and worship God, especially by way of prayer, alms-deeds and fasting.

Over the centuries many quarrels and dissensions have arisen between Christians and Muslims. The sacred Council now pleads with all to forget the past, and urges that a sincere effort be made to achieve mutual understanding: for the benefit of all men, let them together preserve and promote peace, liberty, social justice and moral values.

If we take the council texts on the Muslims and the Jews together, there are some remarkable overlaps in content. According to official Catholic doctrine they can already be the foundations for an Abrahamic ecumene from a Christian perspective. According to these texts all three religions now already agree:

1. In the recognition that there is only the one and only God.

2. In the definition that this God has unchangeable properties: life, mercy, omnipotence and creatorship.

3. In the conviction that this God has not remained silent towards human beings but has spoken, has revealed himself.

4. In the understanding that faith is trust in the will of God after the models of Abraham, Moses and the prophets.

5. In the hope that God will make possible a future day known only to him 'when all the peoples will call on the Lord with one voice and serve him shoulder to shoulder'.

6. In the eschatological expectation that human beings will rise and be judged by a God who recompenses them according to their deeds.

7. In a concern no longer to allow themselves to be dominated by a bad past but in the world today to arrive at 'mutual understanding', to practise 'mutual knowledge and respect', and to meet in 'brotherly dialogue'.

8. In a readiness to work together for the well-being of humankind: for the protection and furtherance of social justice, moral good, peace and freedom for all human beings.

But wouldn't another theological foundation for the relationship between the church and Islam be part of 'mutual understanding', since this foundation has been established with such welcome self-criticism? Is it really enough for a Christian theology – the Catholic theologian Hans Zirker rightly asks – 'first to put Islam with all the other religions . . . and secondly, in addition, to list the individual elements which it shares with the biblical tradition'? Shouldn't there 'above all have been reflection on whether and how the claim of

Christian faith to validity can be seen together with an ongoing history of religion in such a way that this cannot a priori be regarded as simply illegitimate'? How would Christianity have to understand itself 'if it not only perceives the fundamental religious experiences which precede it and to which it owes its existence but also notes seriously those which it has had in its own cultural sphere, indeed its experiences of itself and those which lead beyond itself? For Islam is part of the history of Christianity; although for Christianity it is "another" religion, at the same time it is also an element of its identity.'[13]

So the Council declaration still leaves many theological questions unanswered and thus offers room for a deeper theological reflection, especially as in the case of Islam essential elements of the Islamic self-understanding have not yet even been mentioned: either the role of the Prophet Muhammad or the Qur'an, the role of the faith community (Umma) or the religious law (Shari'a). Here Islam remains a special theological challenge for Christians in particular. It is 'another' religion, yet affirms great parts of the biblical history of revelation. In its faith it is near to Christianity and yet is quite independent. Therefore none of the theological categories so far used by Christians does it justice, whether these are polemical, like 'heresy' or 'demonic human caricature', or meant positively, like 'preparation for the gospel' or 'natural knowledge of God'. No, just as Islam already had a special position in Israel's testimony to itself, an enigmatic hybrid position as a son of Abraham who was set apart and yet blessed, exiled and yet loved, so Christians must also reflect once again about Islam in religious and theological terms, in a new way, different from before, if they are to be serious about their belief that God guides the fates of all peoples and pursues only one plan for realizing his salvation with humanity.

Therefore theologically Islam cannot simply be treated like all the non-biblical religions. It must occupy a theologically constitutive role in the church's reflection on itself if the biblical testimony of faith is taken with full seriousness. And one need only compare Judaism, Christianity and Islam with the non-biblical religions of Asian origin to realize fully the inner affinity of the three Abrahamic religions. Hans Küng has rightly pointed out: 'One need only face representatives of the Indian and Chinese currents of religious systems in ecumenical dialogue in the company of Jews and Muslims to be aware how much is common to Jews, Christians and Muslims, despite all their disputes. They share a broadly similar basic understanding of God, of human beings, of the world and of world history. This is a kind of Abrahamic ecumene, which is founded on a long history and which cannot be obliterated by all the hostility and wars.'[14]

Other representatives of present-day theology also emphasize the special bond between the three great Abrahamic religions. Thus the Catholic Old Testament scholar from Munich, Manfred Görg, has recently pointed out in an urgent plea: 'Abraham is really one of those crystallizing figures in whom one can best bring together Judaism, Christianity and indeed Islam, because Abraham is regarded as "father" of these three great religions. So "blessing" means that through attachment to Abraham, to Abraham's bosom, something like a form of communication comes about which can bind the religions and the peoples together. Thus the promise is aimed at this universal claim that in links back to and remembrance of a figure like Abraham, something quite tremendous happens; that the religions of the nations which are so divided, which in the course of time have again and again forgotten their origin, find themselves again most easily when they concentrate on this exemplary figure of the just man which is quite different from the human rulers who are used as idols.'[15]

But we shall only make progress over a theological link between Judaism, Christianity and Islam if we take with full seriousness the scriptural testimony about Abraham and Ishmael which I brought together at the beginning of this chapter. Here reference should be made to the work of the French Catholic theologian and Islamic specialist Youakim Moubarac, who is indebted to the spirit of his great teacher and pioneering Catholic orientalist Louis Massignon. All his academic life, this great French scholar (1893–1952), who wrote major studies of Islamic mysticism, reflected on the 'Abrahamic mystery' of Islam, and in his love for the depth of Islamic spirituality argued for a Copernican shift in the approach to Islam in Christian theology: from mission to dialogue. We owe to Massignon a saying about the three religions which has become famous: Israel is 'rooted in hope', Christianity 'dedicated to love' and Islam 'centred on faith'.[16] Moreover the epoch-making declaration of the Second Vatican Council about the great importance of the faith of Muslims is greatly indebted to the influence of Massignon, whose understanding of Abraham is expressed in one of his key texts on 'The Three

Prayers of Abraham' (1949).[17] In his spirit, Christian-Muslim dialogue has been carried on since the 1950s by Louis Gardet, Youakim Moubarak, Giulio Basetti-Sani and Herbert Mason.

Of course Moubarac, too, speaks out against levelling down the special relationships in the history of the covenant in the internal relationship between Judaism, Christianity and Islam, as though as a Christian one could construct a special salvation history which by-passed Christ. But he has explicitly pleaded for a theological evaluation of the Genesis texts about Ishmael in the context of God's promise, election and covenant and thus for a consideration of Islam as real 'Abrahamism' in the biblical sense, not merely as 'Ishmael-ism', i.e. as the faith of some 'pagan' people. If we make this theological evaluation, then according to Moubarac we will arrive at a perspective like this. The 'great realities of the promise, the election and the covenant . . . will proclaim God's generosity towards any privilege of tribe and class. In the light of this generosity, not only according to the gospel but also according to the promise given to Abraham, it must be assumed that all are excluded by sin and all redeemed by grace. Moreover there is a change to the Abraham parable of the two sons in the similar parable of the gospel, where the one who has excluded himself subsequently becomes the father's beloved son. Similar considerations relativize, indeed finally evacu-ate, Muslim Ishmaelitism on the same basis as the Jewish sense of exclusiveness and the Christian sense of being an elite. This critical examination of what is said in scripture on the theme of Abraham must necessarily prompt a rethinking of the idea of the uniqueness and consequently narrowness of a so-called sacred history in the relationship as profane and the lack of the possibility of differentiat-ing in it as disastrous. The exemplary character of sacred history itself could lead to the recognition of other examples, instead of veiling them or excluding them.'[18]

In this sense of recognizing 'other examples' in the history of God's blessing, as a Christian one will not only find an ecumene between the three Abrahamic religions of ethical and practical use, but will also have to affirm it theologically. As is well known, God's Spirit, for Christians identical with the Spirit of the risen and exalted Jesus Christ, cannot be domesticated in the church, as scripture already shows. There is this 'mysterious complementarity between the three Abrahamic religions'.[19] And since for Christians the basis for an Abrahamic ecumene lies in scripture, it is not simply a random human matter. Rather, there are deeply religious reasons which argue for such an ecumene. To put it more precisely: an Abrahamic ecumene does not primarily correspond to human strategies, peace programmes or a good social will, but to God's intent with humanity. That means there is all the greater need to support strategies of tolerance, peace, reconciliation and social justice.

So it is particularly important for Christians to listen to the testimony of faith borne by Israel. If they do, they will have to take seriously not only the history and fate of the old covenant people, but also the history and fate of that people which through the proclamation of the Prophet Muhammad as set down in the Qur'an came to believe in the God who is the God of Abraham, Isaac and Jacob and the Father of Jesus Christ. They will constantly remember that the son of Abraham whom Muslims regard as their primal father, Ishmael, contrary to all human will, stands under the special protection and blessing of God – despite his harsh fate as the outcast and abandoned son of Abraham. In interpreting the history of their own faith they will not only never forget that Jesus Christ is a 'son of Abraham' and Christians become children of Abraham through faith in Jesus Christ, but – without blurring the differences – will always treat with great respect the son of Abraham and his descendants whose mother in her greatest need received from God the promise 'I will make you a great people', and about whom scripture unmistakably says, 'God was with the lad'.

Here is the deepest theological reason why Christians must also take seriously the testimony of faith of a further son of Abraham, Muhammad, who shook his people and other peoples out of religious indifference, idolatry, rootedness in this world and social injustice and confronted them with the 'faith of Abraham', in a God who is incomprehensible in his grace and unpredictable in his freedom. For without harmonizing the Bible and the Qur'an and thus concealing the contradictions or speculating on a salvation history which by-passes Christ, they will recognize in the rise of Islam the Spirit of God, who for Christians is the Spirit of the risen and exalted Jesus Christ. Just as the ongoing existence of a living Judaism forced Christians to rethink their theology, so too must Islam, which has continued to exist for almost 1400 years, be regarded as a sign of God not only for Muslims but also for Jews and Christians, one which admonishes them to reflect. So the questions which Cardinal Carlo Maria Martini, Archbishop of Milan, raised in

1990 in connection with the topic 'We Christians and Islam' need to be pursued further by theologians: 'What have Christians to think of Islam? What does it mean for Christians from the point of view of salvation history and the fulfilment of the divine image in the world? Why has God allowed Islam as the only great historical religion to develop six hundred years after Christ, especially as some of the first witnesses regarded it as a Christian heresy, a branch cut off the one identical tree? What meaning in the divine plan can the origin of a religion have which in some ways is closer to Christianity than the other historical religions, and at the same time so militant, so capable of conquest, that some fear that by the power of its witness it can make many proselytes in a Europe which has lost its power and lacks values?'[20]

Abrahamic ecumene: Muslim perspectives

Islam, too, for centuries found it difficult to adopt more than a basically triumphalistic and paternalistic attitude to Christians and Jews. I have already reported the theologically conditioned difference between unbelievers and those of other faiths in the Qur'an and the legally inferior status of Jews and Christians in the context of Muslim society; I have also mentioned later Muslim exegetes who supported the Islamic claim to absoluteness as an exclusive way to salvation with the aid of a theology of abrogation and supersession which in no way fell short of that of Christian theologians.[21] Nor should anyone have any illusions that in present-day Islam, too (especially in the Arab heartlands), there are influential representatives who publicly adopt an aggressive attitude to Jews and Christians, who continue the apologetic polemic tradition of Islamic theology and pursue a policy of total confrontation with other religions.[22]

But none of this should obscure a view of the inner pluralism of contemporary Islam. Here, too, for a long time voices have been raised in support of co-operation between Jews, Christians and Muslims on equal terms. For this they can appeal to the Qur'an itself, which affirms the actual plurality of religions, itself carries on a constant 'dialogue' with non-Muslims and has given clear instructions for good relations in dialogue with non-Muslims. The Qur'anic basis for an Abrahamic ecumene can be found in Surah 3.64:

Say: 'O followers of earlier revelation! Come unto that tenet which we and you hold in common: that we shall worship none but God, and that we shall not ascribe divinity to aught beside Him, and that we shall not take human beings for our lords beside God.' And if they turn away, then say: 'Bear witness that it is we who have surrendered ourselves unto Him.'

Thus according to Fazlur Rahman it is the Qur'an itself which 'envisages some sort of close co-operation between Judaism, Christianity, and Islam and invites Jews and Christians to join Muslims in such a goal' – 'with the aim of balance'.[23]

On this basis, present-day Muslim theologians can argue for what is in fact an 'Abrahamic ecumene' (even if the term seldom appears among them). Here one could refer to a 'cloud of witnesses'.[24] I shall mention just a few. Thus one of the most distinguished Muslim women theologians of our time, Riffat Hassan, who was born in Pakistan and teaches in the United States, argues: 'Anyone who has reads the Qur'an without bias is aware that Islam is truly universal in its ideals. In this context it is interesting to note that whilst the Old Testament frequently talks of the God of Abraham, Isaac and Jacob, the Qur'an never does. It describes Islam as the "Din" of Abraham and the other Prophets but does not describe God as God of Abraham or the God of Muhammad . . . To Muslims, Abraham is the embodiment of the universalism implicit in Islam, and it is the Abrahamic spirit which enables Muslims to become "witnesses for humanity" (cf. Surah 22.78).'[25]

Other Muslim theologians from Germany, Egypt and Tunisia have argued for a co-operative relationship between Jews, Christians and Muslims in this spirit of Abrahamic universalism. Thus the head of the central institute of the 'Islamic Archive in Germany', Muhammad Salim Abdullah, one of the few Muslim dialogue partners available in Germany, writes in his book *Islam. Towards the Dialogue with Christians* (1992): 'It is the awareness of the common heritage of faith which opens up the possibility of feeling what divides us to be less painful, of meeting in peace and friendship beyond what divides us. But the Qur'an also says that one of the most important basic presuppositions for dialogue is that the partners should be equal and have equal rights. Neither should missionize or seek to commandeer the other, to deny him the holiness of his testimony. The one is not to lord it over the other: God alone is the

Lord. God alone establishes convictions and salvation, God alone
makes someone capable of giving testimony; no one can be his
counsellor. The Qur'an admonishes people of the most different
faiths not to sing the praise of God against one another but with one
another.'[26] And as far as an 'Abrahamic ecumene' is concerned:
'Jews, Christians and Muslims can come together as a dialogue
community, as a community sharing a meal or as a competitive
community.'[27]

A 1981 book by two Egyptian Muslim theologians, the Egyptian
Minister of Religion Abdel Munim Al Nimr and the diplomat
Hamdy Mahmoud Azzan, *Islam: The Plea of a Muslim*, also moves
in the same direction. They remark: 'Islam contents itself with
proclaiming the teaching and its message, leaving it completely free
to people whether or not they believe in it of their own free judgment.
Islam commends its faithful to act peacefully towards the "people of
the book" – Christians and Jews. "Always speak courteously with
the 'people of the book' (Surah 29.46)." Muslims are required to live
in friendship with Jews and Christians and to make it possible for
them to honour and worship God in freedom in their own way. Their
places of prayer and religion in an Islamic state are to be protected;
they are guaranteed the same rights as Muslims, and they are to be
equal citizens of such a state. The obligations of Muslims towards
Christians and Jews are binding on them; they have to be responsible
for them before God in this life and the next.'[28]

A pioneer of more recent Islamic-Christian dialogue, the Tunisian
scholar Muhammad Talbi, even uses the word 'ecumenism' directly.
In his contribution to a Muslim-Christian dialogue in 1992 he
declared: 'Certainly we cannot deny our differences. But if we
succeed in toning down our divergences a little and increasing our
convergences without making concessions to what we cannot go
back on, what we cannot be reconciled to and what we cannot
negotiate on, it will help us together to deepen our converging values
of faith, which are not to be treated lightly. In this way we can
support that co-operation which Jacques Berque calls living
together, common effort and mutual ecumenism, an ecumenism
which has its first roots in unshakeable trust in the one who willed
that the universe, supported and made fruitful by people of different
kinds, should have a meaning and be meaningful . . . Let us begin in
the expectation that we shall be enlightened as to our differences –
like Abraham, with our trust in God: in attentive listening to his

word, with a hope which does not know any giving up, which means neither a lack of care nor a sleepy indifference.'[29]

The 'Brotherhood of Abraham' in France. And elsewhere?

It is clear from all these voices that to argue for an Abrahamic ecumenicity is not to paint over or level out the differences which divide Judaism, Christianity and Islam, but to express them in the right spirit. It means that such dialogue should not be carried on with an arrogance about salvation and a feeling of self-satisfaction at being in the truth, but in a spirit of respect for the different testimonies of faith and the different ways of faith – in brotherly and sisterly concern for one another. And how can one better express one's concern than by attempting to learn as much as possible from others, precisely because the brothers and sisters have lived apart for so long? So Abrahamic ecumene is also an ecumene of learning, of studying, of spiritual exploration of one another's religion, culture and civilization. There can be no theological understanding without a comprehensive knowledge of one another and an abiding mutual readiness to learn. There can be no Abrahamic ecumene without taking seriously the self-understanding of the other and listening to the other, rather than simply looking at the other from one's own perspective. That is often wearisome and in the everyday life of a Jew, Christian or Muslim it is inconvenient; but the Abrahamic ecumene cannot be had any cheaper. Those who are committed to it will first fight their own often terrifying ignorance about the other traditions, work to demolish caricatures and prejudices, and not accept from another as certain and final anything that does not correspond to their own self-understanding.

The Fraternité d'Abraham, the 'Brotherhood of Abraham', which has been involved in the work of inter-religious understanding in France since 1967, has produced a splendid testament to this ecumenicity of mutual learning, studying and spiritual exploration. Under the patronage of the leaders of the three great religious traditions in France, this Fraternité d'Abraham has given itself the task of encouraging the 'spiritual, moral and cultural values of the Abrahamic tradition' and 'deepening understanding of one another, protecting and furthering social justice and moral values, peace and freedom'. In a manifesto this organization has described its self-understanding like this:

Three world religions, three monotheistic religions, namely Judaism, Christianity and Islam, refer explicitly to the same patriarch: Abraham. Whether on the basis of tradition, like the descendants of Ishmael and Israel, or whether, like Christians, on the basis of a purely spiritual descent, all regard themselves as children of Abraham. The apostle Paul says: 'All who believe are children of Abraham.' So millions of believers are united in the memory of one and the same person, father of their peoples, a model of faith in the one God, of fundamental significance for their religions. The Qur'an sees him as 'a leader, a man dedicated to Allah, who was elected and guided on the right way'.

In a world which is divided, incessantly threatened and all too often shaken by rivalry and hostility among the nations, it therefore seems more than ever time for all those who see 'Abraham the believer' as the founder of their own religion, indeed of their very selves, to come together as brothers and sisters in a peaceful way. Jews, Christians and Muslims share faith in God, but also faith in God's benevolence, which is extended to all men and women, in his mercy and his generous hospitality. Why should they not then work together to create a world of brothers and sisters? That would be the best testimony to the earnestness and truth of their belief in the God of Abraham, Isaac and Jacob that they could give to others. It would also be the best answer to those who have declared religion to be the opium of the people.

That the affinity of all those who share 'the faith of Abraham the believer' may appear in the hearts of today's masses as a ferment of peace and mutual help which would be capable of provoking enthusiasm and generosity in the service of all truly human concerns – isn't that the most convincing testimony that the world could expect of them? Consequently some Jews, Christians and Muslims have resolved to join together to become aware of all that, from Abraham on, is their common spiritual and cultural heritage, and also to work together for real mutual reconciliation. It concerns those who in whatever form are descendants of Abraham, with the aim of freeing the world from the evils of hatred, fanatical acts of violence, pride in race and blood, and by showing it the authentic and divine sources of a brotherly humanism.[30]

To my knowledge, there is as yet no such permanent, institutionalized Fraternité d'Abraham in either English-speaking or German-speaking countries – though this remark is not meant to disparage the work of numerous dialogue groups, study groups and dialogue centres. But the city of Barcelona, for example, shows how difficult it is to establish such a permanent, institutionalized organization. In connection with the 1992 Olympic Games a special building was erected there for inter-religious services and meetings with the promising name 'Centro Abraham'. But after the Games this building, which was also unique architecturally, did not continue as a centre for inter-religious ecumenicity in the spirit of Abraham; it was converted into a Catholic church. Evidently people in Barcelona have no use for buildings which symbolize the origin of the great religions in the one God – regardless of the fact that thousands of Muslims and hundreds of Jews also live in Barcelona.

In Germany in particular such a Fraternité d'Abraham would be of decisive social significance, given the fragile social situation between Germans and Turks on the one hand and Germans and Jews on the other. In particular, people on all sides committed in the spirit of Abraham (who now already meet in numerous study groups and dialogue groups) could make a more effective contribution towards ensuring that the disastrous seeds of xenophobia, racism, nationalism and fanaticism do not produce shoots again. A publicly visible and effective network of an Abrahamic ecumene could ensure that conflicts were nipped in the bud, specific aid programmes were developed, the work of enlightenment was furthered and a spirit of co-operation, understanding and help was disseminated. Indeed, a concrete political practice in society and politics must follow from the theological need for an Abrahamic ecumene. Here it will be decisive theologically whether Jews, Christians and Muslims stop describing one another as unbelieving, apostate or superseded and begin to accept one another as brothers and sisters in the spirit, together on the way to the God who is greater, after the model of their ancestors Abraham, Hagar and Sarah.

If Jews, Christians and Muslims today accept one another as children of Abraham, this acceptance can be made specific in three great areas: in the sphere of belief in God, in peace work and in spirituality. So to end this book I shall go on briefly to sketch out some outlines here as well.

3. Trust in God beyond intolerance and idolatry

If Jews, Christians and Muslims can accept one another as 'children of Abraham', if in this sense they are capable of an ecumene in the spirit of Abraham, then they will constantly deepen this ecumenical fellowship by reflecting on the meaning of faith in the one true God: the God whom Abraham did not give up in a long life of trust, despite all the pressures. And the book of Genesis tells us of this God of Abraham. Now we can take it up once again and develop what was already hinted at at the beginning of this book on Abraham.

Faith in God without impatience

If we do not just read the Abraham story in Genesis through the lenses of tradition but rather attempt to let Abraham speak as Genesis makes him speak, it becomes clear that Abraham believed in his personal God, whom moreover the book of Genesis always calls the 'God of Abraham'. But Abraham was not what above all the traditions of Judaism and Islam have made him: a militant and intolerant destroyer. Certainly, the book of Genesis unambiguously reports how Abraham worshipped his God, put his trust in him and held fast to him even when this God required the utmost of him: the sacrifice of the son for whom he had had to wait so long and painfully. But there is one thing that the book of Genesis does not report: Abraham's intolerance to other forms of faith, his intolerance towards people who worshipped their god in their own way. The Abraham of Genesis is not an apocalyptic fighter, a fanatical exclusivist, a raging iconoclast.

On the contrary, these primal stories about Abraham display – as we have heard – a marked family atmosphere, without exclusiveness, intolerance or polemic against other religious practices. What prevails is a family religion which was in no way exclusive. Abraham can worship his God without denying others the right to worship their gods. Moreover, right at the beginning of his entry into Canaan he builds an altar to his God (explicitly alongside the cult places of other gods). He follows his God and allows the existence of other gods. We do not hear a word about Abraham having gone through the hill-country of Palestine to root out the altars of other gods, as was later commanded in one of Israel's religious laws (12.2f.). Only through the book of Joshua, at the end of ch.24, which is influenced by Deuteronomy, is for the first time an exclusivism about God introduced into the Abraham story. This matches the experiences of later Judaism, but not the reality of its ancestor Abraham. What follows from this for Jews, Christians and Muslims today?

Freedom from the compulsions of religious systems

Conclusions must be drawn from this for the internal relationship of individual believers to synagogue, church or Umma and for their relationship to the non-Abrahamic religions. Here for reasons of space I can do no more than offer hints. For the Christian tradition, at any rate, reflection on Abraham brings an increase of inner tolerance and a capacity for integration. For the early Christian story of Abraham already draws on the experience of freedom from a purely legalistic way of thinking. Abraham had in fact become the legal private property of a single people. In the spirit of God's freedom Christians burst open this bond, opened the frontier.

So according to the Catholic Old Testament scholar Walter Gross, Christian Abraham theology will do justice to its claim only when it becomes capable of this one thing: 'It needs to open up limits which are too narrow to others who also want to belong but are deterred by these barriers. It is not concerned with demarcation but with gaining more people; and above all, it does not safeguard itself anxiously by precepts of the law, but insists on the freedom of grace: it trusts believers and the divine spirit which is at work in them.'[31] Thus, according to the Catholic New Testament scholar Michael Theobald, Christian Abraham theology derives its power of conviction from the recollection that 'with Abraham the Christian community has no achiever, no successful man, nor even a saint or a pious man as a figure with whom to identify, but simply a sinner who owes what he became, namely righteous, not to his own achievement but to the loving, forgiving and renewing word of God which opens up a future for him. But in this way Abraham is also a figure of integration who does not stand out for his achievements, does not oppress anyone with his holiness but rather points everyone to the grace of God which they all equally need. That is worth thinking about today, not only because the church has split into confessions which lack binding figures to integrate them, but also because of our local communities, which among other things, following sociological laws, often succumb to the temptation to become homogeneous, thus shutting people out of their circle without perhaps specifically meaning to do so.'[32] So this capacity for integration in the spirit of Abraham is the test case for the credibility of the 'Abrahamic ecumene' from a Christian perspective.

A test case for Abrahamic credibility with respect to Islam is beyond doubt the problem of human rights. This can only be hinted at here – without any Christian self-righteousness. For we must not forget that it was the Christian churches which for about 150 years refused to give theological legitimation to the Universal Declaration on the Rights of Man propagated by the American and French Revolutions.[33] But to note this does not free us from the need to refer to the problem of human rights in many Islamic countries[34] – a problem which is even self-critically conceded by Muslims.[35] Thus for example the 1979 constitution of Iran does not have any universal basic law on religious freedom. Religious minorities like the Bahai have virtually no rights there. Particularly also in civil law, especially relating to the person (here Turkey and Tunisia are the exceptions), Islamic law (the Shari'a) is in conflict with the United Nations Declaration of Human Rights, since both Christians and Jews are still prevented by law from marrying Muslim women, whereas a Muslim may marry a Jewish or a Christian women; by law, marriage between Muslims and 'polytheists' is quite impossible.

The problem of 'apostasy' is also a particular burden on inter-religious dialogue.[36] Recent cases, like the death threat on Salman Rushdie issued by Ayatollah Khomeini or the execution of the Sudanese reformer Muhammad Taha (in 1985 in Sudan, under the regime of General Numeri), show a blatant contrast between traditional Islam and universal human rights, which has not been removed even by the 1981 Universal Islamic Declaration of Human Rights made by the Islamic Council for Europe or the Islamic Declaration of Human Rights by the Organization of the Islamic Conference (Cairo 1990, which in part has been further accentuated).[37]

But Abrahamic unity requires one thing in particular: respect for others (particularly dissidents in one's own tradition) in their full human dignity, and a concern to implement human rights. An Abrahamic ecumene which first produced enemies inside or outside and then segregated them or even persecuted them would be a contradiction in terms. In the original biblical record isn't Abraham himself a stranger, an outsider, yet one who is elected by God? Isn't Abraham in all traditions called the friend of God, the man with whom God has a special friendly relationship and who in this way can teach friendship to God? Doesn't the Qur'an say that Abraham was 'clement, most tender-hearted and intent upon turning to God again and again' (Surah 11.75)? And wouldn't the three traditions contradict their own origin if they made Abraham exclusively a friend of the synagogue, the church, or the Umma or a militant champion against enemies within?

No demarcation against non-Abrahamic religions

Indeed, if one takes the spirit of the Abrahamic capacity for integration seriously, then Jews, Christians and Muslims will never demarcate their common faith in a fanatical and intolerant way against other forms of faith. An Abrahamic ecumene at the expense of, say, Hindus or Buddhists, would be a betrayal of the cause of Abraham. To absolutize the Abrahamic religions is contradictory to Abraham. No exclusivist and absolutist policy of religion can be carried on with Abraham. For despite the resoluteness of his confession of his God, the Abraham of Genesis does not call for any aggressive demarcation against other forms of faith, let alone the aggressive annihilation of them. So it is impossible to conceive of Abrahamic ecumene as a monotheistic bulwark against the non-Abrahamic religions, as if these were a priori an expression of reprehensible superstition.

The Christian theologian Theo Sundermeier, who has had considerable experience both in theoretical and in practical mission and dialogue, is therefore quite right in insisting that the Abraham story today must be seen in the context of the pluralism of the religions. So Abrahamic ecumene must not lead to the segregation of the non-Abrahamic religions. This Protestant theologian has rightly pointed out: 'Abraham has no claims to power nor does he project them on his picture of God. He does not seek to rule. He resists striving for power, the deepest human temptation. Anyone who is on the way cannot rule. He puts up his tent at Shechem, according to Luther's translation by the "oak of Moreh". That sounds homely, almost idyllic. The reality is different. He puts up his tent by an oracle tree, i.e. by a Canaanite sanctuary. But here we do not have some zealous man of God cutting down the Donar oak, nor does he make any great detour round the sanctuary of other religions. Here, at the very place where people are accustomed to worship God in another way, he too prays. He does not condemn the sanctuary of the others, but he does not worship the God venerated there either. He hears the voice of *his* God, as later at Bethel. He builds a new altar next to the one that already exists. The common features and the differences become clear. Abraham himself evidently did not see this sharing as a danger, like other generations after him.'[38]

It may be worth reading the Abraham story in Genesis in this way once again, in the interest of the biblical theology of religions which is so urgently needed. Here too we shall make surprising discoveries – first of all in two key scenes: Abraham's encounters with King Abimelech and with the Jerusalem priest-king Melchizedek. The scene with Abimelech king of Gerar (Gen.20.1–18) is surprising in terms of the history of the tradition but also typical of Abraham's readiness for peace. It is the second scene in which Abraham passes off his wife Sarah as his own sister. Why? Out of anxiety that in Gerar there would be 'no fear of God' and that people would kill him because of Sarah's beauty. And indeed Sarah is promptly carried off by Abimelech into his harem. But God – according to this story – reveals the true state of affairs (this woman is married) that same night in a dream and threatens Abimelech with death. Repentant and terrified at the same time, he says to Abraham, 'Why did you lie and deceive me?' Indeed, the king gives Abraham rich presents, so that he now intercedes 'as a prophet' (20.7) for the king before God and dissuades God from punishing him.

This is a strange story, strange because of the surprising change of perspective which it contains. For it is Abraham who first appears in an unfavourable light here. His trick aimed at his survival has brought the innocent king into mortal danger. And it is the pagan, Canaanite king, whom Abraham had at first thought to have no fear of God, who in the end proves to be more godfearing than Abraham. Personally innocent and anxiously concerned to fulfil the will of God, in the end this king is more righteous than Abraham, whom God also requires to excuse the innocent king. Moreover, commentators have rightly spoken of a 'universalistic feature in this story', since here it is shown 'that there can be "fear of God" also outside Israel' and that 'an attitude of reverence can be found even with a Canaanite king'.[39] Furthermore, it is fundamentally 'humiliating for Abraham' to be 'surpassed by the Gentiles in the fear of God'.[40]

However, even more challenging is Abraham's encounter with the high priest of the Canaanite sanctuary at Jerusalem, with Melchizedek (Gen.14.18–20). For here it is indeed striking that Abraham, who has just been successful as leader in a war, not only accepts a blessing and gifts (bread and wine) from such an idolater, but gives this priest of the god El-elyon 'a tithe' of his plunder, which amounts to the recognition of a claim to possession, a right of sovereignty. This is indeed an amazing story, of which Gerhard von Rad already remarked: 'Such a positive, tolerant estimation of a Canaanite cult, outside Israel, is unprecedented elsewhere in the Old Testament.'[41]

Moreover this is the point to introduce a discussion which the American Jewish theologian Jakob Petuchowski sparked off in 1979, in which he even called Melchizedek an 'archetypal ecumenical figure'. For it had also struck Petuchowski that the Bible takes it for granted that in the time of Abraham there was a non-Hebrew priest of God Most High by the name of Melchizedek. Even Abraham does not refuse to pay his respects to such a pagan priest. According to Petuchowski, this raises the theological problem whether according to the testimony of scripture Jew and non-Jew do not have equal religious rights before God. To resolve this problem Petuchowski, too, refers to the rabbinic discussion about the Noachide commandments and the 'just among the nations'. In that case Melchizedek in particular could be understood as one of those who, while not standing in the covenant line which runs through Abraham and Jacob/Israel, is one of the righteous from among the nations through God's covenant with Noah.

Petuchowski concludes: 'The myth of the Noachic covenant can be of great help to us today in an encounter with the world religions. The rabbinic concept of the "righteous among the non-Jewish peoples" (and its legalistic expression in the notion of the "seven commandments of the sons of Noah"' can serve us as a criterion for judging the non-biblical religions. Here it will probably also remain decisive that the rabbis spoke of the "righteous among the nations" – without thus automatically designating all the nations "righteous". The moral criterion is not abandoned . . . Melchizedek was not a Jew, nor is the Christian a Muslim. Nevertheless the Bible calls him "priest of God Most High" and Abraham gives him the tithe. God has his servants and his priests wherever he wants to have them, even outside the biblical religious communities. And Abraham's descendants will have to learn not to refuse respect to these servants and priests of God.'[42]

In the discussion which followed, the Catholic New Testament scholar Franz Mussner explicitly agreed with his Jewish partner and referred once again to the exchange between Melchizedek and Abraham: Melchizedek blesses Abraham and praises God Most High, and through Abraham himself the nations would then receive blessing. But that links the Abraham narratives specifically with the Noah narratives in Genesis 9, so in the light of the Noah narratives it is not surprising that in Genesis 14 a king of Jerusalem, Melchizedek, a priest of God Most High, appears, who is identified with the 'creator of heaven and earth' and with 'Yahweh' the God of Israel. 'The Melchizedek story in Genesis 14 may first seem to be an "alien body", but in the light of the covenant with Noah, universal contexts of salvation emerge which link the creator God and the God of Israel, draw the peoples into covenant salvation, and indicate that traces of truth are to be found in the world religions, represented by Noah and Melchizedek. God also sees his name glorified in the world religions.'[43]

So we will be moved when reading the meditation on Abraham by the Protestant exegete Claus Westermann, the reflections of someone who – as we have often seen in this book – has done more than other Christian theologians through his Genesis commentaries to shed light on the figure of Abraham today. In the framework of a Christian-Muslim religious dialogue Westermann remarked (and is it quite inconceivable that a Muslim or a Jew could assent to this?):

> Abraham stands at the beginning.
>
> He stands at the beginning in three religions, those of Judaism, Christianity and Islam. Could he, because he stands at the beginning of all three religions, take on new significance at a time when the relationship between the religions is changing in a secularized world?
>
> He could take on new significance only if in the three religions a common element could be found in the understanding of the figure of Abraham. That should not be impossible, if we make it clear to ourselves that Abraham was not an Israelite, nor a Muslim, nor a Christian. He was before all three.
>
> Abraham stands at the beginning.
>
> Therefore much about him was different. Different from the

Israelites, different from the Christians, different from the Muslims. Abraham lived as a member and father of a family; the family was the form of society which determined his existence. There was no further form of society for him extending beyond the family. Abraham belonged neither to a tribe nor a people nor to a religious or cultic community extending beyond the family . . .

On his way through time and space, Abraham's life was life with God. In his life, God was necessary and taken for granted. God gave his life a meaning, God was with him.

This relationship with God was so elemental, so natural, so necessary for him that it did not yet need a special cult separate from everyday life, as theologian and priest. Where it is a matter of life and death, theories about God have to fall silent. The only thing that matters is the reality of God. So this was also a relationship with God which had no oppositions. Throughout the history of the patriarchs there is no trace of a clash with other religions, no trace of polemic against other religions.

Abraham stands at the beginning. There was no greater man. He did not have to show any great achievements. But he is the father. His relationship with God was elemental, and therefore it was necessary. It was concerned with survival, survival on the way through time, survival on the way through space. On this way Abraham held firm to God.

God was with him.[44]

Against idolatry old and new

All these scriptural texts about Abraham, all these interpretations from the Jewish, Christian and Muslim side, yet again emphasize impressively that anyone who as a Jew, Christian or Muslim looks at the Abraham of Genesis does not find a situation of battle but a readiness for peace and a capacity for integration. Abraham is a figure on the frontier, a wanderer and a man in search of God. If Jews, Christians and Muslims remember this, Abraham will never become the guarantor of traditionalism, dogmatism and ritualism. In that case, being a Jew, Christian or Muslim in the spirit of Abraham means being on the way to the God who is always greater, who is incomprehensible; it means being open to the demands of a life before God, being open to God's incalculable presence even with others, with people whom one may even have excluded.

Abraham shows that faith is not something that a person 'has' or 'possesses'; faith means living a life before God under the sign of uncertainty, a life which cannot be controlled. Therefore Carlo Maria Martini is right in remarking in a meditative book on Abraham: 'Abraham is the person who seeks God. Abraham is all those who seek God. Abraham is each of us on his or her way to God, each of us who is on the way to following God's word.'[45] And Youakim Moubarac is right in emphasizing an important element for understanding Islam when he links Muhammad's experience with Abraham's experience, an experience which is also important to Jews and Christians: 'Muhammad recognized himself even more deeply in Abraham on the basis of a common religious situation. It is that of the man in the wilderness, a stranger in the world and alone before God . . . Islam was not born in peace in the father's house, nor has it been created to remain in the house of the legitimate wife. "Islam was born in a strange land," says the Hadith, "and it will end as a stranger: blessed are those who confess this destiny among strangers." This way of looking at the promise and the legacy of Abraham as a condition of spiritual existence is not interesting only for Islam.'[46]

But Abraham's tolerance is not cheap – and here lies the element of truth in those traditions (GenR 38, Surah 21) which depict Abraham fighting against the idols. For here Abraham is not fighting against another understanding of God, another religion, but against idolatry: specifically, that means the demonizing of earthly things which in reality prove to be human fabrications. So Abraham's toleration does not extend to idolatry – then or now. On the contrary, anyone who appeals to Abraham will guard against idolatry in the name of the one true God. And idolatry today no longer appears in the form of the worship of carved wooden idols but in new transformations: nationalism, xenophobia, consumerism, racism and sexism. The German Protestant theologian Martin Stöhr, President of the International Council of Christians and Jews, stated this clearly when opening a conference on 'The Blessing of Abraham in the Holy Land Today' (in July 1993, in Haifa, Israel): 'Abraham is not a convenient father. According to the Midrash Rabba and Surah 21, he destroyed the idols, and one day he tore the masks from things which were not of God but human creations. And the idols did not reply. I am convinced that our idols today are no longer made of clay, like those of father Abraham. I assume, rather, that they consist of the raw materials of prejudice, ignorance and anxiety. But they seem to last a long time, and sometimes they even seem very pious . . . In my own country people have recently been serving the idols of nationalism, xenophobia and antisemitism.'[47]

4. Making peace by partition and treaty

Genesis explicitly reports that Abraham was not only a great fighter but also a great peacemaker. How could Christians, Jews and Muslims ever forget this?

How Abraham made peace

If we follow scripture, Abraham makes peace in two ways: by dividing land or through a peace treaty. The second chapter of the story of Abraham (Genesis 13) already reports Abraham's capacity for making peace. For a dispute had developed between the shepherds of Abraham and the shepherds of his nephew Lot over the best pasture in the land. The land had become too small for both, especially as yet other peoples like the Canaanites and Perizzites had settled here. And what does Abraham do? He makes peace by dividing the land:

> Then Abram said to Lot, 'Let there be no strife between you and me, and between your herdsmen and my herdsmen, for we are kinsmen. Is not the whole land before you? Separate yourself from me. If you take the left hand, then I will go to the right; or if you take the right hand, then I will go to the left . . .' So Lot chose for himself all the Jordan valley and Lot journeyed east; thus they separated from one another (13.8f.).

And who could forget the second peace story? It is the foundation legend of Beer-sheba in the wilderness of the Negeb. For when there was a dispute between Abraham and the Philistine Abimelech over a well, Abraham made a treaty with him which he sealed by giving seven lambs to Abimelech:

> He (Abraham) said: 'These seven ewe lambs you will take from my hand, that you may be a witness for me that I dug this well.'

Therefore that place was called Beer-sheba; because there both of them swore an oath. So they made a covenant at Beer-sheba. Then Abimelech and Phicol the commander of his army rose up and returned to the land of the Philistines. Abraham planted a tamarisk tree in Beer-sheba, and called there on the name of the Lord, the Everlasting God (21.30–33).

Making peace by dividing the land and making treaties. Who could mistake the analogies to the present political situation? Jews, Christians and Muslims regard themselves as children of Abraham, but in concrete instances (Bosnia, Israel-Palestine) they do the opposite to their father Abraham. They get embroiled in cruel battles over one and the same land, which they cannot divide. They are incapable of making peace treaties, since they lack the mutual trust and their hearts are full of mistrust, contempt and hatred. The example of Abraham is torn to pieces and disappears like a puff of smoke in exchanges of fire, carpet-bombing and terrorist attacks.

Voices of peace in the spirit of Abraham

And yet even here there are voices of peace in the spirit of Abraham which offer encouragement, voices of Jews, Christians and Muslims. The British Reform rabbi Jonathan Magonet reports how with his fellow rabbi Lionel Blue he saw to it that in the prayer book for the High Holy Days produced by the Reform Synagogues of Great Britain there should also be a poem by the Israeli writer Shin Shalom (Shalom Joseph Shapira), who was born in Poland in 1904 – in 'awareness of the problem of reconciliation between Israel and the Arab world and the need to express this symbolically within the liturgy'.[48] So on the second day of the great feast of Rosh Hashanah the following poem can be heard in all the Reform Synagogues of Great Britain. In it Shin Shalom swears reconciliation with Ishmael, the ancestor of the Arabs on the basis of his experience in Israel:

Ishmael, my brother,
How long shall we fight each other?

My brother from times bygone,
My brother, Hagar's son,
My brother, the wandering one.

One angel was sent to us both,
One angel watched over our growth –
There in the wilderness, death threatening through thirst,
I a sacrifice on the altar, Sarah's first.

Ishmael, my brother, hear my plea:
It was the angel who tied thee to me . . .

Time is running out, put hatred to sleep.
Shoulder to shoulder, let's water our sheep.[49]

One might also recall 20 November 1977. For decades Israel and
Egypt had waged bloody wars with great losses; the last was just four
years in the past. Bitter enmity prevailed between the two countries.
Then to the bewilderment of the world public the Egyptian State
President Anwar el-Sadat made a journey to Jerusalem and addressed the Israeli parliament, the Knesset. Believing Muslim that he was,
Sadat began his speech by recalling what Jews, Christians and
Muslims have in common. 'I come to you today to shape a new form
of life and to bring peace on a firm basis. We all love this land, this
land of God; all of us, Muslims, Christians and Jews who worship
God. God's teachings and commandments are love, honesty,
security and peace.' Then in the course of his speech, quite
deliberately Sadat recalled the figure of Abraham: 'Fate would have
it that my peace mission to you coincides with the sacred Islamic
feast of the sacrifice of Abraham – peace be with him – the ancestor
of the Arabs and the Jews, the servant of God, who sacrificed his own
son, not out of weakness but out of tremendous spiritual strength
and of his own free will. In this way he personified a fixed and
unshakable belief in ideals which have had great significance for
humankind.'[50]

An Abrahamic peace mission: Anwar el-Sadat

Here Anwar el-Sadat deliberately wanted to bring the Abraham
tradition to light in order also to offer it as a model to Jews and
Christians. For him, Abraham stands for an unshakable belief in
'spiritual power', readiness for sacrifice and the maintaining of
ideals. All this was necessary for the people to be led to new shores.
Sadat's journey shows that deep religious convictions can be a
positive influence on Realpolitik. Realpolitik and spirituality need

not be separate spheres, but can combine for the well-being of the nations. Religious faith can be a torch. However, it should not constantly be carried behind politics, but light the way for politics. Anwar el-Sadat is an example of this.

Indeed how earnest the believing Muslim Sadat was over his peace mission in the spirit of Abraham is attested by an unprejudiced contemporary, the former German Federal Chancellor Helmut Schmidt. His memoirs contain a conversation which he had in the 1970s:

> I will never forget a conversation we had for hours. We were going up the Nile, it was dark, and I think we spent the whole night sitting and philosophizing under a starry heaven. That meant that essentially he did the talking and I just kept putting questions. He told me things that were quite unknown to me at that time – that was almost two decades ago. He told me that in the revelation granted to Muhammad which is recorded in the Qur'an all three religions of the book are treated with great respect. I had not been aware that all three mention the same prophets, with two exceptions: the Torah does not contain the Christian and Qur'anic prophet Jesus, and the New Testament does not contain the Islamic Prophet Muhammad. But otherwise almost all occur in the three sacred scriptures. I was particularly impressed by his description of the way in which all the monotheistic religions of the book had received their revelation on Sinai, how we are all children of Abraham. It must be possible for people once again to be made aware that they all come from the same root. Then it must be possible for them to find peace with one another.[51]

Anwar el-Sadat was indeed a politician who had understood that no permanent peace would be possible without bringing in the religious and spiritual dimension of humanity. For without this dimension there will be no trust to give permanence to treaties desired politically and negotiated legally. Indeed a peace policy built on a religious conviction can shape consciences, seize hearts and move former enemies to repent in quite a different way. 'Islam' then ceases to be the enemy of the West and the 'West' the enemy of Muslims, the screen on to which anxieties, warlike scenarios and apocalyptic dramas are projected. Abrahamic ecumene begins with a removal of the enmity between the children of Abraham. Imaginings finally become real encounters.

But a readiness for peace needs its peace symbols. And the Abraham ecumene needs not only a theological foundation and practical implementation but also symbolic representation: places where Abraham is recalled which do not separate the religions but can bring them together in dialogue and prayer. In the land of Abraham there are two places which have great symbolic significance here.

Places of peace for the children of Abraham: Hebron-Jerusalem?

Let us remind ourselves of what Genesis tells us: Abraham died at the age of 175, 'an old man and full of years', and was buried in the cave of Machpelah near Mamre (present-day Hebron), where he had previously purchased a piece of land. And not only his son Isaac but surprisingly also his expelled son Ishmael stood at his grave. With this text (Gen.25.7–11), Israel has handed down once and for all a scene of gripping symbolism, a picture of the reconciliation of brothers who had been made enemies and yet who were capable of standing side by side beside their common father's body.

Moreover in Arabic Hebron alludes to Abraham: it is called al-Khalil, city of the 'friend' of the merciful God. And Abraham's tomb there is caled Haram al-Khalil. This place is of unique significance both theologically and ecumenically, for all three religions. For here, according to tradition, alongside the tomb of Abraham are also the tombs of Sarah, Isaac, Rebecca, Leah and Joseph. Here the three religions have perpetuated themselves in walls and buildings. In the Middle Ages the area with the tombs became a Christian church, built by using the Herodian foundations and walls. In the Muslim-Mameluk era two mosques were added along the two long sides of this former church. Since 1967 there has also been a synagogue between the tombs of Sarah and Abraham.

Today Hebron, al-Khalil, is on the West Bank, in the Occupied Territories. And, as in Jerusalem, theological symbolism (city of the friend of God) and political reality inexorably classh. Here sons of Isaac and sons of Ishmael stand opposite each other armed to the teeth, as bitter enemies. For years – especially since the Intifada – victims of killings have been the order of the day. As recently as 25 February 1994 an Israeli settler ran amok, inflicting a terrible massacre – by the tomb of Abraham and Sarah. With the declared aim of undermining the peace process between Israelis and Palestinians, this fanatic belonging to an ultra-religious splinter group forced his way into the Ibrahim mosque in Hebron and there fired on Muslims at prayer (!) before killing himself. The result was twenty-nine dead and dozens of injured.

A shock-wave of indignation went above all through those groups in Israel which had set their hope totally on the peace process. Measures were taken to ensure that this peace process, which began so hopefully in September 1993 and was on the verge of treaty arrangements, should not once again founder in blood. The Israeli journalist Uri Avnery rightly put the event in a wider religious and political context. 'After the Temple Mount in Jerusalem the Cave of Machpelah is the most sensitive place in the whole country. According to biblical legend the patriarchs and matriarchs are buried there. Abraham, the legendary father of all Jews and Arabs, bought it to bury his beloved wife Sarah there. Today a building stands there which is sacred to both Muslims and Jews . . . On 24 August 1929 sixty-seven pious Jews were killed by Arabs. Many others were then rescued by Arabs, but the Jewish community was virtually wiped out. After the Six Day War a group of right-wing radical settlers entered and were then settled by the Labour Government nearby in Kiriat Arba. But the extreme ultras established themselves in the very centre of Hebron under the protection of the army. Since then this city has been the scene of uninterrupted acts of violence.'[52] However, in the meantime the ultra-orthodox religious splinter group responsible has been classifed by the Israeli governnent as what it really was: a terrorist organization. It has been banned. For their part, Muslim Palestinian terrorists have taken the Hebron massacre as the occasion for continuing their own murderous policy. In a terrorist attack in April 1994, justified as 'vengeance for Hebron', in the city of Afula eight innocent Israeli citizens became the victims of a bomb attack.

And yet there are still countless people, among both Israelis and Palestinians, who are no longer prepared to let peace be bombed to bits by terrorists. And there are countless people on both sides who have not abandoned hope of a religious understanding. Thus recently Shalom Ben-Chorin has given expression to the vision that this very tomb of Abraham might become a place of ecumenical ecounter: Jews and Muslims united like Isaac and Ishmael by the tomb of their ancestor Abraham, after fighting one another for decades in bitter enmity. And we may in fact ask: is it quite inconceivable that despite all the murder and despite all the hatred, one day what Ben-Chorin depicts for us may take place: 'Ishmael and Isaac were not well disposed to each other, but they united by the body of their father and together buried him in the cave of Machpelah in Hebron. This common action has been forgotten today. The cave of Machpelah is a holy place for Jews and Arabs, or really, not the cave itself but the mosque which rises above it; it is claimed by the Arabs, but beyond question must be taken as also belonging to the Jews. No one today thinks of making this holy place of Judaism and Islam today the scene of ecumenical encounter, which would be very much in keeping with biblical tradition.'[53] Indeed, in an interview Ben-Chorin expressed the hope: 'Abraham had two sons: Ishmael the ancestor for the Arabs and Isaac the ancestor of the Jews. They did not love one another. But by the body of their father in the cave of Machpelah in Hebron they mourned together and became reconciled. It is my hope and my prayer that this reconciliation will be repeated.'[54]

But wouldn't another place of peace and ecumenical reconciliation in the land of Abraham be conceivable: the Temple Mount in Jerusalem (Arabic Haram esh-Sharif)? The Catholic theologian Hans Küng urgently commended this possibility in his book *Judaism* (1991).[55] And indeed this place is of towering theological significance, since Jerusalem is the meeting point of the children of Abraham not only for Jews and Christians, but also for Muslims. Here, as is well known, the First and Second Temples stood – at the place which since the time of King Solomon has ben identified with Moriah (Genesis speaks only in general terms of the 'land of Moriah'). This is the place where according to tradition Abraham was to sacrifice his son Isaac. Since 691 a unique building has stood raised above a gigantic bare rock in the middle of the Temple Mount, the Dome of the Rock (Arabic Kubbat al-Sakhra), the third most important sanctuary of Islam after Medina and Mecca. According to present-day Muslim tradition this Dome of the Rock is the place which commemorates the Prophet Muhammad's journey to heaven, on which – as we heard – according to post-Qur'anic tradition he not only met Abraham but also discovered his own physical resemblance to Abraham. So it may not be coincidence that Muslim tradition locates the heavenly journey of the Prophet here (in Surah 17, which is always cited in this connection, the Qur'an does not give a precise location), since for Jews and Christians this place always had a unique connection with Abraham, whose 'religion' Islam claims to be.

For centuries an exclusivist religious policy has been practised here, and still continues today. Extremist Jewish groups are urging the rebuilding of their temple (for the third time, since in the past nineteen centuries two attempts in this direction have failed). Under Crusader rule (1099–1291), Christians – primarily uninterested in this place 'cursed' by Jesus (cf. Mark 13.2) – used the Muslim buildings meanwhile erected here as a residence (the al-Aqsa mosque) or a church (the Dome of the Rock), thus demonstrating the superiority of Christianity to Judaism and Islam. A church instead of the temple! A church in a mosque! For their part, both before and after the period of the Crusades, up to the present day the Muslims have not merely regarded the Temple Mount as a place of pious remembrance of Abraham and Muhammad. The founder of the Dome of the Rock, the Umayyad caliph Abd al-Malik, had this unique building erected with the aim of demonstrating to Jews and Christians at this very place, in space and architecture, the superiority of Islam.

Moreover any visitor to this extraordinarily impressive place will also sense something almost physical: it is loaded with religious and political energy. Muslims are the proud masters of the place, and every Friday it resounds with the mullahs' cry of prayer. Christians enter this place with mixed feelings, since they cannot simply ignore the fate of Jesus, which was essentially bound up with the temple. And even now an orthodox Jew will refuse to visit it, for fear that he might be treading on the innermost Holy of Holies, the precise location of which is unknown. However, every day hundreds of Jews stand beneath the place at the so-called 'Western Wall', and the air vibrates with their prayers. Often even the Temple Mount is the starting point for terrifying violence. As late as 8 October 1990 there was a shocking massacre of Palestinians here by the Israeli security forces, in which twenty Muslims were killed and dozens wounded.

For understandable reasons, Muslims are over-cautious about accepting ecumenical plans for this place, since they fear loss of control over their third most important sanctuary. So perhaps here Christians more freely than others of their Abrahamic brothers and sisters could invite them to reflect. Christians can argue unselfishly without any self-interest for ecumenical awareness, in the conviction that Abrahamic ecumene is the opposite of a mistrustful policy of religion, intent on demarcation or over-trumping. As I have described it, the foundation of Abrahmic ecumene is a theology of universal peace which rests on respect for those of other faiths. Youakim Moubarak rightly remarks: 'Islam invites Jews and Christians to an understanding between the "peoples of the book". In this way the challenge of Islam presents itself as that of a so to speak practical monotheism which is to be inserted into the ordering of times, in expectation of the day of God's judgment. It is incumbent upon Jews and Christians, the one for reasons of hope, the other for reasons of love, to hasten the approach of this day. Islam, which in no way contradicts, invites Christians rather to show themselves honest and faithfully to keep their word; it invites them to come towards the unity of the world in faith in the God of Abraham. Moreover, the fact that the vast majority of peoples who confess this God coincides with the masses of the Third World gives the invitation a special topicality.'[56]

So wouldn't it be conceivable – after a political and legal agreement governing all 'holy places' – for Jews, Christians and Muslims to gather in the Dome of the Rock on special occasions, to reflect on their tribal ancestors Abraham, Hagar and Sarah and pray to a God whom Abraham and Sarah already worshipped, whom Jesus of Nazareth called his Father and whom the Prophet Muhammad also experienced as a merciful God? This prayer would not of course be part of the official ritual prayer on a Friday, Sabbath or Sunday, but would be informal, spontaneous, free, voluntary. So couldn't this unique Dome of the Rock in particular become a place of spiritual peace for Jews, Christians and Muslims who for centuries have sought to demonstrate their superiority here – thus betraying the legacy of their own tribal ancestors? But has such a proposal any prospect of being taken seriously? After the agreement on a first peace treaty between Palestinians and Israelis in September 1993 an encouraging sign has come from the Muslim side. When the German news magazine *Focus* asked King Hussein of Jordan about the proposal made by the Christian theologian Hans Küng that the Dome of the Rock should be seen as a symbol of divine worship and the unity and reconciliation of the three Abrahamic religions, the king replied: 'Jerusalem can be this place of reconciliation. What I imagine is the spirit addressed here.'[57]

5. Praying together for peace and reconciliation

But can Jews, Christians and Muslims pray with one another at all? I
cannot develop any comprehensive inter-religious theology of prayer
here.[58] It is possible only to give some indications of a practical kind.
But they are indispensable, because many people committed to the
inter-religious ecumene are uncertain and hesitant precisely over this
question. Therefore the following theological points need to be
made.

May we pray with one another?

1. Prayers are not 'places' of theological controversy or artificial
theological syntheses. What has not previously been clarified
theologically cannot simply be the subject of a common prayer. One
cannot simply pray away theological differences. Therefore Christians will never expect Jews and Muslims to join in prayers which use
trinitarian formulae. Conversely, Christians cannot be required to
join in prayers in which the Jewish understanding of the law or the
Islamic understanding of salvation is emphasized in a special way.
When Jews, Christians and Muslims pray together, they do so only
to express common convictions. Here those prayers in particular
may be possible and meaningful which ask God's blessing for peace
and the wisdom to regard the differences between the religions more
closely in the light of the common factors which already exist. So
these will be prayers for God's power and wisdom towards
understanding and reconciliation, since we human beings have
continually proved so weak and petty-minded.

2. Elements of other traditions are already taken up and transcended in the prayer practice of the various traditions. Thus Christians
have already been able to join in prayers which are also dear to
Judaism, particularly the Psalms. So it should not be difficult for
Christians to pray with Jews, taking over prayers from the Jewish
tradition. The Jewish theologian Pnina Navè has compiled an
impressive Jewish prayer book of this kind 'for Christians'.[59]
Conversely, Jews should not have any insuperable difficulty in
speaking prayers from the Christian tradition which still indicate
their Jewish origin: for example, the 'Our Father' which the Jew
Jesus taught his Jewish disciples, the structural elements of which the
synagogue has preserved down to the present day in its own life of

prayer. So Jews and Christians can pray together 'like Jesus'. For Pnina Navè, this specifically means: 'Praying as Jesus taught is listening to brothers and strangers. It is a matter of deriving strength and expanding, reflecting and being able to be alone, in order then wholly to live with and influence others. It is readiness for constant service.'[60]

3. But what about the relationship between Jews and Christians on the one hand and Muslims on the other? After all that we have heard about the theological foundations of an Abrahamic ecumene, the answer can only be that if Christians take seriously the fact that Muslims, too, worship the same God, then they can join with Muslims in praying to this God: the creator of heaven and earth, the merciful and gracious governor of history, the judge and perfecter of the world and humankind. The same may also apply to Jews: if they can recognize the presence of the patriarch Abraham in their other brothers and sisters, then they can pray to this God not only with Christians but also with Muslims. For this purpose Annemarie Schimmel, an orientalist with an international reputation, has compiled a book *Prayers from Islam* (1978), structured on the petitions of the 'Our Father'. The then President of the Vatican Secretariat for Non-Christians wrote a commendation for it: 'But these efforts (at collaboration), which are as necessary as they are often difficult, would as it were lack soul were we to leave out of account prayer, in which common faith in the one God finds its living expression. So the presentation to Christians who pray of the treasury of the prayers of Islam in a selection which is both skilfully and carefully chosen is to be welcomed. And it is to be hoped that this book may do good service as an instrument for bringing Christians and Muslims closer together in the Spirit.'[61]

In numerous meetings of the three Abrahamic religions all over the world, in the meantime there have been not only analyses and discussions between Jews, Christians and Muslims but also prayers. So the Christian theologian Walter Strolz has rightly stressed: 'As far as prayer is concerned, we must note firmly that it was precisely as a result of the mutual freeing of the treasury of the prayers of Judaism, Christianity and Islam that future religious dialogues could take on a broader religious and communal foundation.'[62]

Here it is worth recalling one of the most impressive ecumenical events of more recent church history: the peace meeting of the religions in the city of one of the greatest Christians, who is also venerated outside Christianity, in Assisi, the city of St Francis, on 27 October 1986. Religious leaders from all the great world religions, including representatives of Judaism and Islam, gathered with the supreme head of the Catholic Church. There the religions did not yet pray together, but they did pray at the same time.[63] However, there should be no insuperable theological difficulties for Jews, Christians and Muslims if they were to pray to one and the same God, to whom Abraham already prayed, not only alongside one another, as in Assisi, but together.

The Vatican Secretariat for Non-Christians made a necessary and appropriate comment on this question in 1981, speaking of an Abrahamic hospitality.

It can happen that Christians and Muslims feel the need to pray together, though at the same time they may also discover how difficult that is. Evidently each must respect the ritual prayer and the official cult of its partner without wanting to participate in it directly. It is enough to be a sympathetic witness where one is invited, or to be able to be present where one is asked in the name of Abrahamic hospitality. Here true dialogue requires restraint over importunate invitations. They would be only a cause of misunderstanding. Some would see them as a hidden form of proselytism, others as a form of practical syncretism. The same goes for the reciprocal use of the sacred scriptures and the documents of faith. The Qur'an belongs primarily to Muslims and the Fatiha is their own prayer. Similarly the New Testament belongs primarily to Christians, and like the Our Father is the expression above all of their faith. To avoid any attempt at annexation here is to show deep respet for the faith of another. However, one could think that on one side or the other one could find the necessary boldness, following the examples of mystics and saints, to develop common forms of praise and intercession which allow a common experience of prayer.[64]

How we can pray with one another

The key prayer of the Islamic tradition is in fact the opening surah of the Qur'an, the Fatiha. It was spoken in Assisi, as it has been at other ecumenical meetings.[65] Jews and Christians need have no anxieties here if they constantly remember that this prayer belongs primarily to Muslims:

> All praise is due to God alone,
> the Sustainer of all the worlds,
> the Most Gracious, the Dispenser of Grace,
> Lord of the Day of Judgment!
> Thee alone do we worship;
> and unto Thee alone do we turn for aid.
> Guide us the straight way —
> the way of those upon whom Thou has bestowed thy blessings,
> not of those who have been condemned [by Thee],
> nor of those who go astray.

The same is true of the prayer of Abraham contained in the Qur'an:

> O our Sustainer! In Thee have we placed our trust, and unto thee do we turn: for unto thee is all journey's end. O our Sustainer! Make us not a plaything for those who are bent on denying the truth! And forgive us our sins, O our Sustainer: for Thou alone art almighty, truly wise! (Surah 60.4f.)

Jews in Assisi and elsewhere prayed the following prayer. Christians and Muslims should have no reason not to join in it:

> Our God in heaven, the Lord of Peace, will have compassion and mercy upon us and upon all the peoples of the earth who implore his mercy and his compassion, asking for peace, seeking peace.
> Our God in heaven, give us the strength to act, to work and to live until the spirit from above manifests itself upon us, and the desert becomes a vineyard, and the vineyard is seen as a forest.[66]

In Assisi, Christians used one of the most impressive of St Francis' prayers. Would Jews and Muslims have to dissociate themselves from it?

> Lord, make me an instrument of your peace,
> where there is hatred, give love;
> where there is injury, pardon;
> where there is doubt, faith;
> where there is sadness, joy;
> where there is darkness, light.[67]

In this spirit many spontaneous prayers could also be formulated at ecumenical prayer meetings between Jews, Christians and Muslims. One thing is certain: without prayer there can be no real, spiritually deep ecumene, and without spirituality there can be no ecumenicity. It is high time to work on a Jewish-Christian-Muslim prayer book which could be used on ecumenical occasions and into which could flow all the theological and spiritual experiences arising out of the recent years of ecumenical dialogues between Jews, Christians and Muslims. Such a prayer book would be of great practical significance in particular for inter-religious marriages which will grow more frequent in the future.

Such a prayer book might contain a meditation by one of the greatest mystics of Islam, Ibn 'Arabi, who grew up in the Jewish-Christian-Muslim milieu of Spain. It reads:

> To one whose religion is different from mine,
> I shall no longer say,
> My religion is better than yours.
> For my heart is ready to accept any form,
> to be a pasture for gazelles,
> a monastery for monks,
> a temple for idols,
> the Ka'ba for one who has made a vow,
> the tables of the Torah, the scroll of Qur'an.
> For me there is only the religion of love:
> wherever your ascent leads me,
> love will be my confession and my faith.[68]

And such a prayer book could also contain the prayer which Hans Küng has written for an Abrahamic ecumene:

> Hidden, eternal, unfathomable, all-merciful God,
> beside you there is no other God.
> You are great and worthy of all praise;
> your power and grace sustain the universe.
> God of faithfulness without falsity, just and truthful,
> you chose Abraham your devout servant,
> to be the father of many nations,
> and you have spoken through the prophets.
> Hallowed and praised be your name throughout the world.
> May your will be done wherever people live.

Living and gracious God, hear our prayer:
our guilt has become great.
Forgive us children of Abraham our wars,
our enmities, our misdeeds towards one another.
rescue us from all distress and give us peace.
Guardian of our destiny,
bless the leaders and rulers of the nations,
that they may not covet power and glory,
but act responsibly
for the welfare and peace of humankind.
Guide our religious communities and those set over them,
that they may not only proclaim the message of peace
but also show it in their lives.
and to all of us, and to those who do not belong among us,
give your grace, mercy and all good things,
and lead us, God of the living,
on the right way to your eternal glory.[69]

On the way to Abraham's cause

'O followers of earlier revelation! Why do you argue about Abraham, seeing that the Torah and the Gospel were not revealed till [long] after him? Will you not, then, use your reason? Lo! You are the ones who would argue about that which is known to you . . . Abraham was neither a "Jew" nor a "Christian", but was one who turned away from all that is false, having surrendered himself unto God; and he was not of those who ascribe divinity to aught beside him.' Thus the Qur'an, Surah 3.65–67. We have come to the end of this book, but not to the end of the matter. That lies in the future. For an ecumene between Jews, Christians and Muslims is only at its beginnings. And it will come about only if the truth which is expressed in the Qur'an passage that I have cited is taken seriously and Islam is not excluded from it. 'O followers of earlier revelation! Why do you argue about Abraham, seeing that the Torah and the Gospel were not revealed till [long] after him?' Wasn't Abraham earlier than Judaism, Christianity and Islam? Anyone who takes this question seriously must indeed feel it irresponsible before God for those religions which originally wanted simply to bring to light the faith of Abraham to go on drawing dividing lines between themselves, being hostile to, indeed making war on, one another, and appealing to Abraham in the process. The common origin needs to be uncovered as a source of truth.

In other words, there will be an Abrahamic ecumene only when people in all three religions realize that none of the great traditions can claim Abraham only for itself; none can use Abraham to legitimate the superiority of its own tradition. Abraham is greater than all the Jewish, Christian and Muslim pictures of him. Abraham is a believer in God and thus poses a challenge to all traditions which make use of him to draw their own profiles. Thus Abraham is neither a Jew nor a Christian nor simply an adherent of Islam but the 'friend of God' (according to Isa.41.6; James 2.23; Surah 3.125) who can teach friendship with God. And this friendship with God should not be forfeited by making Abraham exclusively a friend of the synagogue, the church or the Umma.

But those who think ecumenically, as brothers and sisters, in the spirit of Abraham, Hagar and Sarah, have parted company with any exclusivism and thus resolved the paradox of the commandeering of Abraham. They have recognized in gratitude how fruitful the tribe of these ancestors has been all down the centuries. They no longer feel jealousy or exclusion, but only joy at how many different children spring from the one stem and how much substance of faith, energy for hope and power of love have come and still come from the one root. They have drawn a line under a theology which reclaims the blessing of the parents only for its own branch.

An ecumenical dialogue between Jews, Christians and Muslims makes sense only if what stands in the foreground is not the use of Abraham for one's own truth-claim but the cause of Abraham, for which all believers are constantly on the way: turning away from false idols (especially exalting oneself above others) and trusting in the one true God who is always greater than any man-made religious traditions and conventions, a God who 'brings the dead to life and calls into being that which is not'. There will be an Abrahamic ecumene only when Jews, Christians and Muslims all understand one another as *hanifs* like Abraham: as those who seek God, trust in God, are given gifts by God. Children of Abraham are not those who have 'an evil eye, an haughty spirit and a proud soul', but those who have 'a good eye, a humble spirit and a lowly soul', as Jewish tradition puts it. Indeed, if according to the Qur'an Abraham was 'gentle, sensitive and penitent', a descendant of Abraham is one who 'has mercy on people'. In short, for Jews, Muslims and Christians, to believe like Abraham does not mean rigidly to cling on to the past and to inherited possesions, but to go forward, to set out 'without knowing where one is going' (Heb.11.8), to 'hope against all hope' (Rom.4.18).

The future of Europe and the Middle East in the third millenium may well depend on whether or not Jews, Christians and Muslims achieve this kind of Abrahamic brotherhood and sisterhood, whether they are capable, like Abraham, of constantly setting out and thus being a blessing for all humankind. The Cambridge Catholic theologian Nicholas Lash has recently emphasized this decisive theological legacy of Abraham: that the obedience of Jews, Christians and Muslims as descendants of Abraham must play a role in bringing blessing and peace to all the families of the nations on earth: 'It is a matter of some urgency that Jews, and Christians, and Muslims should rediscover a sense of shared responsibility for "all the families of the earth", and should set up whatever processes and institutions for mutual education and collaboration seem best suited to enable this duty to be appropriately discharged.'[70]

Indeed, if Jews, Christians and Muslims practise Abrahamic ecumenicity in this sense, the world will be that much richer in friendliness, righteousness and humanity. The year 2000 would provide a unique opportunity for a demonstration of Abrahamic hospitality and brotherhood and sisterhood worldwide – from the church leaders in Rome, Constantinople, Moscow, Geneva and Canterbury to communities wherever the children of Abraham assemble. Christianity could hardly give a better 'birthday present' to the peoples and religions of the earth.[71] It should be given in the awareness that Jews, Christians and Muslims, like Abraham, believe in the God who brings the dead to life and makes extinct relationships fruitful again.

A special word of thanks

This book was orignally sparked off by my professional involvement in *Judaism*, the book which Hans Küng produced in 1991, within the framework of his project 'No World Peace without Religious Peace'. This already contains a brief but most inspiring section on Abraham and his significnce for Judaism, Christianity and Islam and a first theological foundation for the 'Abrahamic ecumene'. I am particularly indebted to Hans Küng for the stimulation that I received here.

But I owe the hope that a book on this topic will make sense, despite all the difficulties, to my Jewish, Christian and Muslim partners in the International Scholars' Annual Trialogue. We have been meeting annually for years, to discuss together basic questions about Judaism, Christianity and Islam. I am grateful to be able to be part of this ecumenical learning process. And I wanted to express gratitude for this by the dedication in this book.

Our enterprise has been made possible, both financially and organizationally, by the National Council of Christians and Jews in New York which can now look back on a history of more than sixty years (it was described in 1991 by the British ecumenist Marcus Braybrooke in his *Children of the One God. A History of the Council of Christians and Jews*). Founded in 1927, in subsequent decades the National Council did pioneering work towards understanding between Christians and Jews. Here great importance was attached to educational work on the basis of the Jewish and Christian communities. However, the Council was an example not only here, but also in its resolute opening up of the dialogue between Christians and Jews into a trialogue between Jews, Christians and Muslims.

In this trialogue, I am particularly grateful to my fellow-Christian and friend Professor Leonard Swidler of Temple University, Philadelphia, for inviting me to the enterprise. In many conversations I have gained inestimable insights here, about Abraham particularly from my Jewish friends Professor Arthur Green of Brandeis University, Boston, and Professor Rivka Horwitz of Ben Gurion University, Beersheba, and also from my Muslim friends Professor Riffat Hassan of Pakistan, at the University of Louisville, and Professor Fathi Osman of Egypt and Los Angeles.

I must also thank Tübingen colleagues who despite many burdens have critically read through individual chapters at my request and given me important advice: Professor Josef van Ess on Islamics, and Professors Michael Theobald and Christian Dietzfelbinger on the New Testament. I am also grateful to members of my family for reading the manuscript: my father Alfred Kuschel of Oberhausen and my father-in- law Ralf Becker of Rottweil. I have also received encouragement and stimulation from my former long-standing colleague Dr Georg Langenhorst (now in Koblenz) and his successor Georg Fröhlich, who has also been a tremendous help both in obtaining literature and working on the proofs. As always I have been able to rely on Frau Ute Netuschil for her patient and admirably skilful technical work on the many versions of this manuscript.

Karl-Josef Kuschel

Notes

Motto, Preface and Prelude

1. M.J.Bin-Gorion, *Die Sagen der Juden, Mythen, Legenden, Auslegungen*, Berlin 1935, 268.

2. G.Kepel, *La revanche de Dieu*, Paris 1991.

3. S.Ben-Chorin, *Die Erwählung Israels. Ein theologisch-politischer Traktat*, Munich 1993, 127.

4. The historical justification for this concern is given in K.-J.Kuschel (ed.), *Christentum und nichtchristliche Religionen. Theologische Modelle im 20. Jahrhundert*, Darmstadt 1994. Cf. similarly H.Küng and K.-J.Kuschel (eds.), *Weltfrieden durch Religionsfrieden. Antworten aus den Weltreligionen*, Munich 1993.

5. M.Braybrooke, *Pilgrimage of Hope. One Hundred Years of Global Interfaith Dialogue*, London 1992.

6. The following publications are already models for this: *Abraham. Père des croyants* (with contributions by Cardinal Tisserant, R.de Vaux, J.Starcky, J.Guillet, P.Démann, J.Daniélou, B.Botte, P.de Menasce, Y.Moubarac, P.Mesnard, Paris 1952); R.Martin-Achard, *Actualité d'Abraham*, Neuchâtel 1969; id., *Abraham sacrifiant. De l'épreuve du Moriya à la nuit d'Auschwitz*, Aubonne, CH 1988; M.Stöhr (ed.), *Abrahams Kinder. Juden – Christen – Moslems*, Frankfurt am Main 1983; B.Antes, 'Abraham im Judentum, Christentum und Islam', in *Christen und Juden. Ein notwendiger Dialog*, Hanover 1988, 11–15; 'Abraham', in *Lexikon religiöser Grundbegriffe. Judentum–Christentum–Islam*, ed. A.T.Khoury, Graz, Vienna and Cologne 1987, 7–11 (with contributions by P.Navè Levinson, G.Evers and S.Balic); *Abraham*, Paris 1992 (with contributions by E.Moatti, P.Rocalve, M.Hamidullah).

7. For the history of research cf. recently M.Kessler and J.Wertheimer (eds.), *Nelly Sachs. Neue Interpretationen*, Tübingen 1994 (which includes my article 'Hiob und Jesus. Die Gedichte der Nelly Sachs als theologische Herausforderung', 203–24).

8. R.Dinesen and H.Müssener (eds.), *Briefe der Nelly Sachs*, Frankfurt am Main 1984 (abbreviated as *Briefe*), 64, 65.

9. *Briefe*, 88.

10. *Briefe*, 37.

11. *Briefe*, 46.

12. *Briefe*, 51.

13. *Briefe*, 65.

14. *Briefe*, 67f.

15. *Briefe*, 214.

16. J.G.Herder, 'Abrahams Kindheit', in *Sämtliche Werke* XXVI, ed. B.Suphan, Berlin 1882, 334–8.

17. N.Sachs, 'Abram im Salz. Ein Spiel für Wort, Mimus, Musik', in ead., *Zeichen im Sand. Die szenischen Dichtungen der Nelly Sachs*, Frankfurt am Main 1962, 93–122: 97. Cf. also the Abraham poem in ead., *Fahrt ins Staublose. Die Gedichte der Nelly Sachs*, Frankfurt am Main 1961, 88f.

18. N.Sachs, 'Letter to W.A.Berendsohn, 2 April 1952', in W.A.Berendsohn, *Nelly Sachs. Einführung in das Werk der Dichterin jüdischen Schicksals*, Darmstadt 1974, 165.

19. *Briefe*, 66.

20. Sachs, 'Letter to W.A.Berendson, 1 September 1946', in Berendson, *Nelly Sachs* (n.18), 135.

21. For the biographical background to the piece cf. R.Dinesen, *Nelly Sachs. Eine Biographie*, Frankfurt am Main 1992, 162–79; similarly G.Fritsch-Vivié, *Nelly Sachs, Mit Selbstzeugnissen und Bilddokumenten*, Hamburg 1993, 79–81.

22. Sachs, 'Letter to W.A.Berendsohn', in Berendsohn, *Nelly Sachs* (n.18), 135.

23. Sachs, 'Abram im Salz' (n.18), 105.

24. Dinesen, *Nelly Sachs* (n.21), 167.

25. Cf. E.Drewermann, *Tiefenpsychologie und Exegese*, Vol.I, Freiburg im Breisgau 1984, esp.187–200.

26. Sachs, 'Abram im Salz' (n.17), 105.

27. *Briefe*, 171.

28. *Briefe*, 116.

29. *Briefe*, 115.

30. *Briefe*, 202f.

31. With this notion Nelly Sachs already anticipates present-day interpretations of Abraham in terms of depth psychology. The most impressive account of these in German is M.Kassel, *Biblische Urbilder. Tiefenpsychologische Auslegung nach C.G.Jung*, Munich 1980, 208–57.

A.   Abraham as the Possession of Judaism, Christianity and Islam

I. Abraham and Judaism

1. There are instances of this in the extended account of research in C.Westermann, *Genesis 12–36*, Minneapolis and London 1985. Cf. also the

most recent histories of Israel or histories of Israelite religion: H.Donner, *Geschichte des Volkes Israel und seiner Nachbarn in Grundzügen* (2 vols.), Göttingen 1984–6 (esp. I, 73–84); R.Albert, *A History of Israelite Religion in the Old Testament Period* (2 vols.), London and Louisville, Ky 1993, 1994 (esp. I, 23–39). However, the most recent Introduction to the Old Testament by the Catholic exegete F.-J.Stendebach (Düsseldorf 1994) still speaks without further explanation of the 'patriarchs' as 'legendary figures', or as ' "fictitious" ancestor figures' (79).

2. Donner, *Geschichte* (n.1), I, 77.

3. Cf. the most recent investigation by F.Crüsemann, *Die Tora. Theologie und Sozialgeschichte des alttestamentlichen Gesetzes*, Munich 1992, 387–93.

4. P.Weimar, 'Abraham', in *Neues Bibellexikon*, ed.M.Görg and B.Lang, I, Zurich 1991, 18.

5. R.E.Clements, 'Abraham', *Theologisches Wörterbuch zum Alten Testament*, ed. G.Botterweck and H.Ringgren, I, Stuttgart, Berlin, Cologne and Mainz 1973, 60f. Cf. also the informative survey on Abraham in the Old Testament by R.Martin Achard, 'Abraham', *Theologische Realenzyklopädie* I, Berlin and New York 1977, 364–72.

6. Crüsemann, *Die Tora* (n.3), 387.

7. Ibid., 393.

8. Thus the convincing account by the Tübingen Old Testament scholar H.Gese, 'Die Komposition der Abrahamserzählung', in id., *Alttestamentliche Studien*, Tübingen 1991, 29–51.

9. J.van Seters, *Abraham in History and Tradition*, New Haven and London 1975; id., *Prologue to History. The Yahwist as Historian in Genesis*, Zurich 1992; id., 'Abraham', *The Encyclopaedia of Religion*, ed. M.Eliade, I, New York and London 1987, 13–17. Similarly H.H.Schmid, *Der sogenannte Jahwist. Beobachtungen und Fragen zur Pentateuch-Forschung*, Zurich 1976. More recently also C.H.Levin, *Der Jahwist*, Göttingen 1993.

10. Thus R.Rendtorff, *Das überlieferungsgeschichtliche Problem des Pentateuch*, Berlin and New York 1977; E.Blum, *Die Komposition der Vätergeschichte*, Neukirchen-Vluyn 1984.

11. Here I am following Gese, 'Komposition' (n.8), 31, and the still standard Genesis commentary by C.Westermann, Minneapolis and London 1985. The results of the more recent documentary hypothesis still hold firm; cf. J.Scharbert, *Genesis 1–11*, Würzburg 1983, ³1990, 9f.; F.-L.Hossfeld, 'Der Pentateuch', in *Höre, Israel: Jahwe ist einzig. Bausteine für eine Theologie des Alten Testamentes*, Stuttgart 1987, 11–68; Stendebach, *Einleitung* (n.1), 73–123.

12. Cf. B.Beer, *Leben Abrahams nach Auffassung der jüdische Sage*, Leipzig 1859. There is rich material on the life of Abraham in L.Ginzberg, *The Legends of the Jews* I, Philadelphia 1925, 207–69.

13. Donner, *Geschichte* (n.1), I, 79. Similarly M.Weippert, 'Synkretismus und Monotheismus. Religionsinterne Konfliktbewältigung im alten Israel', in J.Assmann and D.Harth (eds.), *Kultur und Konflikt*, Frankfurt am Main 1990, 143–79, esp. 144f. Cf. also M.Weippert, 'Geschichte Israels am Scheideweg', *Theologische Rundschau* 58, 1993, 71–103.

14. Albertz, *History* (n.1), I, 32.

15. Donner, *Geschichte* (n.1), I, 80. Cf. Albertz, *History* (n.1), I, 23–39. For criticism of this thesis of Alt's cf. recently M.Köckert, *Vätergott und Väterverheissungen. Eine Auseinandersetzung mit Albrecht Alt und seinen Erben*, Göttingen 1988.

16. Albertz, *History* (n.1), I, 32.

17. Donner, *Geschichte* (n.1), 75.

18. Albertz, *History* (n.1), I, 29.

19. Albertz, *History* (n.1), I, 32.

20. R.Patai, *The Seed of Abraham. Jews and Arabs in Contact and Conflict*, Salt Lake City 1986, 17.

21. Cf. Crüsemann, *Die Tora* (n.3); Albertz, *History* (n.1), II, 466–70.

22. For the theological problem of laughter cf. K.-J.Kuschel, *Laughter*, London and New York 1994 (especially Part II, 'Human Laughter and the Laughter of God. A Biblical Tableau').

23. Scharbert, *Genesis 1–11* (n.11), 146; Westermann, *Genesis II* (n.11), 270, speaks of a 'universalist trait' in the Priestly Writing.

24. Genesis 12.3c need not be translated as a passive; it can also be a reflexive: 'And in you all the families of the earth shall bless themselves' or 'shall wish for blessing with reference to you'. This need not result in an essential difference in content, as Westermann, *Genesis II* (n.11), 152, has emphasized. Cf. similarly W.Zimmerli, *I Mose 12–25: Abraham*, Zurich 1976, 20. Also Scharbert, *Genesis 1–11* (n.11), 128.

25. Westermann, *Genesis II* (n.11), 152, cf. also on Gen.17.19f., esp. 325f.

26. Cf. E.Haag, 'Die Abrahamstradition in Gen.15', in M.Görg (ed.), *Die Väter Israels. Beiträge zur Theologie der Patriarchenüberlieferungen im Alten Testament*, Stuttgart 1989, 83–106.

27. T.Mann, *Joseph and his Brethren*, I, *The Story of Jacob*, Harmondsworth 1978, 4–9.

28. Thus E.Levinas, 'The Trace of the Other', in M.Taylor (ed.), *Deconstruction in Context*, Chicago 1986, 345–59: 348. Cf. K.Ziarek, 'Semantics of Proximity. Language and the Other in the Philosophy of E.Levinas', *Research in Phenomenology* 19, 1989, 213–27.

29. Cf. O.Kaiser, *Der Gott des Alten Testaments. Theologie des Alten Testamentes*, I, Göttingen 1993, 168–76.

30. Unfortunately, within the narrow framework of this study it is impossible to discuss the further great history of the influence of the Abraham stories. That needs a study on its own. However, see S.Kierke-

gaard, *Fear and Trembling. Didactic Lyrics by Johannes D.Silentio*, 1843; M.Buber, 'Abraham der Seher', in *Werke* II (writings on the Bible), Munich 1964, 873–93. Not only Nelly Sachs but also E.Lasker-Schüler, K.Wolfskehl, S.Ben-Chorin and A.Paris Gütersloh have written notable poems on Abraham. For the history of his influence cf. M.Bocian, 'Abraham', in id., *Lexikon der biblischen Personen mit ihrem Fortleben im Judentum, Christentum. Islam, Dichtung, Musik und Kunst*, Stuttgart 1989, 15–24. For the influence especially of the motif of Abraham's sacrifice cf. P.Tschuggnall, *Das Abraham-Opfer als Glaubensparadox. Bibeltheologischer Befund – literarische Rezeption – Kierkegaards Deutung*, Bern, Frankfurt and New York 1989.

31. E.Wiesel, 'Die Opferung Isaaks: Geschichte des Überlebenden', in id., *Adam oder das Geheimnis des Anfangs. Brüderliche Urgestalten*, Freiburg im Breisgau 180, 75–105: 99, 101.

32. Blum, *Komposition* (n.20), 59.

33. A controversy has developed over the question of the role played by the patriarchs in Deuteronomy and the Deuteronomistic tradition. The negative thesis of T.Römer, *Israels Vater. Untersuchungen zur Väter-Thematik im Deuteronomium und in der deuteronomistischen Tradition*, Freiburg and Göttingen 1990, has been energetically refuted by N.Lohfink, *Die Väter Israels im Deuteronomium. Mit einer Stellungnahme von T.Römer*, Freiburg and Göttingen 1991.

34. Cf. N.Füglister, 'Psalm 105 und die Väterverheissung', in Görg (ed.), *Die Väter Israels* (n.26), 41–59.

35. Cf. E.Zenger, 'Der Gott Abrahams und die Völker. Beobachtungen zu Psalm 47', in ibid., 413–30.

36. For the theology of Ben Sira cf. K.-J.Kuschel, *Born Before All Time? The Dispute over Christ's Origin*, London and New York 1992, 196–9 (with bibliography).

37. S.Holm-Nielsen, 'Religiöse Poesie des Spätjudentums', in *Aufstieg und Niedergang der Römischen Welt*, XIX.1, Berlin and New York 1971, 152–86: 164.

38. Cf. the basic study by M.Hengel, *Judaism and Hellenism*, London and Philadelphia 1974.

39. Ibid., I, 72.

40. Abraham himself appears only on the periphery of the Qumran writings, in the Genesis Apocryphon and the Damascus Document. Texts in J.H.Charlesworth, *Old Testament Apocrypha* (2 vols.), New York and London 1983, 1984. Presumably the Testament of Abraham, a legendary elaboration of the death of Abraham, belongs in the same Essene-Qumranic circle. Text in H.Janssen (ed.), *Jüdische Schriften aus hellenistisch-römischer Zeit*, III.12, Gütersloh 1975, 193–256.

41. The Book of Jubilees, in Charlesworth, *Old Testament Apocrypha* (n.40), Vol.II, 35–142.

42. K.Berger, *Das Buch der Jubiläen, Jüdische Schriften aus hellenistich-römischer Zeit*, II.3, Gütersloh 1981, 298.

43. Jubilees 12.17.

44. Jubilees 12.27.

45. Cf. Jubilees 18.16.

46. Jubilees 15.30.

47. Jubilees 22.23f.

48. For the influence on Islam cf. Chapter III below.

49. For the theology of apocalyptic cf. K.-J.Kuschel, *Born Before All Time? The Dispute over Christ's Origin* (n.36), 207–21 (with bibliography).

50. Thus E.Schürer, *Geschichte des Jüdischen Volkes* III (1909), reissued Hildesheim and New York 1970, 260.

51. The Apocalypse of Abraham, in Charlesworth, *Old Testament Apocrypha* (n.40), Vol.I, 681–706.

52. Apocalypse of Abraham 27.3.

53. Apocalypse of Abraham 8.5f.

54. Apocalypse of Abraham 29.17.

55. For research into Philo cf. W.Haase (ed.), *Aufstieg und Niedergang der Römischen Welt*, XXI/1, *Hellenistisches Judentum in römischer Zeit: Philo und Josephus*, Berlin and New York 1984.

56. Philo of Alexandria, *On the Virtues*, in *Philo* VII, Loeb Classical Library (= LCL), translated by F.H.Colson, London and Cambridge, Mass. 1939; cf. also id., *On Abraham*, *Philo* VI, LCL, 1935, 4ff.; id., *On the Migration of Abraham*, *Philo* IV, LCL, 1933, 132ff.

57. C.Colpe, 'Philo von Alexandrien', in *Die Religion in Geschichte und Gegenwart* V, Tübingen [3]1961, 345.

58. Philo, *On Abraham* (n.56), nos. 275f.

59. Josephus, *Antiquities*, I.13.4. For research into Josephus cf. A.Schalit (ed.), *Zur Josephus-Forschung*, Darmstadt 1973; L.H.Feldman, 'Flavius Josephus Revisited. The Man, His Writings and His Significance', in *Aufstieg und Niedergang der Römischen Welt* XXI/2, Berlin and New York 1984, 763–862.

60. Josephus, *Antiquities*, in *Josephus* IV, LCL, translated by H.StJ.Thackeray, London and New York 1930, 7, 1.

61. Ibid.

62. Ibid.

63. Josephus, *Antiquities* I, 8, 2.

64. Cf. D.Georgi, *Die Gegner des Paulus im 2.Korintherbrief*, Neukirchen-Vluyn 1964, 63–82. Similarly G.Mayer, 'Aspekte des Abrahambildes in der hellenistisch-jüdischen Literatur', *Evangelische Theologie* 32, 1972, 118–27.

65. Georgi, *Die Gegner des Paulus* (n.46), 68.

66. Meyer, 'Aspekte des Abrahambildes' (n.64), 125.

67. Josephus, *Antiquities* I, 17.

68. S.Sandmel, *Philo's Place in Judaism. A Study of Conceptions of Abraham in Jewish Literature*, New York 1971, 75.

69. Ibid., 76.

70. Feldman, 'Flavius Josephus Revisited' (n.59), 796.

71. Ibid.

72. Thus aptly, M.Theobald, *Römerbrief (Kap.1–11)*, Stuttgart 1992, 123.

73. Y.Amir, *Die hellenistische Gestalt des Judentums bei Philo von Alexandrien*, Neukirchen-Vluyn 1983, 24.

74. Georgi, *Die Gegner des Paulus* (n.64), 64.

75. For the concept of paradigms and its application to Judaism cf. H.Küng, *Judaism*, London and New York 1992.

76. Cf. the introductory studies by G.Stemberger, *Das klassische Judentum. Kultur und Geschichte der rabbinischen Zeit*, Munich 1979; id., *Der Talmud. Einführung – Texte – Erläuterungen*, Munich [2]1987; id., *Midrasch. Vom Umgang der Rabbinen mit der Bibel*, Munich 1989; similarly P.Navè Levinson, *Einführung in die rabbinische Theologie*, Darmstadt [3]1993.

77. Sandmel, *Philo's Place in Judaism* (n.68), 211.

78. There is a comprehensive survey of the picture of Abraham among the rabbis in P.Billerbeck, 'Abrahams Leben und Bedeutung nach Auffassung der älteren Haggada', *Nathanel* 15, 1899, 43–57, 118–28, 137–57, 161–79; 16, 1900, 33–57, 65–80; similarly H.L.Strack and P.Billerbeck, *Kommentar zum Neuen Testament aus Talmud und Midrasch*, Vol. III, Munich 1926, [6]1975, 186–217; 'Abraham', *Encyclopaedia Judaica* I, Berlin 1928, 374–405; Sandmel, *Philo's Place in Judaism* (n.68), 77–95; R.P.Schmitz, 'Abraham III', *Theologische Realenzyklopädie* I, Berlin and New York 1977, 382–5; F.E.Wieser, *Die Abrahamvorstellungen im Neuen Testament*, Frankfurt am Main and New York 1987, 153–79 (with bibliography).

79. For this complex of problems cf. Kuschel, *Born Before All Time? The Dispute over Christ's Origin* (n.36), 196–206 (with bibliography).

80. The following editions have been used. Quotations from the Mishnah are from *The Mishnah*, ed. H.Danby, Oxford 1930, and from the Talmud from *The Babylonian Talmud*, ed. I. Epstein (The Soncino Talmud), London 1930ff.; *Midrash Tanḥuma*, Vol.I, *Genesis*, translated by John T.Townsend, New York 1989; *Midrash Rabbah, Genesis* I, translated under the editorship of H.Freedman and M.Simon (= GenR); *The Midrash on Psalms*, translated by William G.Brande, New Haven 1959; *Midrash Rabbah. Leviticus*, ed. H.Freedman and M.Simon, London 1939.

81. *Pirqe de Rabbi Eliezer*, translated and annotated by G.Friedlander, London 1916, 29.

82. *Midrash Tanḥuma, Lekh-Lekha*, Gen.3 on Gen.17.1ff., Part V.

83. GenR.64, ch.26.5. For discussion within Judaism on Abraham and the halakhah see the fine study by A.Green, *Devotion and Commandment. The Faith of Abraham in the Hasidic Imagination*, West Orange, New York 1989.

84. GenR 14, ch.2.7.

85. Cf. Pirqe Aboth, 6.10.

86. GenR 48, ch.18.1.

87. Cf. C.Thoma and S.Lauer (eds.), *Die Gleichnisse der Rabbinen*, Part I, *Pesiqta de Rav Kahana (PesK). Einleitung, Übersetzung, Parallelen, Kommentar, Texte*, Bern and Frankfurt am Main 1986, 264.

88. *Midrash on Psalms* (n.80), Psalm 18.29, p.261.

89. Cf. W.Grundmann, '*deixos*', *Theological Dictionary of the New Testament*, ed. G.Kittel, II (1935), Grand Rapids 1969, 39, with reference to bSanh108b. I am grateful for the reference to this text to H.Kessler, who mentions it in his book *Sucht den Lebenden nicht bei den Toten. Die Auferstehung Jesu Christi in biblischer, fundamentaltheologischer und systematischer Sicht*, Düsseldorf 1985, 344.

90. GenR 95, ch.46.28; 64, ch.26.5.

91. GenR 38, ch.11.28; cf. also bPes.118a.

92. GenR 39, ch.12.5.

93. GenR 39, ch.12.1.

94. Cf. IV Ezra 3.13–19.

95. GenR 55, ch.22.1; cf. a variation of this rivalry between Ishmael and Isaac after the appearance of Islam in Targum Pseudo-Jonathan Gen.22.1.

96. LevR 36 (133C).

97. Cf. the basic study by B.J.Bamberger, *Proselytism in the Talmudic Period* (1939), New York 1968; similarly M.Goodman, 'Proselytising in Rabbinic Judaism', in *Journal of Jewish Studies* 40, 1989, 175–85.

98. *Midrash Tanḥuma, Lekh-Lekha*, Gen.3; Gen.14.1ff., Part I.

99. GenR 46, ch.17.1.

100. *Mechilta. Ein tannaitischer Midrasch zu Exodus*. ed. J.Winter and A.Wünsche, Leipzig 1909 reprinted Hildesheim, Zurich and New York 1990, 305: Mishpatim (Nesikin) 18.22.

101. Examples in J.Petuchowski and C.Thoma, *Lexikon der jüdisch-christlichen Begegnung*, Freiburg im Breisgau 1989, 265–8 ('Noachidische Gebote').

102. *Pesikta Rabbati, Discourses for Fasts, Feasts and Special Sabbaths* (2 vols.), translated by W.G.Braude, New Haven and London 1968, 43.4; cf. GenR 53.9.

103. Cf. S.J.D.Cohen, 'The Rabbinic Conversion Ceremony', *Journal of Jewish Studies* 41, 1990, 177–203.

104. Green, *Devotion and Commandment* (n.83).

105. Pirqe Aboth V, 19f.

106. bBezah 32b.

107. D.Hartman, *Maimonides. Torah and Philosophic Quest*, Philadelphia, New York and Jerusalem 1976, 58, 59.

108. Moses Maimonides, 'Der Proselytet. Ein Gutachten', in id., *Ein systematischer Querschnitt durch sein Werk*, ed. N.N.Glatzer, Berlin 1935, 111–15.

109. J.Petuchowski, 'Abraham', *Lexikon der jüdisch-christlichen Begegnung* (n.101), 4.

II. Abraham and Christianity

1. For the picture of Abraham in the New Testament cf. K.Berger, 'Abraham II', *Theologische Realenzyklopädie* I, Berlin and New York 1977, 372–82; F.E.Wieser, *Die Abraham-Vorstellungen im Neuen Testament*, Bern and Frankfurt am Main 1987; J.Siker, *Disinheriting the Jews. Abraham in Early Christian Controversy*, Louisville 1991 (with bibliography).

2. The range of research into the historical Jesus in recent decades can be read off the titles of two studies in English, C.H.Dodd, *The Founder of Christianity*, London and New York 1970, and J.P.Meier, *A Marginal Jew. Rethinking the Historical Jesus*, New York and London 1991 (though a Catholic exegete like Meier of course means this title as an ironical quotation). A fashionable 'eco-psycho' Jesus has been presented by the German journalist F.Alt, *Jesus der erste neue Mann*, Munich 1989.

3. J.Gnilka, *Jesus von Nazaret. Botschaft und Geschichte*, Freiburg im Breisgau 1990, 195.

4. The key function of Ps.110 for early Christianity has been brought out by M.Hengel, 'Die Inthronisation Christi zur Rechten Gottes und Ps 110, 1', in M.Philonenko (ed.), *Le trône de Dieu*, Tübingen 1993, 108–94.

5. L.Schenke, *Die Urgemeinde. Geschichtliche und theologische Entwicklung*, Stuttgart, Berlin and Cologne 1990, 311.

6. Cf. the most recent study by M.Reiser, *Die Gerichtspredigt Jesu. Eine Untersuchung zur eschatologischen Verkündigung Jesu und ihrem frühchristlichen Hintergrund*, Münster 1990.

7. Cf. the basic article by D.Zeller, 'Das Logion Mt 8,11f. Lk 13,28f und das Motif der "Völkerwallfahrt"', *Biblische Zeitschrift* 15, 1971, 222–37; 16, 1972, 84–93.

8. Thus D.Lührmann, *Die Redaktion der Logienquelle*, Neukirchen-Vluyn 1969, 86.

9. S.Schulz, *Q. Die Spruchquelle der Evangelisten*, Zurich 1972, 244.

10. Reiser, *Die Gerichtspredigt Jesu* (n.6), 221.

11. U.Luz, *Das Evangelium nach Matthäus (Mt 8–17)*, Zurich and Neukirchen-Vluyn 1990, 16.

12. Schenke, *Die Urgemeinde* (n.5), 315.

13. W.Gross and K.-J.Kuschel, *'Ich schaffe Finsternis und Unheil!' Ist Gott verantwortlich für das Übel?*, Mainz 1992, 29f.

14. For the picture of Abraham in Paul cf., in addition to the studies mentioned in n.1, especially: C.Dietzfelbinger, *Paulus und das Alte Testament. Die Hermeneutik des Paulus, untersucht an seiner Deutung der Gestalt Abrahams*, Munich 1961; K.Berger, 'Abraham in den Paulinischen Hauptbriefen', *Münchner Theologische Zeitschrift* 17, 1966, 47–89; H.Boers, *Theology Out of the Ghetto. A New Testament Exegetical Study concerning Religious Exclusiveness*, Leiden 1971.

15. Cf. the most recent study by B.Niebuhr, *Heidenapostel aus Israel. Die jüdische Identität des Paulus nach ihrer Darstellung in seinen Briefen*, Tübingen 1992.

16. For the theology of Galatians cf. K.-J.Kuschel, *Born Before All Time? The Dispute over Christ's Origin*, London and New York 1992, 270–7 (with bibliography).

17. For the understanding of the law in Paul, cf. the precise analysis in H.Küng, *Judaism*, London and New York 1992, 487–504.

18. J.Roloff, *Die Kirche im Neuen Testament*, Göttingen 1993, 125.

19. Ibid.

20. Cf. F.Mussner, 'Theologische "Wiedergutmachung" am Beispiel der Auslegung des Galaterbriefs', in id., *Die Kraft der Wurzel. Judentum – Jesus – Kirche*, Freiburg im Breisgau 1987, 55–64.

21. S.Ben Chorin, 'Predigt zu Gal 4,22–5,17', in F.W.Marquardt, *Aber Zion nenne ich Mutter . . . Evangelische Israel-Predigten mit jüdischen Antworten*, Munich 1989, 45–47: 45.

22. Mussner, 'Theologische "Wiedergutmachung"' (n.20), 59f.

23. H.D.Betz, *Galatians*, Hermeneia, Philadelphia 1980, *ad loc*. The remark by G.Ebeling quoted before this comes from his book *Die Wahrheit des Evangeliums. Eine Lesehilfe zum Galaterbrief*, Tübingen 1981, 255.

24. For the theology of Romans, cf. K.-J.Kuschel, *Born Before All Time? The Dispute over Christ's Origin* (n.16), 300–3. In the meantime further commentaries have appeared on this letter: K.Berger, *Gottes einziger Ölbaum. Betrachtungen zum Römerbrief*, Stuttgart 1990; M.Theobald, *Römerbrief* (2 vols.), Stuttgart 1992–93.

25. F.W.Marquardt, *Das christliche Bekenntnis zu Jesus, dem Juden. Eine Christologie*, Vol.I, Munich 1990, 211f. The more recent discussion on Israel and the church has recently been summed up by H.J.Körner, 'Volk Gottes-Kirche-Israel. Das Verhältnis der Kirche zum Judentum als Thema ökumenischer Kirchenkunde und ökumenischer Theologie', *Zeitschrift für Theologie und Kirche* 91, 1994/1, 51–79.

26. N.Brox, ' "Sara zum Beispiel . . ." Israel im 1.Petrusbrief', in P.-G.Müller and W.Stenger (eds.), *Kontinuität und Einheit. Für Franz Mussner*, Fribourg 1981, 484–93: 493.

27. Roloff, *Die Kirche im Neuen Testament* (n.18), 151f.

28. P.Dschulnigg, *Rabbinische Gleichnisse und das Neue Testament. Die*

Gleichnisse der PesK im Vergleich mit den Gleichnissen Jesu und dem Neuen Testament, Bern and Frankfurt am Main 1988, 386.

29. Siker, *Disinheriting the Jews* (n.1), 126f.

30. Roloff, *Die Kirche im Neuen Testament* (n.18), 204, 206.

31. For the theology of the Letter to the Hebrews cf. K.-J.Kuschel, *Born Before All Time? The Dispute over Christ's Origin* (n.16), 349–62. New commentaries have appeared in the meantime: E.Grässer, *An die Hebräer* (EKK, 2 vols.), Zurich and Neukirchen-Vluyn 1990–93; H.F.Weiss, *Der Brief an die Hebräer* (KKNT), Göttingen 1991.

32. Thus H.Stadelmann, 'Zur Christologie des Hebräerbriefes in der neueren Diskussion', *Theologischer Bericht*, Vol.II, Zurich 1973, 135–221: 147.

33. For the function of talk of the pre-existence of Christ and his mediation in creation cf. my *Born Before all Time?* (n.16).

34. Cf. H.Köster, 'Die Auslegung der Abraham-Verheissung in Hebr 6', in R.Rendtorff and K.Koch (eds.), *Studien zur Theologie der alttestamentlichen Überlieferungen*, Neukirchen-Vluyn 1961, 95–109.

35. This is not contradicted by talk in Hebrews about a 'new covenant' which declares 'that the first is obsolete' (8.13). For if we note the context and the line of argument it becomes clear that here Hebrews has taken up a quotation from Jeremiah about the 'new covenant' (31.31–34) and has used it for its own ends. It is not the old covenant which is to be declared obsolete through Jesus, but the Temple cult. Cf. E.Zenger, *Das Erste Testament. Die jüdische Bibel und die Christen*, Düsseldorf 1991, 108.

36. For this complex of problems cf. recently E.Zenger (ed.), *Der Neue Bund im Alten. Studien zur Bundestheologie der beiden Testamente*, Freiburg im Breisgau 1993.

37. For the history of the Johannine community and the christology of the Gospel of John cf. K.-J.Kuschel, *Born Before All Time? The Dispute over Christ's Origin* (n.16), 363–96. Where names in this section appear in brackets, they refer to commentaries on the Gospel of John listed in my book.

38. Thus K.Wengst, *Bedrängte Gemeinde und verherrlichter Christus. Ein Versuch über das Johannes-Evangelium*, Munich [4]1992, 101. Whether the dispute in ch.8 which is of particular interest to us here is an alien body in the Gospel of John shaped by Gnostic dualism and thus is 'in the sharpest contrast' to 'what the Gosepl of John says of Jesus', as C.Westermann recently claims, cannot be decided here, and must be left to specialists: C.Westermann, *Das Johannesevangelium aus der Sicht des AT*, Stuttgart 1994, 31–49.

39. Wengst, *Bedrängte Gemeinde* (n.38), 133f.

40. Ibid., 126, referring to R.Schnackenburg, *The Gospel according to John*, Vol.II, London 1980, 188.

41. Siker, *Disinheriting the Jews* (n.1), 134.

42. Schnackenburg, *The Gospel according to John* II (n.40), 211.

43. Roloff, *Die Kirche im Neuen Testament* (n.18), 305.

44. This process of the disinheriting of Judaism and the Christianizing of Israel has now been well worked on by scholars: K.H.Rengstorf and S.von Kortzfleisch (eds.), *Kirche und Synagoge. Handbuch zur Geschichte von Christen und Juden* (2 vols.), Stuttgart 1968–70; H.Schreckenberg, *Die christlichen* Adversus-Judaeos *Texte und ihr literarische Umfeld (1–11 Jhd.)*, Bern and Frankfurt am Main 1982; id., *Die christlichen* Adversus-Judaeos *Texte (11–13.Jhr.) mit einer Ikonographie des Judenthemas bis zum vierten Laterankonzil*, Bern and Frankfurt am Main 1988. For the image of Abraham in the early church cf. W.Völker, 'Das Abrahambild bei Philo, Origenes und Ambrosius', *Theologische Studien und Kritiken* 103, 1931, 199–207; T.Klauser, 'Abraham', *Reallexikon für Antike und Christentum*, ed T.Klauser, I, Stuttgart 1950, 18–27; R.L.Wilken, 'The Christianizing of Abraham: The Interpretation of Abraham in Early Christianity', *Concordia Theological Monthly* 43, 1972, 723–31; Siker, *Disinheriting the Jews* (n.1), 144–84.

45. K.Wengst, 'Einleitung zum Barnabasbrief', in id., *Schriften des Urchristentums*, II, Darmstadt 1984, 131.

46. Schreckenberg, *Die christlichen* Adversus-Judaeos *Texte* (n.44), 174.

47. Ibid., 178.

48. Texts of the letter of Ignatius are conveniently available in *Early Christian Writings*, Harmondsworth 1968.

49. Ignatius, *To the Philadelphians* 6.1.

50. Ibid., 9.1.

51. For the theology of Justin cf. recently M.Hengel, 'Die Septuaginta als von den Christen beanspruchte Schriftensammlung bei Justin und den Vätern vor Origenes', in J.D.G.Dunn (ed.), *Jews and Christians. The Parting of the Ways, AD 70 to 135*, Tübingen 1992, 39–84.

52. Justin, *Dialogue with the Jew Trypho*, 119.5f.

53. Justin, *Dialogue*, 120.2.

54. Ibid.

55. Justin, *Dialogue*, 131.2.

56. Quoted in Schreckenberg, *Die christlichen* Adversus-Judaeos *Texte* (n.44), 186.

57. Ibid.

58. Justin, *Dialogue*, 11.5.

59. E.Endres, *Die gelbe Farbe. Die Entwicklung der Judenfeindschaft aus dem Christentum*, Munich 1989, 94.

60. Rengstorf and Kortzfleisch (eds.), *Kirche und Synagoge* (n.44), I, 95.

61. Texts in ibid, I.93.

62. Augustine, *Homilies on the Gospel of John* XLIII, 17, Nicene and Post-Nicene Fathers VII, New York 1888.

63. Quoted from P.Brown, *Augustine of Hippo*, London 1967, 318.
64. Ibid., 318f.
65. Augustine, *City of God*, XVI, 16.
66. Ibid., XVI, 28.
67. Ibid., XVI, 26.
68. Ibid., XVI, 35.
69. Ibid., XVI, 37.

III. Abraham and Islam

1. The Qur'an is quoted from the translation by Mohammed Assad, *The Message of the Qur'an*, Gibraltar 1984. For the picture of Abraham in Islam cf. Y.Moubarac, *Abraham dans le Coran*, Paris 1958; H.Speyer, *Die biblischen Erzählungen im Koran*, Hildesheim 1961; J.Hjärpe, 'Abraham IV', *Theologische Realenzyklopädie* I, Berlin and New York 1977, 386f.; J.Bouman, *Gott und Mensch im Koran. Ein Strukturform religiöser Anthropologie anhand des Beispiels Allah und Muhammad*, Darmstadt 1977, ²1989; 'Ibrahim' and 'Ismail', in *Handwörterbuch des Islam*, ed. A.J.Wensinck and J.H.Kramers, Leiden 1976, 192f., 222; R.Paret, 'Ibrahim' and 'Ismail', in *The Encyclopedia of Islam*, new edition, III, Leiden 1979, 980f., and IV, Leiden 1979, 184f.; K.W.Tröger, 'Mohammed und Abraham. Der Prozess der Ablösung des frühen Islam vom Judentum und seine Vorgeschichte', *Kairos* 22, 1980, 188–200; L.Hagemann, *Propheten – Zeugen des Glaubens, Koranische und biblische Deutungen*, Graz 1985, ²1993, 51–64; id., 'Abraham', in *Islam Lexikon. Geschichte – Ideen – Gestalten*, I, Freiburg im Breisgau 1991, 32–5; 'Abraham', in *Concise Encyclopedia of Islam*, ed. C.Glassé, San Francisco 1989, 18f.; M.Hamidullah, 'Abraham selon le Coran et la tradition islamique', in *Abraham*, Paris 1992, 127–67.
2. Cf. the convincing analysis by P.van Buren, *A Theology of the Jewish-Christian Reality*, II, San Francisco 1983, 136–42.
3. Cf. R.Patai, *The Seed of Abraham. Jews and Arabs in Contact and Conflict*, Salt Lake City 1986, 18–33. However, scholars dispute whether the 'sons of Ishmael' mentioned here are the real ancestors of the Arabs. 'Ishmaelites' and 'Arabs' cannot simply be identified like this. Cf. I.Eph'al, ' "Ishmael" and "Arab". A Transformation of Ethnological Terms', *Journal of Near Eastern Studies* 35, 1976, 225–35; id., *The Ancient Arabs. Nomads on the Borders of the Fertile Crescent, 9th–5th Centuries BC*, Leiden 1982, esp. 233–40. There is a critical discussion of Eph'al and a detailed argument for the opposite thesis in I.Shahid, *Byzantium and the Arabs in the Fifth Century*, Baltimore 1989, 332–44.
4. Jubilees 20.12.
5. Josephus, *Antiquities* I, 13,2.
6. *Antiquities* I, 13.4.

7. Examples in H.Schmid, 'Ismael im Alten Testament und im Koran', *Judaica* 32, 1976, 67–81, 119–29.

8. Thus C.Westermann, more clearly in the shorter version than in his larger commentary, cf. *Im Anfang, 1.Mose (Genesis)*, Vol.I, Neukirchen 1986, 258.

9. Cf. the comprehensive study by R.Dagorn, *La Geste d'Ismael d'après l'onomastique et la Tradition Arabes*, Geneva 1981.

10. A.Guillaume, *The Life of Mohammad. A Translation of Ibn Ishaq's 'Sirat Rasul Allah'*, Oxford and New York 1955, 3.

11. T.Nagel, *Staat und Glaubensgemeinschaft im Islam*, Vol.I, Zurich and Munich 1981, 27f.; id., *Der Koran. Einführung – Texte – Erläuterung*, Munich 1983, [2]1991, 88f.; similarly Shahid, *Byzantium and the Arabs* (n.3), 338–49.

12. Guillaume, *Life of Muhammad* (n.10), 99.

13. R.Paret, *Mohammed und der Koran*, Stuttgart, Berlin, Cologne and Mainz 1957, [6]1985; cf. also W.M.Watt, *Mohammad at Mecca*, Oxford and New York 1953, 96f., 158–64; similarly K.Armstrong, *Mohammad. A Biography of the Prophet*, San Francisco 1991, 70f.

14. Cf. Nagel, *Der Koran* (n.11), 86–118 ('Das Leben Mohammads im Spiegel des Korans. Die Entwicklung des prophetischen Selbstverständnisses').

15. There are examples in A.I.Katsh, *Judaism in Islam. Biblical and Talmudic Backgrounds of the Quran and its Commentaries*, New York 1954, [3]1980; N.A.Stillman, *The Jews of Arab Lands. A History and Source Book*, Philadelphia 1979; B.Louis, *The Jews of Islam*, Princeton 1984; J.D.McAuliffe, *Quranic Christians. An Analysis of Classical and Modern Exegesis*, Cambridge 1991; J.Bouman, *Der Koran und die Juden. Die Geschichte einer Tragödie*, Darmstadt 1990.

16. T.Nagel, *Geschichte der islamischen Theologie. Von Mohammed bis zur Gegenwart*, Munich 1994, 19.

17. J.van Ess, 'Muhammad and the Qur'an: Prophecy and Revelation', in H.Küng et al., *Christianity and the World Religions*, London and New York 1986, 10.

18. Speyer, *Die biblischen Erzählungen im Koran* (n.1), 140.

19. Nagel, *Geschichte der islamischen Theologie* (n.16), 27.

20. Jewish parallels: bPesachin 118a; Midrash Numbers Rabba 2.11. Further examples in K.Appel, 'Abraham als dreijähriger Knabe im Feuerofen des Nimrod', *Kairos* 25, 1983, 36–40.

21. Bouman, *Der Koran und die Juden* (n.15), 54.

22. Cf. the comprehensive account by W.M.Watt, *Mohammed at Medina*, Oxford 1956.

23. Cf. Bouman, *Der Koran und die Juden* (n.15), 60–4.

24. Quoted from ibid., 66.

25. Cf. also Guillaume, *The Life of Mohammed* (n.10), 266.

26. R.Paret, 'Ibrahim', *The Encyclopedia of Islam*, new edition, III, Leiden 1979, 980.

27. Id., *Mohammed und der Koran* (n.13), 121.

28. This is the provocative thesis of the Dutch orientalist C.Snouck Hurgronje, *Het Mekkaansche Fest*, Leiden 1880; also in *Verspreide Geschriften*, I, Bonn and Leipzig 1923, 1–124.

29. Thus F.E.Peters, *The Children of Abraham. Judaism – Christianity – Islam*, Princeton 1982, 197; cf. also his very instructive and rich collection, *Judaism, Christianity and Islam. The Classic Texts and Their Interpretation* (3 vols.), Princeton 1990.

30. C.Snouck Hurgronje's theory has been rejected with good reason by Moubarac, *Abraham dans le Coran* (n.1), and also by E.Beck, 'Die Gestalt des Abraham am Wendepunkt der Entwicklung Mohammeds', *Le Muséon* 65, 1952, 73–94. For this controversy see recently W.A.Bijlefeld, 'Controversies around the Quranic Ibrahim Narrative and Its Orientalist Interpretations', *The Muslim World* 72, 1982, 81–94. Objections have been made from the Muslim side by F.Rahman, *Major Themes of the Quran*, Minneapolis and Chicago, esp. 132–70.

31. The Muslim woman theologian Riffat Hassan, who comes from Pakistan and lives in the United States, has therefore rightly requested that because of this statement the sanctuaries of Mecca should no longer be reserved for Muslims but should be opened to 'all people': R.Hassan, 'Feast of Sacrifice in Islam: Abraham, Hagar and Ishamel', in A.Lacoque (ed.), *Commitment and Commemoration. Jews, Christians and Muslims in Dialogue*, Chicago 1994.

32. M.S.Abdullah, *Islam. Für das Gespräch mit Christen*, Gütersloh 1992, 63.

33. Cf. I.Goldziher, *Die Richtungen der islamischen Koranauslegung*, Leiden 1920, 79–81. There are also examples in R.Patia, *The Seed of Abraham* (n.3), 32, and in J.van Ess, *Theologie und Gesellschaft im 2. und 3.Jahrhundert Hidschra. Eine Geschichte des religiösen Denkens im frühen Islam*, V, Berlin and New York 1993, 173f.

34. The degree to which devotion to Abraham during the pilgrimage can take on almost mystical features is made clear by the impressive book by A.Shariati, *Hajj. Reflections on its Rituals*, Albuquerque, NM 1992. F.E.Peters, *The Hajj. The Muslim Pilgrimage to Mecca and the Holy Places*, Princeton 1994, has recently given a comprehensive account of the (Abrahamic) origin and history of the pilgrimage.

35. H.Busse, *Die theologischen Beziehungen des Islams zu Judentum und Christentum. Grundlagen des Dialogs im Koran und die gegenwärtigen Situation*, Darmstadt 1988, ²1991, 85.

36. H.Stieglecker, *Die Glaubenslehren des Islam* (3 vols.), Munich, Paderborn and Vienna 1960–2, 202 (for Abraham cf. II, 196–210).

37. Nagel, *Der Koran* (n.14), 135.

38. S.Hossein-Nasr, 'Islam', in A.Sharma (ed.), *Our Religions*, San Francisco 1993, 427–532: 429.

39. Y.Moubarac, 'Fragen des Katholizismus an den Islam', in H.Vorgrimler and R.van der Gucht (eds.), *Bilanz der Theologie im 20.Jahrhundert*, I, Freiburg im Breisgau 1969, 423–56: 431.

40. C.Colpe, *Das Siegel der Propheten. Historische Beziehungen zwischen Judentum, Judenchristentum, Heidentum und frühen Islam*, Berlin 1990.

41. Tertullian, *Adversus Judaeos* 8, Ante-Nicene Fathers III, Buffalo, 1885; cf. Colpe, *Das Siegel der Propheten* (n.20), 30.

42. There are examples in M.Ayoub, *The Quran and its Interpreters* (2 vols), Albany 1984–1992. Here in I, 264–6, on the inerrancy and sinlessness of Abraham.

43. There are texts in the following source books: G.Weil, *Biblische Legenden der Muselmänner. Aus arabischen Quellen zusammengetragen und mit jüdischen Werken verglichen*, Frankfurt am Main 1845, 68–99; F.Wüstenfeld (ed.), *Geschichte der Stadt Mekka. Nach der arabischen Chroniken bearbeitet*, Leipzig 1861, 2–10; M.Grünbaum, *Neue Beiträge zur semitischen Sagenkunde*, Leiden 1893 (on Abraham, 89–132); M.Lings, *Mohammad. His Life, Based on the Earliest Sources*, Cambridge 1983, 1–5. F.E.Peters, *A Reader on Classical Islam*, Princeton 1994, esp.13–20, 35–42, offers a good collection of the classical texts.

44. W.M.Watt, *Der Islam*, I, Stuttgart and Mainz 1980, 124.

45. Guillaume, *The Life of Mohammed* (n.10), 186. The further development of the tradition has been investigated by A.Schimmel, *Und Mohammed ist sein Prophet. Die Verehrung des Propheten in der islamischen Frömmigkeit*, Cologne and Düsseldorf 1981, Ch.VIII, 'Die Himmelsreise des Propheten'. The Hadith traditions on Abraham have been collected by sources in A.J.Wensinck, *A Handbook of Early Mohammedan Tradition. Alphabetically Arranged*, Leiden 1927 (c.v. Ibrahim).

46. Cf. S.Z.Abedin, 'Ahl Adh-Dhimma: Andersgläubige aus islamischer Sicht', *Moslemische Revue* 68, 1992, 65–82; similarly K.Duran, 'Die Muslime und die Andersgläubigen', in *Der Islam. Religion – Ethik – Politik*, Stuttgart, Berlin and Cologne 1991, 125–52.

47. H.Zirker, *Islam. Theologische und gesellschaftliche Herausforderung*, Düsseldorf 1993, 87.

48. Ibid., 86.

49. Ibid., 89.

B. Perspectives for an Abrahamic Ecumene

I. Presuppositions for an Ecumenical Awareness

1. L.Gardet, *Connaître l'Islam*, Paris 1958; G.C.Anawati, 'Christentum

und Islam. Ihr Verhältnis aus christlicher Sicht', in A.Bsteh (ed.), *Dialog aus der Mitte christlicher Theologie*, Mödling 1987, 197–216: 207.

2. M.Baar, *Nahost – Auftakt zum Weltbrand oder Weltfrieden? Erbschaftstreit zwischen Ismael und Isaak um Volk, Land und Segen*, Bad Liebenzell [2]1984.

3. Cf. N.Daniel, *Islam and the West, The Making of an Image* (1960), reissued Edinburgh 1989; L.Hagemann, *Christentum und Islam zwischen Konfrontation und Begegnung*, Altenberge 1983; C.Colpe, *Problem Islam*, Frankfurt am Main 1989, 11–38; W.M.Watt, *Muslim-Christian Encounters. Perceptions and Misperceptions*, London and New York 1991; J.Waardenburg, *Islamisch-Christliche Beziehungen. Geschichtliche Streifzüge*, Würzburg and Altenberge 1992.

4. Cf. recently H.Zirker, 'Die Muslime und der Jude im fingierten Religionsgespräch: Zu Nikolaus von Keus' *De Pace fidei*', in id. *Islam, Theologische und gesellschaftliche Herausforderung*, Düsseldorf 1993, 87.

5. The visible expression of the Christian claim to universality is the World Conference of Protestant missionary societies held in Edinburgh in 1910, where the slogan was 'the evangelization of the world in this generation'. Cf. my contribution to *A Global Ethic. The Declaration of the Parliament of the World's Religions*, London and New York 1993, 77–106.

6. K.Cragg, *The Pen and the Faith. Eight Modern Muslim Writers and the Quran*, London 1985.

7. Hans Küng, *Global Responsibility*, London and New York 1991.

8. The text of the declaration, drafted by Hans Küng, appears in *A Global Ethic* (n.5).

9. Ibid., 17.

10. Ibid., 31.

11. Ibid., 23, 26.

12. Cf. D.Novak, *The Image of the Non-Jew and Judaism. An Historical and Constructive Study of the Noahide Laws*, New York and Toronto 1983; id., *Jewish-Christian Dialogue. A Jewish Justification*, London and New York 1989.

13. Cf. J.J.Petuchowski, 'Noachidische Gebote', in id. and C.Thoma (eds.), *Lexikon der jüdisch-christlichen Begegnung*, Freiburg im Breisgau 1989, 265–8.

14. The most recent impressive example is E.B.Borowitz, *Renewing the Covenant. A Theology for the Postmodern Jew*, Philadelphia and New York 1991, 188.

15. *Gates of Prayer, The New Union Prayerbook*, New York 1975, 703–5.

16. This formula, 'Force them to come in (the church)', used by Augustine (*Sermon* 112.8) against heretics, had disastrous effects on the attitude especially of the mediaeval church to all non-Christians. Cf.

P.Brown, *Augustine of Hippo*, London 1967, Part III, ch.21, 'Disciplina': 'Augustine may be the first theorist of the Inquisition' (240).

17. Y.Moubarac, 'Fragen des Katholizismus an den Islam', in H.Vorgrimler and R.van der Gucht (ed.), *Bilanz der Theologie im 20.Jahrhundert*, I, Freiburg im Breisgau 1969, 423–56: 424.

18. *Christliches Bekenntnis und biblischer Auftrag angesichts des Islam*, Bielefeld 1984.

19. P.von der Osten-Sacken, *Grundzüge einer Theologie im christlich-jüdische Gespräch*, Munich 1982, 168. M.Theobald, *Römerbrief* I, Stuttgart 1992, 315f., has once again demonstrated impressively that on the basis of these insights it is also no longer possible to justify an old-style church mission to the Jews.

20. The texts can be found in R.Rendtorff and H.H.Henrix (eds.), *Die Kirche und das Judentum. Dokumente von 1945–1985*, Paderborn and Munich 1988. Similarly U.Schwemer (ed.), *Christen und Juden. Dokumente der Annäherung*, Gütersloh 1991. They are interpreted and given a context in K-J.Kuschel, 'Die Kirchen und das Judentum', *Stimmen der Zeit* 117, 1992, 147–62; R.Rendtorff, *Hat denn Gott sein Volk verstossen? Die evangelische Kirche und das Judentum seit 1945. Ein Kommentar*, Munich 1989.

21. *Dokumente 1945–1985* (n.20), 457.

22. Cf. the most recent study by J.Zehner, *Der notwendige Dialog. Die Weltreligionen in katholischer und evangelischer Sicht*, Gütersloh 1992.

23. *Was jeder vom Islam wissen muss*, published by the Lutherisches Kirchenamt der Vereinigten Evangelisch-Lutherischen Kirche Deutschlands and the Kirchenamt der Evangelischen Kirche im Deutschland, Gütersloh 1990, 184. Cf. also the study *Religionen, Religiosität und christliche Glaube*, produced by the Arnoldsheim Conference and the Lutherisches Kirchenamt of the VELKD, Gütersloh 1991, which has objective information and aims at co-existence.

24. *Was jeder vom Islam wissen muss* (n.24), 182.

25. Ibid., 177, 180.

26. For the Vatican II declaration on the religions cf. recently M.Ruokanen, *The Catholic Doctrine of Non-Christian Religions according to the Second Vatican Council*, Leiden, New York and Cologne 1992.

27. M.Abdul al-Ra'uf, 'Judaism and Christianity in the Perspective of Islam', in Isma'il Raji al-Faruqi (ed.), *Trialogue of Abrahamic Faiths*, Brendwood, Maryland 1982, 22–29: 28.

28. A.Sachedina, 'Is Islamic Revelation an Abrogation of Judaeo-Christian Revelation', *Concilium* 1994/3, 94–102: 101.

29. Cf. the informative volume edited by L.Swidler, *Muslims in Dialogue. The Evolution of a Dialogue*, Lewiston, NY 1992; similarly J.Hick and E.S.Meltzer, *Three Faiths – One God. A Jewish, Christian, Muslim Encounter*, Albany, NY 1989; A.Falaturi, J.J.Petuchowski and W.Strolz

(ed.), *Drei Wege zu dem einen Gott. Glaubenserfahrung in den monotheistischen Religionen*, Freiburg im Breisgau 1976.

30. S.Hossein Nasr, 'Islam', in A.Sharma (ed.), *Our Religion*, San Francisco 1993, 522.

31. S.Balic, *Ruf vom Minarett. Weltislam heute – Renaissance oder Rückfall? Eine Selbstdarstellung*, Hamburg ³1984, 108f.; id., *Der Islam im Spannungsfeld von Tradition und heutiger Zeit*, Altenberge 1993.

32. F.Rahman, 'Islam', in M.Eliade (ed.), *Encyclopedia of Religion*, Vol.VII, New York 1987, 303–22: 321.

33. Cf. the thorough study by A.T.Khoury, *Toleranz im Islam*, Munich and Mainz 1980; id., *Der Islam. Sein Glaube, seine Lebensordnung, sein Anspruch*, Freiburg im Breisgau 1988, ²1993, esp. 193–209; similarly W.Kerber (ed.), *Wie tolerant ist der Islam?*, Munich 1991.

34. Cf. K.Rudolph, 'Juden – Christen – Muslime: Zum Verhältnis der drei monotheistischen Religionen in religionswissenschaftlicher Sicht', *Judaica* 44, 1988, 214–32.

35. This notion is also taken up in the constructive book, inviting dialogue, by M.Borrmanns, *Wege zum christlich-islamischen Dialog*, Frankfurt 1985, 12.

36. Ibid., 9, 12.

II. What Abrahamic Ecumene Cannot Be

1. For the history of ecumenism cf. my brief study, K.-J.Kuschel, *Leben im ökumenischen Geist. Plädoyer gegen die Resignation*, Ostfildern 1991.

2. J.Neusner, *Jews and Christians. The Myth of a Common Tradition*, London 1991, esp. 120f.

3. It has been noted that for example at a Christian-Muslim encounter sponsored by the World Council of Churches in Broumara (Lebanon), a text was approved which no longer simply spoke of religions but only of traditions. It is printed in A.von Denffer (ed.), *Dialogue between Christians and Muslims*, III, *Statements and Resolutions*, Leicester 1984, 5–11.

4. R.Mayer (ed.), *Der Babylonische Talmud*, Munich 1963, 97.

III. What Abrahamic Ecumene Can Mean

1. In this connection I gratefully recall a conversation with Thomas F.Stransky, Director of the Tantur Institute in Jerusalem, on 23 March 1994 at the Crown-Minow Conference in the University of Notre Dame, Indiana. In it, Fr Stransky drew my attention to the politicizing of Abraham, Hagar and Sarah in the present Israeli-Palestinian conflict. What we have here, he argued, is not a portrait of Abraham himself but the exploitation of Abraham for pedagogical, political and indeed military purposes. The way in which a biblical figure is thus exploited in present-day Israel in particular

would be worth a separate study. A first attempt at this has been made by J.Schoneveld, *Die Bibel in der israelischen Erziehung. Eine Studie über Zugänge zur Hebräischen Bibel und zum Bibelunterricht in der israelischen pädagogischen Literatur*, Neukirchen-Vluyn 1987 (on Abraham, 134–63).

2. C.Westermann, *Genesis 12–50* (1975), Darmstadt [3]1992, 45.

3. Cf. the instructive article by the Jerusalem Jewish theologian who works at the Shalom Hartman Institute, T.Mark, 'The Issues of Jewish-Christian Dialogue Today', *Studies in Interreligious Dialogue* 3, 1993, 5–11.

4. G.von Rad, *Genesis*, Old Testament Library, London and Philadelphia, [2]1972, 224.

5. C.Westermann, *Genesis 23–36*, Minneapolis and London 1985, 344. For the theological relevance of Ishmael cf. also M.Hayek, *Le mystère d'Ismaël*, Paris 1964.

6. D.Hartman, *A Living Covenant. The Innovative Spirit in Traditional Judaism*, New York 1985, 31.

7. D.S.Flusser, 'Christianity', in A.A.Cohen and P.Mendes-Flohr (eds.), *Contemporary Jewish Religious Thought*, New York and London 1987, 61–6: 62.

8. Cf. P.Lapide, 'Das jüdische Verständnis von Christentum und Islam', in M.Stöhr (ed.), *Abrahams Kinder. Juden – Christen – Moslems*, Frankfurt 1983, 1–28; similarly A.H.Friedlander, 'Sind die Juden erwählt?', *Judaica* 43, 1987, 131–41; S.Ben-Chorin, *Die Erwählung Israels. Ein theologisch-politischer Traktat*, Munich 1993.

9. All the quotations are from I.Greenberg, *The Jewish Way. Living the Holidays*, New York 1988, 71f.

10. M.Wyschogrod, 'Islam and Christianity in the Perspective of Judaism', in Isma'il Raji al-Faruqi (ed.), *Trialogue of Abrahamic Faiths*, Brendwood, Maryland 1982, 13–18: 18.

11. On a visit to Israel in January 1994 in connection with our trialogue meeting I came to know the activities of the Al-Liqa Centre in Bethlehem, which is a meeting place for Muslim and Christian Palestinians, and also the activities of the Rainbow Group in Jerusalem.

12. There is more on this in my article 'Die Kirche und das Judentum', *Stimmen der Zeit* 117, 1992, 147–62.

13. H.Zirker, *Islam. Theologische und Gesellschaftliche Herausforderung*, Düsseldorf 1993, 27, 36.

14. H.Küng, *Judaism*, London and New York 1992, 17.

15. M.Görg, *In Abrahams Schoss*, Düsseldorf 1993, 174.

16. Cf. the introductory study by G.Basetti-Sani, *Louis Massignon. Christian Ecumenist*, Chicago 1974; id., *The Koran in the Light of Christ. Islam in the Plan of History of Salvation*, Chicago 1977, 3–39.

17. English text in H.Massignon (ed.), *Testimonies and Reflections. Essays of Louis Massignon*, Notre Dame, Indiana 1989, 3–20.

18. Y.Moubarac, 'Das christliche Denken und der Islam. Haupterkenntnisse und neue Problemstellungen', *Concilium* 12, 1976, 349–58: 355 (never published in English).

19. Thus recently, with reference to Massignon, C.Geffré, 'La portée theologique du dialogue islamo-chrétien', *Islamochristiana* 18, 1992, 1–22: 9.

20. C.M.Martini, 'Wir und der Islam', CIBEDO 5, 1991, 1–11: 5. Developments since the Council have been sketched out by L.Hagemann, 'Katholische Kirche und Islam', in *Islam-Lexikon*, ed. A.T.Khoury et al., Freiburg im Breisgau 1991, 430–8. It is worth paying particular attention to the statements by Pope John Paul II about the faith of Abraham which united Jews and Christians and about Abraham's hospitality.

21. Cf. J.Waardenburg, 'World Religions as seen in the Light of Islam', in A.T.Welch and P.Cachica (eds.), *Islam. Past Influence and Future Challenge*, Edinburgh 1979, 245–75.

22. Examples in A.T.Khoury and L.Hagemann, *Christentum und Christen im Denken zeitgenössischer Muslime*, Altenberge 1986. Similarly M.Ayoub, 'Muslim Views of Christianity. Some Modern Examples', *Islamochristiana* 10, 1984, 49–70.

23. F.Rahman, 'Islam', in M.Eliade (ed.), *Encyclopedia of Religion*, Vol. VII, New York 1987, 321.

24. Examples also in Khoury and Hagemann, *Christentum und Christen* (n.22), 173–89. The contributions by Muslim theologians working in Germany, A.Falaturi, 'Christliche Theologie und westliches Islamverständnis', and E.Elshahed, 'Die Problematik des interreligiösen Dialogs aus muslimischer Sicht', in H.Häring and K.-J.Kuschel (eds.), *Hans Küng. Neue Horizonte des Glaubens und Denkens. Ein Arbeitsbuch*, Munich 1993, 651–62; 663–72, are written in the same spirit.

25. R.Hassan, 'Feast of Sacrifice in Islam: Abraham, Hagar and Ishmael', in A.LaCoque (ed.), *Commitment and Commemoration. Jews, Christians and Muslims in Dialogue*, Chicago 1994.

26. M.S.Abdullah, *Islam. Für das Gespräch mit Christen*, Gütersloh 1992, 66f.

27. Ibid., 139.

28. H.Mahmoud Azzan, *Der Islam. Plädoyer eines Moslems*, Stuttgart 1981, 10.

29. M.Talbi, 'Hören auf sein Wort. Der Koran in der Geschichte der islamischen Tradition', in A.Bsteh (ed.), *Hören auf sein Wort. Der Mensch als Hörer des Wortes Gottes in christlicher und islamischer Überlieferung*, Mödling 1992, 119–50: 149, 150. The treatment of Abraham by M.Talbi, 'Foi d'Abraham et foi islamique', *Islamochristiana* 5, 1979, is equally impressive.

30. CIBEDO has been providing information on Christian-Muslim dialogue in Germany since 1987; *Islamochristiana*, the journal of the

Pontifical Institute for Arabic and Islamic Studies in Rome, has been providing information on the international sphere since 1975.

31. W.Gross, *Glaubensgehorsam als Wagnis der Freiheit. Wir sind Abraham*, Mainz 1980, 67.

32. M.Theobald, *Römerbrief*, Vol.1, Stuttgart 1992, 136.

33. Cf. K.-J.Kuschel, 'Wie Menschenrechte, Weltreligionen und Weltfrieden zusammenhangen', in H.Küng and K.-J.Kuschel (eds.), *Weltfrieden durch Religionsfrieden. Antworten aus den Weltreligionen*, Munich 1993, 171–216.

34. Cf. the most recent study by J.Schwartländer (ed.), *Freiheit der Religion. Christentum und Islam under dem Anspruch der Menschenrechte*, Mainz 1993.

35. Thus e.g. M.Arkoun, 'Der Ursprung der Menschenrechte aus der Sicht des Islam', in H.Küng and K.-J.Kuschel (eds.), *Weltfrieden durch Religionsfrieden* (n.33), 53–66; B.Tibi, 'Im Namen Gottes? Der Islam, die Menschenrechte und die kulturelle Moderne', in M.Lüders (ed.), *Der Islam im Aufbruch? Perspektiven der arabischen Welt*, Munich 1992, 144–61.

36. Cf. the most recent study by J.C.Bürgel, *Allmacht und Mächtigkeit. Religion und Welt im Islam*, Munich 1991, esp.345–59 (on the cases of M.Mahfuz, S.Rushdie and M.Tacha). For the most recent case, that of the Egyptian Nasr Hamid Abu Zaid, who has been accused of critical interpretation of the Qur'an, cf. the account by B.Heine, 'Neue Koranforschung', *Orientierung* 58, 1994, 73f.

37. In addition to Schwartländer's book *Freiheit der Religion* (n.34), cf. id. and H.Bielefeldt, *Christen und Muslime vor der Herausforderung der Menschenrechte*, Bonn 1992.

38. T.Sundermeier, '"Mission nach der Weise Abrahams". Eine Predigt über Gen.12, 1–9', in E.Blum, C.Macholz and E.W.Stegemann (eds.), *Die Hebräische Bibel und ihre zweifache Nachgeschichte. FS Rendtorff zum 65.Geburtstag*, Neukirchen-Vluyn 1990, 575–9: 577f. On the same topic, N.Lohfink, 'Die Religion der Patriarchen und die Konsequenzen für eine Theologie der nichtchristlichen Religionen', in id., *Bibelauslegung im Wandel. Ein Exeget ortet seine Wissenschaft*, Frankfurt am Main 1967, 107–28. More recently: W.Bühlmann, *Wenn Gott zu allen Menschen geht. Der biblische Glaube, die Weltreligionen und die Zukunft der Menschheit*, Mainz 1992.

39. von Rad, *Genesis* (n.4), 229.

40. C.Westermann, *Am Anfang, 1.Mose (Genesis)*, Vol.I, Neukirchen-Vluyn 1986, 221.

41. von Rad, *Genesis* (n.4), 180.

42. J.J.Petuchowski, *Melchisedech. Urgestalt der Ökumene*, Freiburg im Breisgau 1979, 36, 37.

43. F.Mussner, 'Nachwort. Bemerkungen eines christlichen Theologen', in Petuchowski, *Melchisedech* (n.42), 40.

44. C.Westermann, 'Der Gott Abrahmas', in A.Bstseh (ed.), *Der Gott des Christentums und des Islams*, Mödling 1978, 141–3.

45. C.M.Martini, *Abraham. Der Weg eines Suchenden*, Munich, Zurich and Vienna 1985, 14.

46. Y.Moubarac, 'Fragen des Katholizismus an den Islam', in H.Vorgrimler and R.van der Gucht (eds.), *Bilanz der Theologie im 20.Jahrhundert*, Freiburg im Breisgau 1969, 433.

47. I am grateful to Professor Martin Stöhr for making the English text accessible to me.

48. From a lecture given by Rabbi Dr Jonathan Magonet in a trialogue conversation in Cologne, 1–2 December 1992. I have it under the title 'Abraham and Judaism. Tradition and Significance from the Beginnings to the Present'.

49. The text is printed in *Forms of Prayer for Jewish Worship*, published by The Assembly of Rabbis of the Reform Synagogues of Great Britain, Vol.III (Prayers for the High Holy Days), London 1985, 891.

50. Anwar el-Sadat, *Unterwegs zur Gerechtigkeit. Auf der Suche nach Identität: die Geschichte meines Lebens*, Vienna and Munich 1978, 381, 384.

51. H.Schmidt, 'Wir haben die gleichen Propheten', *Die Zeit*, 2 April 1993.

52. U.Avnery, 'Am Grabe Abrahams', *Der Spiegel* 9/1994, 158.

53. Ben-Chorin, *Die Erwählung Israels* (n.8), 127.

54. Id., 'Israels Luft macht radikal', *Der Spiegel* 35, 1993, 150.

55. Küng, *Judaism* (n.14), 578–80.

56. Moubarac, 'Fragen des Katholizismus an den Islam' (n.46), 453.

57. *Focus* 45, 1993, 261. Cf. also Crown Prince Hassan Bin Talal, *Search for Peace. The Politics of the Middle Ground in the Arab East*, London 1984, a book by the king's brother, who is deeply committed to inter-religious dialogue.

58. Cf. W.Strolz, *Heilswege der Weltreligionen I, Christliche Begegnung mit Judentum und Islam*, Freiburg im Breisgau 1984, esp. Ch.VI, 'Beten in den monotheistischen Religionen'; similarly P.Neuenzeit, *Juden und Christen auf neuen Wegen zum Gespräch*, Würzburg 1990 (here especially P.Fiedler, 'Gemeinsames Beten von Christen und Juden', 173–94).

59. P.Navè, *Du unser Vater. Jüdische Gebete für Christen*, Freiburg im Breisgau 1975; cf. also P.Navè-Levinson, *Einblicke in das Judentum*, Paderborn 1991, 227–39; the brief dialogue with the apostle Paul on Christians, Jews and Muslims is particularly attractive here.

60. P.Navè, *Du unser Vater* (n.59), 105.

61. A.Schimmel, *Denn Dein ist das Reich. Gebete aus dem Islam*, Freiburg im Breisgau 1978, 5f.

62. Strolz, *Heilswege der Weltreligionen* I (n.58), 117.

63. The Assisi texts are published in *Assisi: World Day of Prayer for Peace*, Vatican City 1987.

64. M.Borrmanns, *Wege zum christlich-islamischen Dialog*, Frankfurt 1985, 149.

65. Cf. 'Christen und Muslime beten. Eine gemeinsame Gebetsstunde', in A.Bsteh (ed.), *Hören auf sein Wort. Der Mensch als Hörer des Wortes Gottes in christlicher und islamischer Überlieferung*, Mödling 1992, 151–65.

66. *Assisi: World Day of Prayer* (n.63), 128.

67. Ibid. (n.63), 144.

68. Quoted in Bsteh (ed.), *Hören auf sein Wort* (n.65), 186.

69. Küng, *Judaism* (n.14), 581f.

70. N.Lash, 'Hoping against Hope or Abraham's Dilemma', *Modern Theology* 10, 1994, 233–46: 245.

71. According to a report by the Catholic news agency of 14 June 1994, at the last plenary meetings of Roman Catholic cardinals a 'Pan-Christian meeting' in Jerusalem and a 'Peace Meeting with Jews, Muslims and Christians on Mount Sinai' was considered for the year 2000.

Index

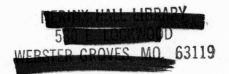
ERONX HALL LIBRARY
5 0 E. LOCKWOOD
WEBSTER GROVES, MO. 63119